DAZZLING
AND
DIVINE

To Louise,
A faithful guide
to many a sojourner.

Mark
4-28-04

DAZZLING
AND
DIVINE

A CONTEMPLATIVE JOURNEY IN CHRIST

BY MARK SIBLEY JONES

AUSTIN, TEXAS

DAZZLING AND DIVINE:
A CONTEMPLATIVE JOURNEY IN CHRIST
BY MARK SIBLEY JONES

Cover Artist: Temple Lee Parker
(see:www.tanglewave.com)
Cover graphics: Michael Qualben
Copyright © 2003 Mark Sibley Jones
First Printing: 2004
Printed in the United States of America

Several Scripture translations warrant acknowledgment with appreciation. Scripture quotations from the *Holy Bible, New International Version NIV* © 1973, 1978, 1984 by International Bible Society. Used by permission Zondervan Publishing House. When noted, Scripture quotations are from the *Holy Bible, New King James* (NKJV), Thomas Nelson, Nashville, TN © 1982 and from the *Holy Bible, King James Version*, The World Publishing House, New York City.

Used by permission: ICS Publications, Institute of Carmelite Studies, Washington, D.C.
Used by permission: The Liturgical Press, St. John's Abbey, Collegeville, MN.

Published by
LangMarc Publishing
P.O. Box 90488
Austin, Texas 78709
1-800-864-1648

Library of Congress Control Number: 2004102258

ISBN: 1-880-292-696   U.S.A. $24.95/Can.$29.95

DEDICATION

TO MARLENA AND CARLI

CONTENTS

.

INTRODUCTION: THE JOURNEY

With each nightfall Daniel felt more hopelessly lost. Days before, he had embarked on a solo hunting trip in the Alaskan wilderness, feeling confident and self-sufficient. With an unexpected storm and perpetually overcast skies, it was impossible to get his bearings sans the compass he'd forgotten to pack. Would he find his way out before his provisions expired? Emerging from a dense forest into the afternoon light of a clearing, the hunter saw a welcome sign of hope: the back side of a sign post! Nearing the sign, he saw the beginning of a dirt road. With new energy in each step, he came around to the front of the sign just as a motorist slowed to a stop on the road. Showing a relieved grin, the hunter looked upon the exasperated face of the driver, and then at the sign, which he could now read. "End of Road." To one lost man, the sign was a nuisance at the end of a long day of frustrating map searching and wrong turns; to the other, a herald of salvation.

* * *

Life is a journey. This statement is both a popular cliché and a profound truth. The meaning you assign to life's road signs is unique to your perspective. The pages you are about to read reflect the perspective of my soul's journey with Christ and my desire to offer a way for others to authentically discover their journey. This journey of mine over the past several years has been enriched by a cross fertilization of the Christian contemplative tradition and the evangelical movement with the emphasis both bring to a personal relationship with God. The result is a mystical, exegetical syllogism of the spiritual life and its development. Mystical in the sense that the experience of God is primary; exegetical in that the Scriptures provide the primary basis for interpreting this experience.

Teresa of Avila and John of the Cross were sixteenth-century Roman Catholic mystics who are among the most influential writers on contemplative prayer. In *The Interior Castle*, Teresa described her vision of the spiritual life as a crystal castle with many dwelling places where pilgrims experience the presence of God at different levels according to where they are in their unique relationship to God. These seven "mansions" are "dwelling places" of progressive enlightenment in a person's journey within his or her own soul, culminating in union with God.

For John, in *Ascent of Mount Carmel* and *Dark Night of the Soul*, the journey in Christ is depicted as emerging through an ascetic purging darkness of faith and eventually coming to a point where one finds his or her own way with Christ. Persecuted as a reformer of his church, the *Dark Night of the Soul* was John's exposition of the "Spiritual Canticles," a poem of his loving relationship with Christ written during his imprisonment.

Though contemporaries of the Protestant Reformation, Teresa and John were in a different theological universe from Protestant and evangelical forerunners. They lived in the context of sixteenth-century Spanish Inquisition Catholicism and were reformers in their own right. I'm reminded of the original meaning of "Protestant," which is "to profess." Though in a different context, Teresa and John carried on a mission similar to the early proponents of the Reformation: to profess the truth that believers may have a personal and direct relationship with God.

The works of Teresa and John have become cherished guides in my journey of relating to God. Their personalities come through in their writings and make their aspirations all the more real. I identify with John's melancholia and his struggle to find a place in the world. His gift for analysis inspires me. Teresa's bent toward emotion invites me to step beyond mere logic and experience God with my whole self. Her vivacious- ness challenges me to step out of my introversion and find connections between my contemplation and com- munity.

This important spiritual task of connecting one's experience to the larger world is the impetus of this book. Here I seek to connect my personal experience to communities of faith. What develops is in some ways a running journal of conversations and readings I have encountered along the way. It is not meant to be a textbook survey of the literature, theories and theolo- gies of spirituality—much less Teresian and sanjuanist (of John of the Cross) spiritualities—but a reflection on the sources and thoughts that have influenced me.

While my studies of Teresa and John sparked my creation of this particular model, the paradigm emerged out of my reflections on my own path and seeing the universal realities of my experience reflected in the stories of countless persons as well as in the classics. For example, years ago I shared with a spiritual growth group that I felt I'd come to the "end of the paved road" in my spiritual journey, meaning that the teachings of my church seemed to provide no guidance for where my experience with God was going. Years later I discov- ered this to be a key concept in John's *Ascent*, the place beyond which there is "nada." Lo and behold, others had proceeded me on this path! It has been a process similar to that of Carl Jung discovering archetypal im- ages in the statements of his patients that corresponded to ancient writings. Likewise, I experience a connection with the larger historical community of God's children. This connection, in some fashion, is the experience of everyone who leads a contemplative life and finds that their awareness is enhanced by the awareness of others.

Sojourns at the bedside of hospital patients, holy moments in the counseling office with clients, and sacred conversations with fellow seekers in their work places and churches have borne out the applicability of this model of spiritual experience. Those with whom I have shared this paradigm—in spiritual direction, retreats, and workshops—consistently report how their spirituality is opened in fresh ways. It is deeply satisfying when I hear someone describe how their prayer life has become more intimate, the Scriptures read with new insights, and stuck places in spiritual development met with new meaning. My one prayer and purpose for this book is to help my traveling companions grow in the knowledge and love of God as we journey together.

Overview

Succinctly, my model depicts two cycles: a discipleship cycle and a contemplative cycle. The discipleship cycle includes the experiences of being distracted by Christ, dazzled by Christ, and discipled by Christ. The contemplative cycle includes the experiences of dwelling in Christ, being desired by Christ, and our destiny in Christ. The bridge between the two cycles is the experience of being disillusioned by Christ. The seven chapters of the book elaborate on each of these experiences.

Discipleship: A Familiar Cycle. The adult journey of faith often includes a struggle with distraction, which is typically seen as a negative force: the world distracting our focus from God. Chapter one, **"Distracted by Christ"** reframes distraction as a necessary process and describes how God begins to get our attention, distracting us from the world. The paradox of distraction occurs as we open ourselves to the initiative of God. This significant step of growth leads to a profound experience of God.

"Dazzled by Christ," discussed in chapter two, is a place of wonderment and new energy. God finally gets our attention, and we are enthralled. We discover new spiritual realities beneath the surface of our lives.

Chapter three details the posture of being **"Discipled by Christ."** Christ calls us beyond the spectacular and into relationship. Out of our excitement, we may seek out methods and rules, thinking that our piety will maintain our high road with God. We then discover that Christ is not calling us to methods but to relationship.

Most Christians, I believe, live their lives in a cycle of distraction-dazzlement-discipleship. As discipleship grows rigid and stale, a recapitulation to distraction occurs. We are renewed in our faith with new methods of following Christ. This cycle is the basic ebb and flow of spirituality as we wax and wane in our devotion. With each successive circuit, we grow deeper in our devotion and wiser in the art of sojourning.

Disillusionment: A Turning Point. Many disciples, however, experience a new wave in their process of discipleship. They describe it as a revolution in their faith—a desert, dry place, trial, or total change of perspective—that John termed the "dark night." From this point there is no clear path, no method. It is a place where the experience of prayer changes dramatically from talking to being.

Chapter four delineates this place of being **"Disillusioned by Christ."** In disillusionment our images (or illusions) of God do not hold up any longer and must be cast aside for new constantly changing, and eventually obsolete, images. Our spirituality is stripped of elements that are not authentic to ourselves. We may even come to a point of disappointment and anger with God. We may feel shunned and repressed by our churches, which often point the disillusioned back to distraction ("get your eyes off the world"), dazzlement ("look at what God is doing!") and discipleship ("try harder, get on fire for God, repent"). Disillusionment is vital to our spiritual growth; we cannot progress further on the journey without it. A journey of illusion, after all, is no journey.

Contemplation: Beyond Imagining. "Dwelling in Christ" is a place where we lay to rest old images of God only to see them resurrected into new ones we couldn't have imagined! It is a place of experiencing spiritually the crucifixion and resurrection in Christ that may of us identified with at our conversion or baptism. It is a struggle to the death. Either God dies (and we continue in our old illusions of God), or we die (to the old False Self). In dying we leave behind the methodology of discipleship and are simply journeying with Christ (or inviting Christ on our journeys!). Old ways of praying can be tedious; we long for communion, not just talking to God. The journey becomes an interior one, as Teresa put it, "Soul, you must seek yourself in Me and in yourself seek Me."

Chapter six, **"Desired in Christ"** recaptures the ancient characterization of the desire for spiritual union with God as an intense romance. Christ desires us-to have a relationship with us and will be not be denied any part of us-so much so that it may be unnerving when we begin to discover how much! This union of soul and Spirit is envisioned in chapter seven, **"Destiny in Christ."** Drawing from the historical Christian notion of becoming one with God, this chapter focuses on our destiny in Christ: often referred to as glorification, union with Christ, or being "in Christ."

* * *

Imagine a bicycle—a fine vehicle for journeying—as a symbol of the model. The front wheel is the Discipleship Cycle. That is the wheel we steer, using our intellectual powers to guide us. Discipleship is like that; we want to be in control. The rear wheel of this paradigmatic bike is the Contemplative Cycle. It is where the power is—the wheel we pedal using our largest muscle groups, our most natural power. What holds the two cycles together is the cross frame, the part we sit on. Imagine the frame as Disillusionment, learning to trust. We trust the frame to hold us. It is the most passive aspect of riding a bike.

* * *

Classically the spiritual journey has been depicted as moving through definable stages, steps or progressions. Teresa of Avila's Interior Castle images the journey inward, into the soul. Others have likewise described the journey into the self until one encounters another Self. John of the Cross, in *Ascent of Mount Carmel*, portrays the journey as a climb. John Bunyan's *Pilgrim's Progress* allegorizes the journey as moving forward in faith and virtue. The journey is all at once a journey inward, a journey upward, and a journey forward. According to the creative genius of the respective guide, the journey deepens to the mother lode of precious faith, matures the delicious fruit of the Spirit, scales the heights, traverses sea and desert, and stretches out to the horizon.

Generally these models allow for a conception of spirituality that is both linear and process-oriented. By linear I mean a straightforward way of thinking that moves from one point to another and then to another. Linear thinking takes us from beginning to end; from cause to effect. Process-oriented thinking does not rely so much on movement from point to point, but rather sees unfolding processes or developments. I like to think of the distinction between the two as the difference between running a race and dancing.

Stage paradigms, as illuminating as they may be, are bound to break down. After all, what bike doesn't get a flat occasionally (unless you never ride it)? Take the well-known stages of grief by Elizabeth Kübler-Ross as an example. Anyone who has worked with grieving persons has come to appreciate Kübler-Ross' insights as well as the limitations of her stages: shock, denial, bargaining, and so on. Not everyone goes through the stages in predicable fashion, however. Sometimes it seems a stage is missed, or repeated. The value of such a model is to help us see that grief is a process, not an event, and to honor the unique way each person grieves.

One critique of many spiritual growth paradigms is that they, like the stages of grief, cannot capture the creative and individualistic movements of the soul. I agree, but I wonder how many of us would perceive the uniqueness and individuality of our journey without the form of some paradigm? Universal models, although "one size fits all," help us discover our individuality.

Certainly John of the Cross recognized this essential fact. John describes the ascent of Mount Carmel as "Nada, nada, nada . . . (nothing, nothing, nothing) and even on the Mount nada . . . Hereon out, there is no road because for the just man there is no law." John certainly captures the essence of the unfolding journey of a person with Christ. Having no road does not mean there is no journey; having no road means there is no *definable path* for the journey. Anyone who embarks on the journey will eventually discover this fact. There comes a point of departure from the known to the unknown, from the defined to the indefinable; from the beaten path to the way only you will go. There is always more. If it were not for the paved road of spirituality I was taught as a child, I might not perceive that there is more when I come to the end of the pavement. This book is my attempt to describe that "more" even as I realize that my description cannot do justice to the journey, the "nada" of each person's path.

DISCIPLESHIP:
A FAMILIAR CYCLE

1

DISTRACTED BY CHRIST

Dark subliminal shapes rise from the misty night as the evening relinquishes its first vestiges of deep mystery. The traveler peers into the night fearfully searching the formless images. Cuddled into a nest of boulders, he quietly breathes, waiting for daybreak. Vespered hours wear on cryptically. The traveler nurses his hopes that the dawn will bring answers. "Where am I?" he yawns.

The brilliant light startles him. Awakening from perilous sleep, the traveler shakes at the sight of towering evergreens. Ghosts of his long vigil, they worship the sky with scents of dew-laden gems. A laughter comes from the remaining shadows, mocking the torments of the nocturnal demons. Into this world he is born to search and wander.

MSJ

If I say, "Surely the darkness will hide me and
the light become night around me," even the darkness will not be dark to you; the night will shine
like the day, for darkness is as light to you. Psalm
139:11-12.

* * *

We've heard the words before, but not the message.
This time, we hear. Our attention may be captured in
many different ways. A scary crisis awakens us to the
unpredictability of life. More subtly, an unsettling rest-
lessness may creep up during the best of times. It is
uncanny.

The visit of distraction could just as well be an
unexpected encouragement during depression, or a
boredom that sets in just when we're starting to reach
our goals. An inexplicable resentment rises from the still
waters of contentment, or a breathtaking vista appears
over the horizon on the road to nowhere. The wind
changes. The mid-day sun darkens. A shooting star
flashes in the corner of our eye. Whatever it is, it gives us
pause. A godly pause.

Distraction is about focus. Many Christians struggle
to keep their focus on Christ. They lament their inability
to stay with the program of their prayers and devotions.
They know what it is like to be focused and long for the
inspiration and creativity they have experienced on
occasion. Service came naturally, prayer was warm and
meaningful, and the way was clear. They had the courage of Bunyan's valiant warrior in *Pilgrim's Progress* to
storm the gates of God's palace, defying all the worldly
obstacles and demonic enemies who would prevent
their entrance into salvation. Now, they have lost the
time, the energy, the concentration, the direction, the
courage. How to get back on track?

C.S. Lewis describes how the novice deals with
distraction in prayer by seeking to "thrust it away by
sheer willpower and . . . continue the normal prayer as

if nothing had happened." By accepting the distraction as our present problem and making it the main theme of our prayers and endeavors, says Lewis, we will move closer to God.[1]

Jesus modeled this distractibility by responding to an anonymous sickly woman who distracted him by touching his robe on a crowded street. On another occasion, he allowed children to come to him and presented them to his hearers as object lessons in faith. To enter the kingdom of heaven, he emphasized, we must come as one of the little ones. Could he have been saying that we should be as distractible as children, or as distractible as himself?

Distraction originates from outside us but resonates within. Christ stands at the door of our heart and beacons us to let God into our lives. The response comes from within. We need Christ's distraction to discover our purpose.

The challenge of distraction is to let go of our compulsions of holding onto Christ and instead allow Christ to lead us into a new awareness of God. Trust that God knows how to get your attention! For Abraham it was a starlit night when God revealed to him that his descendents would be as numerous as the stars in the sky. For young Samuel, it was a call in the night from God with a message for the nation to repent. For Elijah it was a gentle whisper reminding him that God's power was not just in the sensational. For John the Baptizer it was the Spirit as a descending dove revealing Jesus as the Christ. What is it for you?

* * *

"I thought so," said Worldly Wiseman to Christian in *Pilgrim's Progress*, "and it is happened unto thee as to other weak men, who, meddling with things too high for them, do suddenly fall into thy distractions . . ."[2]

Merry-go-round Christianity teaches us that if we con-
centrate hard enough and strain far enough, we may
grab the brass ring. If we miss it, it is because we lost our
focus. The gospel, on the other hand, is about God
appearing in the midst of life, captivating our attention.
It is not that we are normally so focused on Christ and
then are distracted by life in an unguarded moment. It is
more likely that we are so very much tuned in to the
issues of life that Christ is the one who is distracting.

There are basically two ways of thinking about the
locus of God which result in two different ways of
approaching God. One concept is the aloof God who is
barely heard. God's voice competes with all the other
sounds of life. God is like a faint star that can only be
seen on a clear moonless night when we drive away
from the city lights, and then only with a powerful
telescope. We must work and sacrifice to move toward
this faint God. This is the common God.

Another way of thinking is that God is immanent.
God is so powerfully present that any awareness of God
can overwhelm us. God pursues us and moves toward
us in all of life, like Francis Thompson's "Hound of
Heaven." God is willing to pay any price and make any
sacrifice to get our attention. God is a blazing sun that
illumines our world and energizes all that moves. God
is a mystery that pervades everything.

Our lack of awareness of God is not from God's
faintness but perhaps from our having become ever
defensive against God's overwhelming presence. The
ancient Hebrews called this the *shekhinah* of God, and
they believed that anyone who looked on the face of
God would die. Truly, such an awareness of God is
tantamount to a death, for it changes us so radically.

Prayer, conversely, may also be seen as an attempt
to reach the distant God, much like using a radio telescope to contact distant life forms in the universe. If we
dare believe in the immanence of God, however, we

may see prayer as cracking open the door of our soul to take a peek at the brilliance that surrounds us. This is the God of Abraham, Moses, Elijah and Jesus. This is the God of good news.

For Teresa, God is so close at hand that we only need to look inside to see the beauty of God.

> . . . we consider our soul to be like a castle made entirely out of a diamond or of very clear crystal, in which there are many rooms, just as in heaven there are many dwelling places. For in reflecting upon it carefully . . . we realize that the soul of the just person is nothing else but a paradise where the Lord says He finds His delight . . . it [is] almost impossible for us to understand the sublime dignity and beauty of the soul.[3]

Distraction is a vitally important place in the spiritual journey—one we serendipitously come back to again and again—because it is where we learn to let God take the initiative.

Navigating the Distraction

Distraction is a paradox. The value of distraction as a place on the journey of Christ is its ability to help us break out of our ruts and pick up the trail of God's new direction. These distractions are what James Hillman, in *The Soul's Code,* refers to as "trivial gusts that take you off course and seem to be delaying your projected arrival in the teleological harbor." Don't point your compass "too fixedly on the far horizon," he warns. These accidental gusts have purpose, which can be seen only by the purposive eye. Life is about learning to make the little corrections in our course as a consequence of these gusts—adjustments that shape the form of our soul.[4]

Making these course adjustments is one of the arts of the spiritual life. We set our course, then alter it; set it, then alter it—always with an eye on the horizon where our home port lies. This is the Discipleship Cycle: altering course and setting the sail. The process is ongoing. In the next two chapters I will elaborate more on the cycle of distraction-dazzlement-discipleship. Suffice it to say for now that we recapitulate to distraction from discipleship when we enter again into a new period of growth and discovery.

What Kind of Distraction is That?

There is true distraction and false distraction. True distraction is the call of God, to God. False distraction binds us from being aware of God.

In Jesus' Parable of the Two Sons, a man's youngest son asks for his inheritance and goes to a far country, parties hearty with his wealth, and squanders it. Broke and starving at his pig farm job, the son comes to himself and leaves for home with a plan to be his father's servant. Upon his arrival he is welcomed home as a son in a great celebration, except by his older brother who opts out of the party in pouty jealousy.

There is a big difference between the two parties in the parable. The son's party was thrown for his fair-weather friends in a binge of extravagance. The father's party, though very extravagant, was one of grace and love, thrown for his son "who was dead and now is alive."

True distraction leads to true celebration—dazzlement—where there is more openness to God. False distraction leads to increasing obfuscation.

In discerning the difference between true and false distraction it is often helpful to consider the nature of our vision, piety, and friendship. Is the distraction enlightening or obscuring? Does it produce an affection for God or a devotion to religious teachings about God? Our companions, are they sojourners or detractors?

Vision

Distraction is about viewing life in a new light. That light shines from God and can overcome any depth of darkness. Many biblical examples depict the onset of physical blindness at a time of potential distraction by God, as if the physical blindness symbolized a spiritual darkness.

Lostness. Spiritual blindness comes in various forms. There a blindness of the soul that is so pervasive that a person is completely devoid of God's light. It is a veil that covers the heart. In Teresa's words,

> No night can be so dark, no gloom nor blackness can compare to its obscurity. Suffice it to say that the sun in the center of the soul, which gave it such splendor and beauty, is totally eclipsed . . .[5]

The dark soul not only lacks the light of God but also may try to prevent others from being illuminated as well. It becomes a case of the blind leading the blind and both falling into the ditch.

I observed a similar dynamic with a couple who were seeking treatment for the wife's fainting spells. Each time the wife began to describe how she would faint on an occasion, the husband would interrupt with some empty reassurance, such as, "It's probably nothing." No medical reason for the fainting could be found, and the husband's unwillingness to look at it seriously was keeping the couple from discovering the meaning of the spells at a deeper level.

Preoccupation. Teresa describes another kind of blindness, the "semi-darkness" of one at the entrance of the Interior Castle, like that of a person coming into a brightly-lit room with "eyes clogged and half closed with dust." "These fierce and wild beasts," which she describes as fears preventing us from our journey, "blind the eyes of the beginner, so that he sees nothing but them." This soul is yet "worldly and preoccupied with earthly riches, honor and affairs."[6]

"Today, as in Teresa's time," writes Rosemary Broughton in *Praying with Teresa of Avila*, "external affairs and realities can very easily lure us into ignoring our own soul." She continues: "Even when we acknowledge the fact (or the possibility) that we may possess a soul, we rarely think of entering into it, or we candidly admit that we do not know quite how to do this."[7]

Teresa is here describing distraction in the classic sense, allowing ourselves to be preoccupied with concerns and interests to the extent that we neglect our souls. It is as if we have so many issues cluttering our foreground vision that we can't see the more salient issues in the background.

Pride. Paul warns against being "wise in your own conceits." The prideful soul sees only the light of its own reflection. The distraction of God becomes refracted to the extent that it takes on the image of the self. What we think of as godly is little more than our own self-conceit. While in spiritual maturity, the self is sanctified to the point that "to live is Christ," the prideful soul will come to this conclusion when there has really come no such union.

The prophet Isaiah gives a graphic portrayal of how the prideful soul worships its own reflection and the works of its own hands. A carpenter cuts down a tree. Half the wood is used for firewood with which he cooks his meal and warms himself. By the firelight, warmed and filled, he whittles the remaining stock into an idol and worships it. "A deluded heart misleads him," Isaiah warns, "he cannot save himself, nor say, 'Is not this thing in my right hand a lie?'" (Is. 44:20). Prideful false distraction leads ultimately to worshiping the created rather than the Creator.

Of course, the "deluded heart" does not know it is deluded. The idolater thinks of himself or herself as deeply spiritual. John of the Cross describes this delusion as the "habit of pride."

These beginners feel so fervent and diligent in their spiritual exercises and undertakings that a certain kind of secret pride is generated in them that begets a complacency with themselves and their accomplishments …they develop a somewhat vain—at times very vain—desire to speak of spiritual things in others' presence, and sometimes even to instruct rather than be instructed.[8]

When I first began to focus in earnest on learning the art of meditation, I would often find myself feeling so good at it! Of course, my self compliments were merely distractions from the real point of it all: to meditate. Ironically, blindness can be a beginning of spiritual enlightenment. The first step toward light begins with an awareness of darkness. Christ distracts us from our darkness by illuminating our lives with flashes of grace.

Piety

Piety is defined as "devotion to religion."[9] False distraction leads to a devotion to religion rather than a devotion to Christ. It is a compulsive satisfaction in the means of the distraction rather than the Distracter, like being more fascinated by a person's house than the person and what their home reveals of them.

Pietistic false distraction may take the form of pleasure or guilt. John of the Cross warns against the "vice of lust," such as the emphasis on "the pleasure human nature finds in spiritual exercises."[10] We may discover a joy or ecstasy that comes with experiences of deep prayer, praise, worship and even certain acts of service. The temptation is to focus on the pleasure of this joy rather than on the relationship with Christ that produces it.

There is a distinction here between the self compliments I just described and finding "pleasure" in prayer.

There is certainly nothing wrong with enjoying prayer and worship. I've had some great times in prayer. In fact, I've had some downright intoxicating prayer experiences. The wisdom that John voices is to not focus so much on the emotional by-products of prayer as on the process of prayer itself.

A true piety is the development of good disciplines of prayer which create time and space for God to distract us further.

Friendship

John and Teresa both note the importance of spiritual friendships and point to the hazard of maintaining friendships based on "lust rather than from the spirit."[11] For John, the test of a spiritual friendship is that it increases one's remembrance and desire for God. A friendship resulting in a colder heart toward God and remorse for this coldness has come from false distraction. Teresa encouraged her readers to seek out friendships with those who have traveled further on the journey and will "aid her greatly and draw her to join them."[12]

Many of my most significant divine distractions have come through others. A phone call, a certain phrase, some mysterious timing. It is in this way that we incarnate the presence of God to one another.

Learning to be Distracted

This locality on the journey of Christ is a distraction zone. It is a passage of detours and delightful excursions. Those who claim to have mapped out their journey with Christ in advance had better check their compass. Life is full of wide, clearly-marked roads that lead to self-absorption and self-deceit. The soul's path is on no map. Uncharted, unclaimed and unnamed, it is nonexistent—until you embark upon it. It is your road with your name on the sign.

Distractions are the comets of the night sky. The expert astronomers know the orbits of the planets and the coordinates of the constellations. With legions of huge telescopes they study the heavens nightly. But, every now and again comes a new comet. Some have been discovered by amateur stargazers with mere binoculars. Coming out of nowhere, they evoke our awe and fear.

You don't have to be a rocket scientist or theologian to be encountered by God. In the spiritual universe of the soul, the star maps are drawn by the surveyors of religion, but the most exciting discoveries are made by the explorers of experience. One knows the book of God; the other knows God. One knows the laws of God; the other, the love of God. One knows how things should be; the other wonders how things could be.

Distraction is an intersection of colliding views of God and life. At this crossroad staid predictability gets sideswiped by mystery.

Distraction is invitation. Think back to the precursors of the significant events in your life. Were they planned or discovered? Your first encounter with the person you married. A big break in your career. A turn in your health. First encounters with persons who now are good friends.

Some of the greatest, most inspiring stories I've ever heard are about how things turned out differently than planned. Jesus told one of those stories:

> A certain man was preparing a great banquet and invited many guests. At the time of the banquet he sent his servant to tell those who had been invited, "Come, for everything is now ready."
>
> But they all alike began to make excuses. The first said, "I have just bought a field, and I must go and see it. Please excuse me."

Another said, "I have just bought five yoke of oxen, and I'm on my way to try them out. Please excuse me."

Still another said, "I just got married, so I can't come."

The servant came back and reported this to his master. Then the owner of the house became angry and ordered his servant, "Go out quickly into the streets and alleys of the town and bring in the poor, the crippled, the blind and the lame."

"Sir," the servant said, "what you ordered has been done, but there is still room."

Then the master told his servant, "Go out to the roads and country lanes and make them come in, so that my house will be full. I tell you, not one of those men who were invited will get a taste of my banquet." (Luke 14:16-24)

This parable is steeped in first-century tradition about the Messianic Banquet. After the Messiah sets all things right, the people of God will enjoy eternal fellowship at the Lord's table. Quite a party. All Jews worth their salt longed for the day.

Jesus gives his story a twist. When the servant comes around to yell out, "Come and get it," the invited beg off. What a weird way to respond!

According to invitation customs, the guests had already been invited. The servant is only announcing that the time has come. To decline at this juncture is a faux pas of enormity. You don't just say no at a time like this. What the busy-ness of the guests reveals about their relationship with the host is plain to see. It is thumbing-the-nose time.

A tradition exists about what this story means. It is clear. God invites. People refuse. God gets mad. Moral: don't make God mad. That's the colloquial Christian culture of distraction. Don't do it. It's bad to be distracted. It makes God mad when we get distracted. Stay focused and God will love you and you'll get to go to the party.

Matthew's version of this story is even more harsh: the inconsiderate wretches are condemned. They are also depicted as murderers. Throw the wicked, inconsiderate, distracted, murdering wretches into hell (Matt. 22). That'll teach them to let their minds wander!

Whoa! Jesus has another scenario. God is already throwing the party and along comes an invitation. Wanna come? It'll be fun! Sometimes we're just too engrossed in our stuff to hear the invitation. But, God is a distracting God. God knows how to get our attention, Teresa says:

> For often when a person is distracted and forgetful of God, His Majesty will awaken it. His action is as quick as a falling comet. And as clearly as it hears a thunderclap, even though no sound is heard, the soul understands that it was called by God.[13]

Hear that? It is the sound of music and laughter. You can just barely hear it above the racket of street noise. Among the clatter of banging and hammering rises the sound of . . . a tambourine. Who is singing? You go back to your work. Yet, again you raise your head and listen to the appealing sounds. Go, check it out! It's a party!

I must admit that I identify with the three distracted guys in Jesus' story. It isn't like they were doing evil. They were intent on the stuff of life: land, oxen, and spouse. I feel very creative when it comes to putting God off. I convince myself that I have more important matters to attend.

As Pascal put it, the root of all evil is our inability to sit still. We create objects of our desire and become attached to them and the illusions we create about them. Pascal's theory of distraction, or *divertissement*, is that we are doomed to *activity* itself. According to Thomas Merton, we use distractions to numb our spirits because of our incapacity for contemplation, which is our highest activity. "Only Christ . . . could save time from being an endless circle of frustrations," from the "vanities" of "ceaseless and sterile activity." It is Christ who distracts us from the vanity of our preoccupations.[14]

When taken in the light of first-century Palestinian life, the three "excuses" were really vocations, or callings. The *field* represents the vocation of finding and making our place in the world. The *oxen* portray the vocation of subsistence and livelihood: career, vocation, budgets, and food. The *spouse* represents the vocation of relationships, of family and covenant. Any person not focused on these things would have been considered irresponsible.

Land, beasts and spouse: each calling to a level of involvement, interaction and interrelationship. A farmer works the land, plowing and digging; planting and harvesting. Driving a team of oxen with hands to the reins—prodding, feeding, watering, bedding and healing—required being up-close and personal. A wife was more than a romantic partner. She would be a companion and fellow laborer, sharing interdependently in the enterprise of life.

The irony of distraction is that we feel Christ is calling us away from our *callings:* our vocations of place, livelihood and relationship. We can't possibly go to a party when there is so much to take care of, so much duty to uphold. The playful cajolery of Christ sounds more like a temptation or a seduction.

Christ is not calling us from our place in the world, our livelihood and relationships, but from seeing these as who we are and finding our highest pleasure and purpose in them. We make it an either/or proposition. Either I follow Christ or my vocation. Christ calls to a both/and. When Christ is at the center of our vocations, he transforms them.

Distraction is counter-intuitive. We may feel that distractions are what take us away from our focus on God. There is a bit of grandiosity in this: that we feel we are so centered in God. Our sense of security in our own ability to maintain our focus on God may be a pride that leads to a fall. In truth, God comes to us out of the dark—out of the blue—and we may not be open to the distraction, to what God is saying to us because it is so counter to what we think or believe.

The invited guests could not see past their vocations to the banquet of the Messiah. A story like this told in the home of a well-known Pharisee had obvious connotations. Pharisees were the most pious of religious people. Nothing keeps us from fellowship with God like a good hearty religion. Religion is about destination; Christianity is a journey.

Christ calls us to let go of our compulsions—our ways of holding onto God and godliness—and to let God hold onto us. The master in the banquet parable told his servant to compel people to come to the party, "make them come in." This compelling refers to the ancient custom of taking invited guests by the arm and bringing them into the house, even pulling them in. "Yes, yes, come in! Sure, but it can wait. You must come in—just for awhile, okay?"

Bunyan depicts this drawing invitation in *Pilgrim's Progress* as Christian's arrival at the true beginning point of his journey: the Wicket Gate. At that point, the gatekeeper, Goodwill, pulled him forcibly through lest he become a target for the devil's arrows at this crucial threshold.

What a picture of grace! God's invitation has a compelling force; we are drawn into God's house.

There is a progression to Jesus' parable. First and initially, the Israelites of standing were invited. Before telling the story, Jesus had observed how his fellow guests were concerned about sitting in the seats of status. No doubt, Jesus' depiction of the invited guests in the parable had a double meaning for those sitting with him at the table. Paradoxically, in the story it was the guests of status who refused to come to the party.

Secondly, when the invited guests reneged on their RSVP, the host invited the marginalized Israelites—those with handicaps—who were religiously ostracized by the Pharisees. Religion demands perfection and condemns shortcomings. Levitical law allowed no place in the Temple for the physically and mentally imperfect. Christ calls us to accommodation. This was a radical move in the culture of the day (a move we're just beginning to make in our day).

Thirdly, and most iconoclastically, the travelers were compelled into the party house. This group may have included the most unworthy sort by Pharisaic standards: the Gentiles. People of different race and language at God's party? Unspeakable! Can't you hear the fabric of society tearing?

As previously uninvited guests on their way to somewhere else, the last two groups were required to make the greatest adjustment in response to the invitation. Unlike those who had time to prepare, these downcast and outcasts had to respond on the spur of the moment. Their capacity for distraction was greater. It is yet another way Christ turned the world upside down. The first shall be last and the last shall be first. The focused are shut out and the distractible are pulled in.

The spiritual journey begins with our making space for God, not at our initiative, but at God's. God throws quite a party, if you're willing to be distracted. Distraction is not only a virtue of the spiritual life, it is an indispensable quality.

The distracting Spirit is like the wind rustling in the trees. Leaves are very distractible. If we are distractible, we will be easily moved by the Spirit of God.

Vocations of Distraction

The three vocations of place, livelihood and relationships referred to in the above parable can be seen as a paradigm for distraction. In looking at the developmental aspects of these vocations, we see the signs and seasons of moving into adulthood. Through the distracting call of Christ our vocations are transformed from self-oriented compulsions to avenues of discovering our significance in God's universe.

Making Our Place in the World

First there is the field: the vocation of making our place in the world. How we make our place in the world measures our relationship to God. I imagine a young man receiving his share of the family farm, a woman being endowed with family heirlooms, or a man expanding his business.

I remember the feeling of purchasing my first home. As a thirty-year-old doctoral candidate, I took a pastorate in a traditional, urban neighborhood of my hometown. I felt a profound settledness. It was my place, not a landlord's house, nor my parents' home. The age of Jesus at the outset of his ministry, I was carving out my own niche in the world. Would the Son of Man, who had "no place to lay his head," call me away from such a place? Five years later, I discerned that God was calling me to leave. Not only did I leave this place, but I gave up having a place of my own while I finished an internship in counseling. The crisis of adjustment for my family was stressful. I now have a deeper appreciation for the difficulty the invited guest had in leaving a field to go to God's party.

We must make our place in the world. We will do it either in a manner that enhances our lives spiritually or in a way that detracts from our true humanness. Place-making requires the elements of time, depth and creativity. Time enough to establish oneself. Depth enough to put our roots down to the water tables of community. Creativity enough to fashion our place as an expression of our truest nature.

I've met persons who seem to have never fully landed. They are caught up in dream-chasing to the extent that they carry through with few of their creative notions. The stories of their lives are disjointed series of half-written fairy tales without the depth of meaning found in a cohesive narrative. This is distraction in its negative, shadow sense.

As in many spiritual realities, truth exists between the extremes. At the other extremity of distracted place-making are root-bound individuals. They are so tied to the earth of their place that they can no longer make it their own. Their place is defined by mothers and fathers, mother-figures and father-figures, in such a way that it stifles their own self-definition. The chief symptom of their stagnation is a persistent, simmering anger. Sometimes masked in depression, the bitterness can be heard in the cynical powerlessness of their language and self-assessments. Otherwise, it spells out a choking moralism and judgmental disposition toward others, especially toward the free-spirited. Their story is the story of their clan: canonical, sacred, unquestioned, hiding shameful wounds behind secrets and secret sin. Like the age-old incantations of a ritual, the spell-binding story defines the person and his or her place in life.

Our life's story is the account of our finding our place in the world. Jesus told the story of a person who found a treasure hidden in a field, reburied it and gladly went and bought the field. This kingdom parable is a picture of distraction. Do we find the kingdom or does it find us? Did the man become a treasure hunter or a treasure finder? Did he compulsively go digging in fields the rest of his life or did he settle down on his treasured field? The treasure is not the field of our lives, but what we find in the field. Our place in this world is the gift found in distraction. The serendipity of the find became the story of the man's life—The Man Who Found the Treasure in the Field. Likewise, our story reflects our basic disposition toward our place in life: hunting or finding.

While hiking in the Texas hill country, I was discussing with my wife Thomas Moore's book, *The Enchantment of Everyday Life*. Moore refers to the ancient religious practices of discerning the spirits of a place before deciding to build. Just then, Marlena pointed to a large flat rock under our feet on the trail. The rock's natural indentations formed the clear picture of a face—to us a scowling face. "Looks like we just met one of the spirits of this place," I remarked as I took a photo. The developed picture sits on my desktop, but now the rock's face is more inviting and happy. Perhaps the rock was reflecting *my* spirit at the time.

One's story can either reveal or conceal. I grew up in a religion that valued stories. It was important to be able to "give a testimony" of God's work in our lives, past or present. In the formality of this storytelling, I heard the self-descriptions of my fellow congregants. Some testimonies were full of stock phrases and cliché meanings, finished and polished in neat packaging, designed to impress and uphold carefully-crafted self images. They either whitewashed the obvious or hurtfully broadcast secrets in a public confessional. Other testimonies had a richness and individuality—works in progress—bearing the signature of grace. These stories rang true with an authentic tone, giving greater light into the soul of the storyteller.

Our story portrays our place in the world and our aspirations for enriching our place. A good story enlightens both teller and hearer to the sense of journey. The story of a life-enhancing place carries both the thread of meaning spun from the wheel of generations and the recipes of healing potions distilled from the laboratory of life's experiments. It offers a bookbinding for the journey's saga of mountains and valleys, conflicts and covenants. It is a display case for artifacts of legends and a drawing board for blurry blueprints of visions. Standing in such a place is like attending a celebration.

For Israel, the place of greatest distractibility was the Exodus, a life-defining journey from slavery to promise. This story embodies the soul of the nation and many stories were spun from this central legend: stories of mighty kings and captivities, victory chants and lamentations.Israel's greatest figures were sojourners. Abraham, a "stranger in a strange land." Sarah, the mother of a nation. Moses, the leader of the migration, and his mother who courageously cast him afloat in the Nile to be found by Pharaoh's daughter. Elijah, the prophet who discovered God in the stillness of Horeb. Daniel, who in Babylonia discovered that God's power and presence is not limited to a certain land. Though focused on the land, Israel's soul was not in the land, but in the journey of God with the people who traversed the land. The Scriptures record the epic of God's recurrent distraction of the nation from their land to the journey— and the many heroes who caught sight of the vision.

The outset of the journey of Christ could be described as a call to begin forming the story of one's relationship with God. As our story forms, so our place in the world takes shape.

Making a Living

The second excuse mentioned in the story of the banquet is the team of oxen: the vocation of making a living. No casual acquisition, a team of oxen was a pair of matched beasts of burden with such power a man could move mountains in behalf of the family's subsistence. The ancient culture was heavy on a man to make a living. "But if any provide not for his own, and specially for those of his own house, he hath denied the faith, and is worse than an infidel" (I Tim. 5:8 KJV).

It is precisely this crisis of livelihood that confronts us at midlife. In light of the passing of time, we begin to question the meaning of our work. Does it fit us well? Are we stressed out over it, and why? Some people decide to retool with education and embark on a new career. Others find ways to redefine their work, integrating their growing self-definition into what they do for a living. Work becomes more interwoven with the fabric of life in an enriching way.

A juncture for better or worse, midlife can also be a season of disintegration when the meaning of life, much less work, escapes us. I have met many on the journey who have not transcended this crisis. Self-destructive behavior often results—at work or home—as if their call to distraction is more like the seducing sounds of the mythological Sirens who lured ancient sailors into ruin. It is imperative to discern the call of Christ from the compulsions of myth.

Myths are stories and symbols that carry the meanings and values of culture. Often we are not conscious of these myths that influence us so profoundly. Every family has myths that are passed from generation to generation but are stories never told. It is as if these untold stories create a compulsion that we are powerless over and doomed to act out. The role of the son or daughter, the drive to succeed or fail, the meaning of pregnancy, abuse, addiction: all can be the subject of mythic compulsions.

In Homer's *Odyssey*, the songs of the voluptuous Sirens enticed sailors to their treacherous shores. Odysseus ordered his crewmen to plug their ears and lash him to the mast so they could resist these ruinous enchantments. But these Siren compulsions could be

transcended. The music of Orpheus aboard ship with
Jason and the Argonauts was more enchanting than
even that of the Sirens. In response, the Sirens cast
themselves into the rocky waters.

This myth portrays something of the nature of myth
itself—and the power of distraction. We, like Odysseus,
in seeking freedom from the forces that bind us, are
bound to re-enact over and again the drama of our
mythic compulsions. But Christ, like Orpheus, sounds a
tune that is eternally more spellbinding and enrapturing. In hearkening to the call of Christ, and being subdued by it, we are freed from our compulsions and the
myths that produce them.

We will hear a call in midlife surrounding vocation.
Will it be the distracting call of God urging us to health
and faith or the destructive call of social myth?

Shadowy myth produces compulsions of extremes.
We are either adrift in isolation or moored at the harbor
of culture. We are either lost to ourselves or self-absorbed. We are either bound in powerlessness or deluded into thinking we are society's sovereign. The
vocational call of Christ frees us from these extremes.
Three distinctive qualities of Christ's calling are community orientation, the enhancement of identity, and
the clarification of authority.

Christ calls to community. Distraction becomes destruction when divorced from the matrix of community,
as the story of Samson and Delilah illustrates. Samson
knew he had a power, but he lacked the gifts to discover
its purpose. His culture applauded his violent pursuits
and even credited his behavior to the Spirit of God. He
lacked a community that could provide an interpretive
culture within which he could discern the true meaning
of his gifts. The culture of the Judges-era Israel is documented in the refrain, "In those days Israel had no king;
everyone did as he saw fit." Without an interpretive,
integrating culture, Samson's life was like a mighty

sailboat with no rudder, acting on pure instinct. He identified the source of his power as on top of his head, rather than in his heart. With his head shaved, he was blinded. When vocation comes solely from others, it can be taken away by others.

The medieval guilds are a picture of how vocation, identity and community are naturally linked. Many names derived from these guilds, such as Smith, Cooper, and Carpenter, give evidence of how identity is garnered from vocation and community. In contrast, the mythic compulsion of self-employment holds that we choose our own vocation as solely an expression of individualism. A key to striking a balance between the rule of culture and the freedom of the soul is identity. We must discover who we are, and that discovery can take place only in the context of relationships and shared history.

Christ calls to identity. Samson lived his life as a man whose purpose was imposed upon him by parents and society rather than discovered from within. His life was that of the terrorist: carrying out the political agenda of a nation under the dictates of a foreign power.

Rather than being a man of great strength, Samson was a strong man. His strength was his identity rather than his identity being his strength. He had split off his *being* from his *doing*. The mythic compulsion of dissociation tempts us to define ourselves by our doing, to separate our living from livelihood.

In the modern American psyche, self-esteem and livelihood go hand-in-hand. The term vocation (from the Latin *vocare*, "to call") captures this mythic compulsion. We use it to describe the way we make a living: carpenter, computer programmer, or sales representative. We think of ourselves most easily in terms of what we do for a living. We are what we do.

As Jesus called Peter the fisherman to be a "fisher of men," so Christ invites us to transcend our livelihood but not deny it. Many New Testament writers found their highest calling in being a "bond slave of Jesus Christ." By seeing themselves as servants of Christ, they maintained a perspective on work that allows for deep spiritual meaning. Paul made tents at night so he could do ministry during the day. The body, for Paul, was a "tent" and his mission was to weave for others a heavenly tent by sharing the gospel of Jesus Christ. The two were not separate—work and identity—but linked. Our work does not define us, but reflects our self-definition. Identity is based on relationship with Christ. Yet, meaningful work expresses our personal mission—to give glory to God—as stated in the Rule of St. Benedict.

Christ calls to authority. From the rock of identity flows the spring of authority. Authority is the power to make a difference, to express our gifts and claim our place in the world. Livelihood and authority are bound up together.

Authority is recognizing our limits as well as our powers. Culture, at its best, provides a structure of authority that enhances creativity and freedom. Without the circumference of authority, we are left to our natural inclination to be sovereigns in our own realms— the mythic compulsion of power. Power struggles are a major symptom of this mythic compulsion. Distraction is opening ourselves to a transcendent power that transforms our self-sovereignty into servanthood.

Samson had power but no authority. He could kill people but not govern them. He sought revenge, not justice. He sought love and received manipulation. He tore down magnificent buildings but left no abiding structures to carry on his mission.

Our vocation of livelihood is a channel for our creative, nurturing, and self-defining gifts. Christ distracts us from the mundane tedium of the work-a-day world to a sense of giftedness; we *possess* gifts and we *are* gifts. From our sense of giftedness we can offer ourselves to others as companions of the journey in a community that creates a shared history.

Making and Maintaining Relationships

Marriage was the third excuse offered by the invited guests in Jesus' story: the vocation of making and maintaining relationships. Relationships require a dynamic balance of inclusion and exclusion, of saying Yes and No. Here the man welshes on one social commitment for the sake of another, choosing to be with his newly-wed wife rather than attend the banquet of a friend. His fault lies not in maintaining a healthy boundary around his relationship with his family but in seeing the banquet as violating that boundary.

Some of Jesus' harshest teachings reflected this difficult distinction. As if to hammer home this element of the Messianic Banquet story, Luke follows it with one of Jesus' most pointed statements, "If anyone comes to me and does not hate his father and mother, his wife and children, his brothers and sisters—yes, even his own life—he cannot be my disciple" (Luke 14:6). Rather than a discounting the importance of family, Jesus was emphasizing the spiritual foundation of all relationships.

As a marriage and family therapist, I echo the current emphasis on strengthening family life in our society. For years, the indicators of divorce rate and the number of children growing up in "broken" homes has indicted the American family. Did Jesus downplay this emphasis on strengthening the family?

As with the other vocations of distraction, Jesus did not come to destroy but fulfill. Christ does not exclude good family life; He saves it. Christ distracts us from our focus on our family to the deeper meaning of relating.

Our most profound sense of identity comes from family. Our DNA—characteristics of appearance, personality and temperament—derive from our parents. Just as significant, if not more so, the formative atmo-

sphere of our childhood family life also plays a important role in influencing our styles of relating. Studies
show that we replicate our family-of-origin relational
patterns, not only in our families-of-creation but in the
workplace. How can we deny our family?

One of the marks of solid adult development is
making the transition from family-of-origin to family-
of-creation. The old rules and norms of our childhood
family are evaluated and new rules are written, for
better or worse. As a counselor in proximity to a nursing
school, I hear this clash of rules often in the stories of my
female nurse clients seeking a professional identity in a
male-dominated medical world. Trying to juggle their
self-expectations of being a good professional, good
mother, good wife—and unconsciously, a good daughter—they are overwhelmed. The inner voice of parents
says to stay home and raise the kids and make a home
for their husband. Yet, their aspirations for a career cuts
short their time. The callings feel mutually exclusive as
if success in career means failure at home, not because
they are indeed failing but because they cannot measure
up to all these lofty ideals. A sense of alienation from
God and feelings of anger toward God soon ensues,
unless these women find more self-affirming feminine
images of career and calling.

As I listen to the stories of my depressed counselees,
I can hear the haunting voice of my own guilt. I am an
empathic listener in the counseling office. Am I this
good a listener to my family? How can I justify the long
hours at work when I should be spending more time at
home? Do I use work as a way of avoiding family life?

The Gospels paint a surprisingly antagonistic picture of Jesus' relationship with his family. His birth
uprooted the family. They moved out of the country to
save his life from Herod the Great, who had all the little
boys of Bethlehem slain in his attempt to annihilate the
"King of the Jews." I wonder if Herod's horrible para-

noid act is reflected in Jesus' sense of self as one who "did not come to bring peace, but a sword" (Matthew 10:34)?

The tension between Jesus and his mother appears in the almost humorous account of the family leaving him behind in the temple during a pilgrimage to Jerusalem. Finding him in the temple, Mary expressed her grief and relief. Even at age twelve, Jesus rebuts his scolding mother by asking, "Why were you searching for me? Didn't you know I had to be in my Father's house?" (Luke 2:49).

Jesus' first miracle is set in the context of an apparent manipulation by his mother to rescue a short-sighted host who did not provide enough wine for a wedding banquet. "Woman, what do I have to do with you?" was Jesus' response.

At one point, Jesus' mother and brothers were obviously convinced that he was insane and came to take charge of him. When told that his family had come to see him, Jesus referred to his disciples, "Here are my mother and my brothers! Whoever does God's will is my brother and sister and mother" (Matthew 12:49).

Is this Jesus, who supposedly never married or had children, to be our model of family relationships? The question is meant to create a dilemma's horn. Obviously, the Gospel accounts of Jesus' family life are obscure at best; there are other indications of warmth and commitment. What I believe Jesus taught and modeled in his relationships with family was a deep form of spirituality, as well as a flair for yanking the chain of his audience. The distraction of Christ is to a relationship with God where nothing else, and no one else, interferes. When we are free to love God, then we are free to love others.

Marriage, too, is a journey. It is a life-long sojourn of two growing, developing persons. What happens when one partner moves into a deeper relationship with Christ than the other partner? Or, when one moves away from their relationship with Christ? How can spouses share a common faith, yet maintain their spiritual individuality?

Frederick Buechner describes the marriage made in heaven as "one where a man and a woman become more richly themselves together than the chances are either of them could ever have managed to become alone."[15] Christ calls us to come outside of ourselves, transcending our self-absorption, to a place where we can find our true selves in God.

The parable of the party, like so many of Jesus' teachings, confronted the xenophobia of the culture and speaks to our struggles to relate to persons of difference. Only as we develop a sound sense of who we are can we respectfully relate to others. Relationship then becomes less about uniformity between two persons and more about celebrating uniqueness and personhood.

In Erik Erikson's model of psychosocial development, intimacy follows identity. For Erikson, identity is the crisis of adolescence; intimacy the crisis of young adulthood. A developmentally successful adolescence prepares us for developing the capacity for intimacy, which is so important for marriage.

Paul calls for a mutual submission of husband and wife to one another based on a mutual commitment to Christ in Ephesians 5:21, "Submitting to one another in the fear of Christ." Those who try to impose a hierarchical interpretation on this passage miss this central thesis. One of the greatest challenges to the spiritual journey is marriage—maintaining an intimate connection while growing uniquely in our relationship with God. Paul recognized this and saw marriage as a metaphor of spirituality and faithfulness. Faithfulness in marriage is rooted in our faithfulness to the transcendent nature of marriage as God's design, as shared history, and as an acknowledgement of the goodness of committed companionship.

In making and maintaining relationships, we express the true nature of God as relational—as traditionally understood as a unity of Father, Son, and Spirit. In Christ our relationships take on new and sacred meaning.

Community in Distraction

The spiritual journey is more than just a personal matter. We are called into a community of sojourners. It follows that distraction is also a community phenomenon as Christ calls us, as part of a group, to God into a new way of being. While this book is primarily about our individual journey in Christ, I want to touch on some of the dynamics of groups in distraction to the extent that these dynamics affect our relationship with Christ.

Loss of Focus

In my experience, and according to many group dynamic theories, groups actually spend just a fraction of their time and resources accomplishing the objectives for which they were formed. This lack of focus can be seen as a nonproductive waste or the necessary precursor to effective group work. Periods of unfocused mulling can indicate an emerging movement of the Spirit.

The early church languished in disarray following the ascension of Christ, or so it appeared. In fact, they were waiting for the infilling of the Holy Spirit, as Jesus had instructed. At Pentecost, the church found its focus.

Spiritually, groups need a period of creative chaos in order to make room for a fresh movement of God. Old structures of group identity and norms wane as the labor pains of a new structure are felt.

During this season of decomposition, group members are wise in discerning whether the nondirectedness is a matter of group dysfunction or a stirring of God. There is a knack to sensing the difference. If the dispersion of group focus follows quickly after a major decision, it could be symptomatic of a premature action, mistaken direction, or a breakdown in group cohesion. Seasoned sojourners, however, have a sense of the cyclical nature of distraction in group process. It just seems time for a fresh breeze of the Spirit. Settledness, stirring, fervency and waning: all are important aspects of the spiritual rhythm of groups.

Conflict

A conflict arose in the early church because the Greek-speaking widows felt left out of the daily distribution of food. The apostles' response is a classic one in conflict management. They saw the conflict as an opportunity to enhance the quality of the community and opened up the leadership of the church to include Greek-speaking persons. In so doing, they avoided many of the pitfalls groups get into during conflict.

Conflict is an occasion for discovering a new meaning for a group's existence or adapting to a new direction in God's leading. According to Bruce Tuckman's theory of group process, conflict is a normal part of group life. For Tuckman, groups naturally go through a repetitive cycle of forming, storming, norming and performing. Storming is a way for groups to establish norms, or agreed-upon behaviors, which make effective group work possible.[16]

In society, when storming is done well it is called elections; when it is done poorly, it is called terrorism. Faith-based groups often have built-in ways of looking at conflict which virtually guarantee that the conflict will be acted out destructively. By espousing a theology that conflict is sinful, a group is locked into a destructive manner of conflict. First it is suppressed, then it is inevitably expressed as judgmentalism or coercion.

Seeing conflict as a signal that the group is changing frees us to refrain from blaming and judging others. Groups in positive distraction have found a way to utilize conflict as a natural, wholesome, and integral part of group re-formation and vitality.

Christ is Calling

The journey of Christ waits for us. Those who keep journals of their reflections often observe a thread that runs through various entries. Christ continually leads the way if we are open to follow.

The journey of Christ is a paradox: the more we follow a set path, the further we drift off course. The psalmist prayed that God would lead us in the "paths of righteousness," the worn, well-known trails of God's guidance. Jesus defined the way as a relationship with him, "I am the way." It is not the path that we are to follow, but the Pathfinder. We naturally assume that we are to discover and create the way, as if cutting a trail through a jungle. There is some truth to this. The journey is one of discovery and co-creation. We do blaze our own trails with Christ. As soon as we begin to plot the path, however, we've already drifted off course.

One common construing of the journey of Christ is that it is like flying by instruments. As long as we attend to the dials in front of us and respond accordingly, we'll make it to our destination. The dials of direction are the Scriptures, the inner witness of the Spirit, community wisdom, and so on. There is truth to this. But, what is the destination that we're striving for? Heaven? Perfection? Self-esteem? Success?

Christians of the flying-by-instruments school inevitably become distraught by their inability to stay on course. They fall asleep at the wheel. They start looking at the scenery out the window. They fly through overcast skies and get scared. They receive conflicting signals from the dials. Sooner or later they lose their focus on the instruments. Then what? How can we keep from being distracted *from* Christ?

Jesus said, "Take my yoke upon you and learn from me." The yoke is designed for two. Christ invites us to be yokefellows, to journey with God. The journey is not about the destination, it is about the yoke that binds two together. It is about relationship. The destination, if you must have one, is union with Christ.

The paradox is this: not that we are distracted *from* Christ, but that we are distracted *by* Christ. One of Jesus' metaphors of his own saving purpose was a shepherd who leaves the flock to seek out the one lost sheep. We, like sheep, have gone astray, says Isaiah. We live in a perpetual state of focus, not on Christ but on the issues of life. It is not we who seek out Christ; Christ seeks us out and distracts us away from our preoccupations. Jesus said, "My sheep know my voice." Shepherds lead their flocks; sheep follow out of a sense of familiarity. Perhaps what Jesus meant was that our following Christ is contingent on knowing that we are Christ's followers.

Right in the middle of our busy, preoccupied lives Christ calls. Christ calls to us, and the moment we lift our heads to listen, the journey begins.

Prayer of Distraction

My prayer for today is that no thing will have such brilliance as Christ,

That no interruption will seem as a discontinuity, but rather a leading of the Spirit,

That no memory will seem as a wound, but as a reminder of God's healing,

That no fear will seem as a fortress against hope, but as an occasion for God's deliverance,

That no attraction will seem as an allurement from righteousness, but as a celebration of the beauty of God's creation,

That no conversation will seem as idle words, but as a moment for God to speak,

That my heart will be still in the peace of God,

That my mind will be clear with the light of God, and

That my soul will be satisfied with the goodness of God.

Amen.

Reflection

When did you first become aware that Christ wanted to have something to do with you personally?

What is your number one preoccupation?

How do you suppose Christ gets your attention? How does Christ distract you?

To what or whom is Christ inviting you?

In what ways would you describe your life's journey?

What is your calling? In what ways does your work reflect that calling?

How has your image of God changed?

Have you ever felt pursued by God? What do you remember of that experience?

Who are your fellow sojourners? Detractors? Are you a sojourner or a detractor?

When Christ invites you to "sit still" what illusion keeps you involved in activity?

Describe an experience when you have been distracted from darkness by a "flash of grace."

When does your focus on what is "good" show out a graced distraction by God?

What is your personal authority? How do you claim your power? . . . or live with your limitations?

If you are part of a religious group, how does that group deal with the "storming" phase? Does this phase lead to coercion and judgmentalism or new life and grace for the group?

Endnotes

1 Lewis, C.S., *The Screwtape Letters*, (Old Tappan, N.J., Fleming H. Revell Company, 1976), p. 125.

2 Bunyan, *Pilgrim's Progress* (Grand Rapids: Spire Books), p. 11.

3 Teresa of Avila, *The Interior Castle* in Kieran Kavanaugh and Otilio Rodriguez, trans., *The Collected Works of St. Teresa of Avila*, Vol. 2, (Washington, D.C.: ICS Publications, 1980), pp. 283-284. Unless noted, all references to Teresa's writings will be taken from ICS Publications texts.

4 James Hillman, *The Soul's Code* (New York: Random House, 1996), pp. 203-207.

5 Teresa of Avila, Robert Van De Weyer, trans., *The Interior Castle* (London: HarperCollins, 1995), p. 10.

6 *Castle* (Van De Weyer), p. 16.

7 Rosemary Broughton, *Praying with Teresa of Avila* (St. Mary's Press, 1995), p. 33.

8 John of the Cross in Kieran Kavanaugh and Otilio Rodriguez, trans., *The Collected Works of St. John of the Cross*, (Washington, D.C.: ICS Publications, 1991), p. 362. Unless noted, all references to John's writings will be taken from ICS Publications texts.

9 Webster's Dictionary

10 *Dark Night*, p. 367.

11 *Dark Night*, p. 369.

12 *Castle* (Van De Weyer), p. 24.

13 *Castle*, p. 367.

14 Thomas Merton, *The Ascent to Truth*, pp. 21-24.

15 Buechner, Frederick, *Whistling in the Dark*, Harper SanFrancisco, 1993, p. 87.

16 Tuckman, B.W., *Psychological Bulletin*, 63, (1965), pp. 384-399. Tuckman, B.W., and Jensen, M.A.C., *Group and Organizational Studies*, 2, (1977), Stages of small group development revisited, pp. 419-427.

2

DAZZLED BY CHRIST

Morning sun rays glisten on the water's surface like festival lights dancing in time with his pounding heart. Approaching the crystal lake, the traveler sees matted reflections of sky and trees stretch out to the distant bank. A long-legged figure hangs below him as he studies the water's edge—his own reflection contemplating his gaze.

With water cold and sweet, he slakes his thirst with hand cups. His knees feel clammy as he rises from his prayerful descent to the muddy bank.

As the concentric ripples expanded from where he had wounded the glass surface, darkness swims in the underworld. Through his mirrored and rippled face, the eyes of a silent host appears and then darts into the unknown below.

MSJ

He leads me beside quiet waters, he restores my
soul. Psalm 23:3-4.

* * *

A woman approached the village well in the heat of
the day. On this day a visitor met her, a rabbi journeying
from the south. Their conversation took the form of a
game, with move and countermove, covering the gamut
of her life. He knew the story of her racial and gender-
borne oppression, a cascade of broken marriages, empty
religion; spiritual longing. With each sentence the rabbi
revealed her secrets and circumvented her defenses
until all her tactics of avoidance lay in the dust. Upon
the dry barrenness of her soul came a refreshing water
of life not drawn from the well but from deep within.
Her testimony brought a whole town to Jesus, "He told
me everything I ever did" (John 4:39).

Witnessing his signs and wonders, Jesus' bedazzled
followers were astonished at what God could do. As
Jesus went about teaching, preaching and healing during the beginning of his ministry, the news got out and
people flocked to him. They were amazed at this teaching because of his authority and authenticity.

Dazzlement is a beginning or new beginning of
Christ's ministry in our lives. New converts are swept
off their feet in a novel way of being and living. Stagnant
disciples, distracted once again by the initiative of God,
are renewed in their enthusiasm and interest in Christ.

In dazzlement, we are invited to "Taste and see that
the Lord is good." The experience of God is sweet
indeed, as Teresa described it:

> So desirous is He that we should seek Him and
> enjoy His company, that in one way or another He
> never ceases calling us to Him. So sweet is His voice,
> that the poor soul is disconsolate at being unable to
> follow His bidding at once . . . no one could ever wish
> for a better friend.[1]

Dazzlement is the feeling that life makes sense; that the pieces fit. We are so captivated by Christ that everything else pales. It is a finding and being found out; knowing and being known. Dazzlement is connection with the engine room of creativity: it is the wind in your unfurled sails.

Cultivating a sense of dazzlement is key to a meaningful and growing relationship with Christ because it refreshes us and inspires us to continue the journey. Otherwise our relationship with the Water of Life turns to hard religious stone.

Dazzlement is a taste of all the other places on the journey. It is our taste of distraction that gets us into dazzlement. It is our dazzlement that leads us into discipleship, for the dazzled follow Christ like a disciple. It foretells disillusionment for it contains the experience of the "wound of love" and a struggle with the shadow side of life.

Dazzlement is an invitation to a new dwelling place in Christ. We are called from the False Self to the True Self; to authenticity. This taste of authentic living is as exciting as it is radical.

Dazzlement is a foretaste of being desired by Christ—of his marriage chamber—for it is a place of infatuation, not so much with Christ as with the new life in Christ. It is a taste of our destiny, for we are awed by the glimpse of the potential of knowing and loving God.

> I am *Yours* and born for you,
> What do *You* want of me? . . .
>
> Yours, you made me,
> Yours, you saved me,
> Yours, you endured me,
> Yours, you called me,
> Yours, you awaited me,
> Yours, I did not stray.
> What do *You* want of me?[2]
>
> Teresa

Dazzlement and Shadow

I choose the term dazzlement to describe this place on the journey because the word connotes the effects of brilliant light and a sense of being charmed or profoundly impressed. Just as shadows are defined by light, so Christ's light reveals the shadow of life. Shadow is the part of us that we do not know nor find acceptable. The origin of the emerging reality of Christ in our life, the shadow holds surprises. As we are distracted by the light above, Christ emerges from the shadow below. It is a dawning in the soul; an awakening.

To talk about interior light is to talk about interior darkness. Just as the shadow defines the object illuminated, so the emerging light of Christ demarcates the unknown regions that lie within. The temptation of dazzlement is to believe that the light—and darkness— are outside of us rather than within. Extrinsic illumination is powerless to bring about change; real change occurs from the inside out.

Throughout history the sea has been a mythological symbol of this unknown dark region of the soul as well as the beginning place of creation. While we long to ascend to the heights in our quest for knowledge, we rarely descend into the abyss in our explorations. Nothing is so defiant of light as the deep.

The New Testament story of Simon Peter's call provides a rich figure for how dazzlement arises from the shadow. Peter was a fisherman, a man whose livelihood entailed drawing from the depths. There he met the Tour Guide of the Deep.

> One day as Jesus was standing by the Lake of Gennesaret, with the people crowding around him and listening to the word of God, he saw at the water's edge two boats, left there by the fishermen, who were washing their nets. He got into one of the boats, the one belonging to Simon, and asked him to put out a little

from shore. Then he sat down and taught the people from the boat.

When he had finished speaking, he said to Simon, "Put out into deep water, and let down the nets for a catch."

Simon answered, "Master, we've worked hard all night and haven't caught anything. But because you say so, I will let down the nets."

When they had done so, they caught such a large number of fish that their nets began to break. So they signaled their partners in the other boat to come and help them, and they came and filled both boats so full that they began to sink.

When Simon Peter saw this, he fell at Jesus' knees and said, "Go away from me, Lord; I am a sinful man!" For he and all his companions were astonished at the catch of fish they had taken, and so were James and John, the sons of Zebedee, Simon's partners.

Then Jesus said to Simon, "Don't be afraid; from now on you will catch men." So they pulled their boats up on shore, left everything and followed him. (Luke 5:1-11)

In the story, Jesus asks Peter to put his boat "out into deep water." Jesus had been teaching from the boat, enlightening the people with his message. Now he would bring something up from the deep, a harvest from the shadow. Peter had fished long hours in the darkness of night. Now he would see his catch in the light of day.

Shadow is a term used by Carl Jung to describe the dark and unconscious side of ourselves, which is not necessarily evil but cut off from our awareness. His dreams were haunted by the recurring image of a fish-skinned Bible, which he interpreted as a symbol of the unconscious since fishes are mute and unconscious. Perhaps it is not only the muteness of fishes that portended them as symbols of the shadowy unconscious in Jung's dreams, but that they dwell in the watery underworld, beneath the surface, much like the unconscious forces in the psyche.

The shadow is what we do not want to know about ourselves, lest we are undone by it. It is what is unknown and unloved. But, it is also the source of creative energies, locked away awaiting liberation. Into this shadowy deep Jesus pushed Peter.

Symbols of Shadow

Scripture and mythology contain many symbols of the shadow, both as a region of darkness and as a source of creation.

Shadow as the Abode of Evil and Death

In Genesis, the symbol of the sea is connected with the idea of the deep: the Abyss or the unfathomable bottomless pit. The concept was expanded in later Hebrew thought. In the sea lurked the Leviathan, the dragon Rahab, the sea monster and the sea serpent alluded to in Job, Psalms, and Isaiah. In New Testament times, the pit was construed as the underworld, the place of the dead and the abode of demons.

The demons possessing the Gerasene man, in Luke's Gospel, asked Jesus to send them into a nearby herd of pigs rather than to the fearful Abyss. When Jesus consented, the demoniac pigs ran into the Lake of Gennesaret—the same sea from which Peter netted his miraculous catch of fish—and drowned. Ironically the demons returned to the Abyss after all.

Our shadow is the abode of evil and death. It is where we sequester the unacceptable aspects of our lives, which we fear would undo us if they were known.

Shadow as the Wellspring of Creativity

The Hebrews knew that evil and death lay in the sea but that the sea was also the source of creation, as stated in Genesis 1:2, "the earth was formless and empty, darkness was over the surface of the deep, and the Spirit of God was hovering over the waters." The chaotic forces were contained by the movement of God. This concept of the primordial existence of the unformed sea in the beginning of creation is echoed in the creation myths of several cultures: Mesopotamian, Indo-Iranian, Greek, Finnish, Mexican, and some of the Native American tribes.[3]

The Old Norse runic myth of the well of Mimir offers some similar metaphors for the shadow. The ancient Scandinavians considered this mythic well to be the source of poetic wisdom. The well was beside Yggdrasil, the World Tree, whose roots reached to the underworld and was guarded by the sea giant Mimir, the Wise. Odin, the god of war and death, hung himself for nine days on Yggdrasil as a self-sacrifice to obtain wisdom and inspiration from the well. Additionally, in exchange for a drink from the well, he gave one of his eyes to Mimir.

Three parallels exist between this myth and the place of dazzlement. First, the source of the well is drawn from the watery depths of the underworld. Here again is the connection between deep knowledge and deep water. The source of self-knowledge lies in what we do not know—in the murky depths of the unconscious—out of reach. Through Christ we may access this deep place within.

Second, the prize of the well is poetic wisdom. Not just insight, but a special kind of insight: the ability to see metaphorical truth. Poetry is an expression utilizing rhythm and image. To gain such wisdom implies a feel for the pulse and deep meanings of life. A prize indeed.

I've come to believe that the closer we get to the spiritual realm, the more we enter the arena of metaphor. From listening to the stories of patients who have had near death experiences, I've found their reports to be highly metaphorical. Green foliage, blue river, music, spatial images of seeing themselves in one place and others in another place, light, darkness. Symbols abound. It is no wonder that when John wrote the Revelation, he almost exclusively used symbol. The apocalyptic literary tradition is steeped in the use of symbol to express spiritual realities. It is the milieu of these emerging images that creates opportunities for new awareness and ways of being. Dazzlement is learning the imagery of our soul.

Third, the well is guarded by a giant who requires sacrifice for access to the well, namely life and sight. I see this myth as depicting the paradox of self-knowledge. In order to achieve true insight, Odin sacrificed himself to himself and gave up half his sight. The myth conveys a profound truth: to achieve insight we must learn to see with the inner eye and face our true self.

Such an inward look can be painful and overwhelming but ultimately leads to freedom. It is only with God's help that we can face the inner reality of our soul. It is there that Christ meets us. We fear, and sometimes hate, what we do not know about ourselves. Christ knows and loves, and God's "perfect love drives out fear, because fear has to do with punishment." To know God we must first know ourselves. Our blocks to self-knowledge also block the light of God.

For Teresa, humility is self-knowledge. Only as we know ourselves can we relate honestly with God and others. The chief requirement for attaining self-knowledge, Teresa suggested, is courage.

Knowing that courage is a prerequisite to self-awareness, Jesus' response to the awestruck Peter in the boat is "Don't be afraid." An interesting response to a guilt statement! Christ knows what is in the deep (unknown and unloved by us) and this frightened Peter. But, with the strength and comforting presence of Christ, we can take a long, loving look at ourselves.

There is no shortcut to self-awareness. The secrets of the self are so well guarded that we might kill to protect them, or die to reveal them. Adam and Eve ate of the Tree of Knowledge and it cost them dearly, as God had warned, "The day you eat . . . you shall surely die."

Hillman refers to the Kabbalistic symbol of the tree of life, taken from the Garden of Eden story, as a portrait of self-awareness. A form of thirteenth-century Jewish spirituality, the Kabbalah was probably a literary influence in Teresa's portrayal of the soul and the journey into the inner self. For Hillman, the tree with its roots growing down depicts the connection of the soul to the unseen regions that provide rootedness and groundedness in true, authentic selfhood.

The fear of self-knowledge is the fear of judgment and condemnation. It is the belief that the One who truly knows us will then reject us. We, too, will be sent to the Abyss. Christ brings the evil spirits out of our depths and judges them. But, there is a difference between judgment and condemnation. The spirits of the Gerasene man were evil because they were self-destructive. With self-awareness, we get in touch with our own self-destructive nature and redeem it. Paul says, "if we judged ourselves, we would not come under judgment," and that God's judgment is a discipline "so that we will not be condemned with the world."

Interestingly, Jesus' term for Hell was Gehenna, the city trash dump, a place where the Jerusalem population discarded their refuse. Our temptation may be to see our shadow as the trash dump of our souls. Christ emerges from the shadow, however, with treasures in hand. What a paradox! We look for Christ in the light of what we find acceptable about ourselves, but Christ emerges from the dark!

Robert Bly provides a rich metaphor for the paradox of what emerges from the shadow in his recounting of the Brothers Grimm story, *Iron John*. A whole village is terrified by the mysterious and deadly powers of a pond in the woods, from which no one returns. When a brave hunter drains the pond, a wild man is found at the bottom. The wild man is caged by the townspeople but escapes with the king's son. As the story progresses, the true character of Iron John unfolds. Rather than being a horrible monster, he is really a sage who teaches the young boy how to live.[4]

Iron John depicts the task we all must eventually face of descending into the murky depths of our psyche and accept what we find there. Thomas Keating depicts it as taking the lid off the sewer hole and looking inside. We may indeed find evil, which we must offer up to God. But, we must not be too quick to judge. What initially may appear as an evil of great destruction will evolve, in the light of grace, into a true virtue.

Like the hero in *Iron John,* Moses stood at the Red Sea and parted it, both revealing its depths and making a passage. The nation passed through the sea to salvation, a passage celebrated in the epics of Israel. As Pharaoh's charioteers pursued, they were drowned by the crashing waves as the sea closed in over them. The sea that offered salvation when laid open by God also brought destruction when defied by those who ignored God. It is dangerous to defy the shadow.

Matthew 13 contains eight of Jesus' parables about the hidden kingdom. All convey the theme of treasure emerging from the earth: seeds that fall upon rich and poor soils, weeds sown among the wheat, a mustard seed, yeast in dough, a treasure found in a field, a pearl of great value, good and bad fish caught in the same net, and treasures brought from the storeroom—old and new. "The knowledge of the secrets of the kingdom of heaven has been given to you," Jesus told his disciples. Learning to value what Christ brings forth from the shadow is the key to dazzlement.

Signs of Dazzlement

Dazzlement, in its most redemptive form, goes far beyond mere excitement or bewilderment. Dazzlement lays bare the deep issues of our soul, and it is this self-revealing quality that defines its importance in the spiritual journey. Without this emergence of self-awareness, we would blindly grope. Peter's response to Jesus illustrates the salient features of true dazzlement.

Awe

Only that which is greater than us can awe us. Peter was frightened by what Jesus knew. Perhaps he thought, "If Jesus knows what is in the sea, then he knows what is in me!" It was a fear of the unknown depths and of the God who knows what is down there that engulfed Peter with awe.

The Wisdom literature of Scripture repeats the admonition that "the fear of the Lord is the beginning of wisdom." More than just fright, the word connotes a sense of awe. It is awesome when Christ emerges from our unconscious with something within us that God wants us to discover.

Dazzlement is awe at what emerges from the depths as well as the view from the heights. It is like standing on the rim of the Grand Canyon, seeing both enormous depth and distance at the same time. It is at once an acrophobic height as well a marvel of unimaginable forces and timelessness that could displace such vastness in the earth.

The same Peter who was astonished at what Jesus could surface from the depths of the sea is also the Peter who saw the transfiguration of Jesus on the mountain top. Dazzlement is about these highs and lows. On the one hand, we fear what is emerging from the unknown; on the other hand, we rise in ecstasy to the heights of wonder.

Dazzled worshipers, without self-consciousness, are caught up in praise and meaningful stirrings at the experience of God's greatness. Concomitantly, they are brought down in conviction of their sinfulness once their self-consciousness returns. Isaiah, in a vision of dazzlement, "saw the Lord . . . high and exalted," and responded, "Woe is me!"

Dazzlement feels like a dangerous place. Some of us are so defended against awe that we resist any stirring of the depths lest we lose our composure. Others are so predisposed to the histrionic that we view and portray dazzlement as something of supreme value in itself and as the ultimate validation of true Christianity. Both are two sides of the same coin; for one, dazzlement is too much of a threat and for the other, it is too much of an end. A balanced view of dazzlement sees it not so much as a norm for the journey, but a place that reveals something we need to know as we travel in the plains and valleys of life: that God is always beyond what we "ask or imagine, according to his power that is at work within us."

Guilt and Shame

Only that which is bright can reveal our darkness. Peter's nets caught what Jesus was bringing to the surface. Anytime Christ brings something to the light within us that has been kept in darkness, a disturbing sense of exposure ensues. We instinctively want to distance ourselves not only from that which has been revealed, but from the one revealing it. Peter voiced his sense of alienation, "Go away from me, Lord; I am a sinful man!" The light was too bright.

After spending forty days on Mount Sinai with God, Moses descended with the Law and a face so bright that the people asked him to put a veil over his face. They didn't like that heavenly glow. The law revealed not only the glory of God, but the sinfulness of the people as well.

What Christ reveals is as much a reflection of our-selves as it is a reflection of God. "And we, who with unveiled faces all reflect the Lord's glory, are being transformed into this likeness with ever-increasing glory, which comes from the Lord, who is the Spirit" (II Cor. 3:18). "Reflect" in this verse has the double meaning of "contemplate." We both reflect the glory of God to others and contemplate God's glory in self-reflection.

Seeing our reflection, whether in the water of shadow or the brilliance of the mountaintop, we can respond in a number of ways. First, we may find it hard to look. We may not like what we see and turn away.

Second, we may be dazzled into self-absorption, like Narcissus, falling in love with our own reflection. Or, thirdly, like Bunyan's Christian, we may be so fo-cused on the Celestial City ahead of us and preoccupied with Fear coming up behind us that we fall right into the Slough of Despond. In that shame and despair, we may get bogged down until we learn with Bunyan that "Shame tells me what men are; but it tells me nothing about what God, or the word of God, is."[5]

Fourthly, we may take a long, courageous and lov-ing gaze; seeing ourselves through the eyes of Christ who truly knows us and loves us.

A long, loving look at ourselves through the lens of grace enables us to achieve some balance in our self-image. In light of the acceptance of Christ, we can be honest with ourselves about our inner darkness and yet claim the virtues that also reside within. Donald Capps, in *Deadly Sins and Saving Virtues*, presents the tradi-tional schema of the deadly sins and the corresponding virtues in a way that supports such a balanced self-view.

Capps seeks to integrate the deadly sins and saving virtues with the developmental psychological model of

Erik Erikson. In so doing, Capps defines the sins and virtues as being in a dynamic relationship. The deadly sins are "genuinely deadly—as malevolent powers," but for each sin there exists a corresponding virtue, a "vital strength that issues out of an effective negotiation of the crisis of a given stage of life."[6]

Erikson described the human journey as a series of developmental crises at definable stages throughout life. Shame and guilt, for Erikson, are issues that we struggle with in our infancy, childhood, and throughout life. The outcome of our early struggles sets the stage for our life's journey. For this reason, it is common for adults to experience a re-emergence of old, childhood crises. There is healing to be done.

Crisis

Only that which creates an opportunity for change can call us to decision. At this point we come to a fork in the road: the choice between new and old. This pivotal point hinges on our response to the new self-awareness Christ presents. Will we turn our face in shame and run, or will we accept the acceptance of God and embrace our new awareness? The route of shame leads to condemnation; the route of openness leads to grace and growth. If we face ourselves in the mirror of God's acceptance, we can then embark on a deeper level of self-acceptance and renewal. If we contemplate ourselves in the reflection of God's grace, we see the face of Christ.

Augustine pictured the grace of God as a bright light shining into our darkness. In the shame and fear of exposure, we run from the searching light until we are overcome by it. Yet, Augustine found himself drawn to the loving and lovely nature of God. In Augustinian terms, Capps describes the crisis created by the emergence of grace in *Life Cycle Theory* and *Pastoral Care*:

The issue for Augustine is no longer Adam's question, "How can I conceal my shame?" The question now is, "How may God become known to me?" And the answer is that as we cross the boundary from avoiding shame to embracing it, accepting it as the most intimate part of ourselves, we create the inner climate in which God becomes revealed to us . . . What Augustine has done in the Confessions is to make the "self" of which we are most profoundly ashamed the very core of our Christian identity.[7]

For Teresa, the second mansion in her *Interior Castle* is a place to grapple with the evil within us and to learn not to rely on "consolations" for our assurance. Dazzlement is not just about pleasant surprises, though it is a pleasant surprise.

Kierkegaard described this pivot point as a crisis of decision: whether to leap into the unknown of our potentialities or to shrink back in angst or anxiety about our existence. In anxiety, we become closed to new experiences and perceptions, narrowing our focus to only that which is certain and familiar. In faith, however, we open ourselves to new possibilities, to unknown opportunities that await us.

Maslow likewise depicts this crisis of our potential as a block to our self-actualization: "We fear our highest possibility (as well as our lowest ones). We are generally afraid to become that which we can glimpse in our most perfect moments . . . and yet we simultaneously shiver with weakness, awe and fear before these very same possibilities.[8]

Jung describes how dazzlement comes with a temptation to turn away from the new that is emerging—our True Self—and opt out for something false. Christ comes to us out of our shadow, and we instinctively push God away.

. . . the acceptance of oneself is the essence of the moral problem and the epitome of a whole outlook upon life. That I feed the hungry, that I forgive an insult, that I love my enemy in the name of Christ—all these are undoubtedly great virtues. What I do unto the least of my brethren, that I do unto Christ. But what if I should discover that the least amongst them all, the poorest of all the beggars, the most impudent of all the offenders, the very enemy himself—that these are within me, and that I myself stand in need of the alms of my own kindness—that I myself am the enemy who must be loved: what then? As a rule, the Christian's attitude is then reversed; there is no longer any question of love or long-suffering; we say to the brother within us "Raca," and condemn and rage against ourselves. We hide it from the world; we refuse to admit ever having met this least among the lowly in ourselves. Had it been God himself who drew near to us in this despicable form, we should have denied him a thousand times before a single cock had crowed.[9]

For Jung, this "state of being at war with oneself" creates a neurotic "inner cleavage," or "dissociation of personality."

What drives people to war with themselves is the intuition or the knowledge that they consist of two persons in opposition to one another. The conflict may be between the sensual and the spiritual man, or between the ego and the shadow. It is what Faust means when he says, "Two souls, alas, dwell in my breast apart."[10]

I hear this language of dissociation from persons who are struggling with this integration. They refer to "my human side," as if to say they have another side. What other side do we have besides our humanity? Divinity? We may be spiritual beings as well as physical beings, but we are human—only human; gloriously human. The incarnation of God in Christ teaches us that spirit and body are a unity. To be true to ourselves we must honor both—we are both. The journey of Christ is a journey of humanness as we discover who we are and seek to live out that self-awareness more authentically. In reflecting on Thomas à Kempis' *The Imitation of Christ*, Jung asks if Christ is calling us to "copy his life," or if Christ is calling us to live our lives "as truly as He lived his in all its implications?"[11]

Creative Energy

Only that which is new can make the old obsolete. A weary Peter washed his nets after a long night of fruitless fishing. Looking up, he sees a young rabbi walking along the shore and overhears his teaching as a crowd forms. The rabbi then chooses Peter as an object lesson and invites him to cast his nets on the other side of his boat. Respectfully indulging the strange humor of the minister, Peter obliges with a small protest. Soon the water churns with fish and the boats are nearly swamped by the enormous catch.

Peter's astonishment got him into his shadow. The catch was more than his sinking boat could hold, like old wineskins that cannot hold the new wine of the kingdom.

Christ has a way of sinking our boats—our familiar modes of moving through life—and forcing us to look to God for a new vehicle. The old structures of life cannot support the new realities of God's dynamic creations. From the depths Peter also gleaned a renewed energy. Animated in his astonishment, he falls at Jesus' feet.

The sea is a source of creation as well as shadow. From the shadow, Christ calls us from our laborious tedium to creativity. The old structures cannot withstand the new power. "Therefore, if anyone is in Christ, he is a new creation; the old has gone, the new has come!"

In Luke's Gospel, Elizabeth's baby, John, "leaped in her womb" when Mary, pregnant with Jesus, greeted her. Mary, by taking on her mission as God-bearer, was saying Yes to something incredible. In dazzlement, something leaps within us, something yet unborn.

Meister Eckhart likened the creative emergence of Christ within us as pregnancy: "I dreamt that I, even though a man, was pregnant, pregnant and full with Nothingness like a woman who is with child . . . and that out of this Nothingness God was born . . . the fruitful person gives birth out of the very same foundation from which the Creator begets the eternal Word and it is from this core that one becomes fruitfully pregnant . . . We are all meant to be mothers of God.[12]

Eckhart's words came alive to me during a conversation with a pregnant friend. I was telling her how stuck I was feeling at a point in writing this book. The book had become a Jeremiah-like calling—something I had to do and yet I didn't feel up to the task—I couldn't not write it. She stated that she felt the same way with her upcoming delivery! Contemplating that conversation and the words of Eckhart, which my friend shared with me, I began to see pregnancy as a threefold metaphor for the emergence of creative energy. First, in pregnancy the body changes and restructures itself for the indwelling creation. This may have been what Jesus sought to convey to Nicodemus, "you must be born again." Jesus sensed the emergence of new life in Nicodemus, not only through womb water, but of the Spirit. As the new life of Christ grows within us, we are changed.

Second, pregnancy is not a static place. We will have to deliver. The closer the due date, the more uncomfortable we become. The birthing is thrust upon us.

Third, no one else knows what the pregnancy means to us. It can be a cause of celebration or grief, or a strange mixture of myriad meanings and feelings. Knowing this about the birth wind of the Spirit that "blows wherever it pleases," I hesitate to prescribe a formula for spiritual development. Though constantly progressing toward new birth, the journey's meaning remains always a personal mystery to each of us. "It is ineffable," says Eckhart.

Identity and Purpose

Only the creator can define the purpose of the created. Christ called Peter to a radically new self-awareness and purpose: "from now on you will catch men." The words of this call deserve some unpacking. "From now on" and "fisher of men" are significant terms for Luke. Literally, "from the now," Luke's term emphasized that God's ultimate and eschatological purposes are being fulfilled in history. It conveys the sense that God is taking initiative and that the mission of God is grounded in divine action.[13] Dazzlement is the sense that "Wow! It's happening!"

In redefining Peter's vocation from a fisherman to a "fisher of men," Jesus was drawing from a historical meaning of the term as being the avant-garde of a new movement. Taken together, these terms are a signal that something profound is occurring. At this moment God is creating a new world order!

Our encounters with Christ are life-changing at the deepest levels. Christ gives us a new name and a new awareness of our purpose.

What emerges in the spiritual journey of Christ is a new identity. We take on a new way of being. Dazzlement is a place of receiving a new name—a new means of recognition.

Developing the Art of Dazzlement

Dazzlement is the natural outgrowth of distraction. As Christ draws our focus onto Himself, we are innately taken by the new life of creativity and integration that emerges. Not a skill or method, dazzlement is an art— the art of wonder. While dazzlement is the work of the

Spirit, I believe we can develop certain dispositions that enhance our experience of this place.

Cultivating a Sense of Awe

For most adults, the childlike, naïve wonder at experiencing life is socialized into oblivion. Nurturing that inner child enables us to develop a basic level of trust in God's goodness and the goodness of any given moment in relation to Christ.

One Saturday afternoon while making homemade bread, my daughter invited me into the wonder of bubbles in a bottle of oil. The show was stopped for a moment as we stood gazing at the tiny transparent orbs floating in the bottle I suspended just above our faces. For just an instant, I flashed back to a faint feeling of childhood wonderment at the simple but fascinating discoveries of life and felt a shared sense of commonality with my smiling child in that fascination.

If the awe of God is the beginning of wisdom, then dazzlement is the origin of further self-awareness and growth, with the ultimate goal of union with Christ. Living in awe is being open to the beyond.

Dazzlement is having our focus off ourselves and on Christ. Peter displayed this quality one stormy night at sea in Matthew 14. Christ appears to the disciples as he walks on water and bids Peter to walk with him. Gripped by the call, Peter steps out of his boat and walks on the stormy waters to Christ. This is transcendence, which is another way of talking about dazzlement. Peter had a knack for the transcendent, seeing beyond the moment in his impulsive reach for God.

Living Authentically

Another aspect of artfully living out our dazzlement is to seek to live out of our true self, as that is revealed by Christ. As the psalmist prayed, "Surely you desire truth in the inner parts; you teach me wisdom in the inmost place." Christ calls us to live authentically in relationship with God, self, and others, what Buber termed the I-Thou. I-Thou living is relating to others as significant in and of themselves, not just as an object of our interest.

To live truly in relationship, we must be honest and gracious to ourselves, as Jung reminds us. This means reckoning with our shadow and learning to love what is unlovable about ourselves. Look to the shadow, not the best foot you put forward, for the source of grace and creativity.

After the crucifixion, the depressed disciples went back to the life Christ had called them from: to their vocations of fishing. Once again the rabbi appeared on the shore in the morning and once again the nets were overfilled with a miraculous catch after a fruitless night. Discerning immediately that it was Jesus on the shore— the resurrected Christ—Peter jumped into the water and made for shore.

This was a significant leap. Peter cast himself into the abyss of shadow. Not fearing the unknown. Not tiptoeing across. Not sinking in a panic. He *jumped* into grace.

On shore, Peter would soon hear the three probing questions from Christ echoing and redeeming his three denials. Do you love me? Do you love me? Do you love me?

Living authentically is to surrender to the distraction and dazzlement of Christ, trusting that Christ pursues a relationship with our True Self.

Making a Good Thing Last!

The experience of God in this place of dazzlement is a temporary surge of creative energy. Dazzlement is a wave; ride it as long as it lasts. Soon enough, in the distraction-dazzlement-discipleship cycle, the energies of dazzlement will eventually give way to the ordering compulsions of discipleship.

This waning of dazzlement does not necessarily reflect some failure on our part. It is inherent in the gospel story itself.

James William McClendon, Jr. points out the difficulty of New Testament writers in describing the extraordinary and unprecedented transformations Christ brought to their lives. They were forced to draw from "other spheres of life in order to indicate the new thing" they were experiencing.[14] There were no words adequate for telling the story.

> Yet time goes by; the new world does not simply pass over into the expected age to come but hovers, waiting for an end that in one sense is present but in another is not. Consequently, terms newly minted to express faith's new possession grow old, and they and the practices that witnessed to the new awareness ossify into a tradition as much in want of redemption as the old had ever been . . . How can religious communities that have shaped themselves to maintain and preserve Christian life be open to the hot breath of the Spirit that creates them, open to the onset of the new that comes in Christ?[15]

Dazzled Christians are likewise speechless in conveying the extraordinary nature of their new experience and learnings. New images, allusions, and terms must be invented, or borrowed, to enable them to relay their experience. As soon as these language devices are contrived, the nature of discipleship sets in: a way of experiencing God in a more ordered, comprehensible fashion. In the meantime, it is this creative floundering that defines dazzlement.

Drawing a distinction between new and old is a way Christians have historically described the uniqueness of this dazzling place in the spiritual journey. Yet, as McClendon reminds us, it is not so easy to define the line between new and old. The old is passing away, yet the old still remains. The new is coming, and has already come. In the New Testament, this difference in time is described using two words: *chronos* and *kairos.*

Chronos is the creation of humankind based on the order of the universe—an order that is God's creation. In chronological time, we think of time as duration or sequence. *Chronos* is the quantity of time.

Kairos is the time of God. It is the "fullness of time," the right time. In *kairos* time, we think of time in terms of season or opportunity. *Kairos* is the quality of time.

Distraction and dazzlement entail *kairos* time. It is time to have a breakthrough with God. In God's timing, we are moved by the Spirit. *Chronos* is transformed into *kairos.* We can even lose all sense of time as we are caught up in a new experience of God.

One thing that works against dazzlement is a tendency to allow our lives to be governed by human-made order rather than God's movement. This may have been one aspect of what Paul meant by worshiping "created things rather than the Creator."

The art of dazzlement is knowing when it is harvest time. Other seasons in the ebb and flow of the spiritual life exist in their own goodness, such as wintry wet and dormant times when energies are low and the movement of our spirit is beneath the surface. But there are also seasons of ingathering and reaping the fruit of our endurance. Wisdom is to accept this rhythm of the spiritual life and make the most of the season.

Living on the Foundation of a Solid Faith

Dazzlement can be a time of radical change when we are willing to follow Christ. Our following, however, may be more out of astonishment than loyalty. The seasoned follower of Christ has learned that not every season is harvest season. Harvest is the end of a process of sowing and cultivation, not the beginning.

Teresa instructed her sisters not to build their spirituality on mere positive feelings "a poor way to start building so precious and great an edifice." Rather, the beginning of the spiritual life is to doggedly bring one's will in to conformity with God's will.[16]

Teresa's words are timely. First, beginnings in the spiritual life are best focused on the destination of our relationship with Christ rather than any payoff of a better life. Second, the basis of Christian faith is in the desire to do the will of God, not astonishment. Teresa cautions against a faith based on "interior consolations," or peaceful and pleasant experiences. The spiritual journey, says Broughton, is marked with ups and downs: "those who start to practice prayer often experience a strange exhilaration, a new peace, a more vivid life." But, she continues, "As with any exercise, prayer may seem laborious and unproductive at the beginning."[17]

The principle I am trying to convey here on maximizing dazzlement is balance. On the foundation of a solid faith, dazzlement can be a fruitful and celebrative season. As a foundation for faith, however, dazzlement provides little stability.

As a miracle worker who could feed thousands with a single lunch basket, Jesus certainly knew how to engender dazzlement in his followers. Jesus, however, challenged the trailing masses by saying, "you are looking for me, not because you saw miraculous signs but because you ate the loaves and had your fill."

Reality for Jesus' followers is the realm of the Spirit, not the flesh. He went on to give hard sayings that anyone who follows him eats not only his bread, but his flesh and blood, as well. Confronted with such a high cost of discipleship and centering one's life totally on Jesus, the followers lost much of their interest.

Christ invites us to shed our secondary agendas and simply follow him. For Jacob, as for most of us, this took a lifetime. After taking his brother Esau's birthright and blessing, Jacob fled for his life from Esau's revenge. At Bethel he realized he was in the presence of God and tried to cut a deal: If you'll protect me, God, then I'll worship you. Years later, fleeing from another furious relative, Laban, Jacob had the famous encounter with God when he wrestled all night with the angel. This more authentic struggle with God resulted in a profound personal transformation.

True dazzlement ultimately leads to a truer discipleship. If we have really been apprehended by Christ and enthralled with Christ, we will seek to live the surrendered life as a follower. We will live more out of awe and authenticity, appreciating the timing of God.

Community in Dazzlement

In the Bible the church is depicted as a structure of dazzlement: a matrix of dynamic and faithful relationships wherein people experience the presence of God. The New Testament concept of church has its roots in the tabernacle and temple of Israel. A tent-like portable structure that served as the meeting place between God and God's people during the Exodus from Egyptian slavery, the tabernacle traveled as the people traveled. The temples built in Jerusalem were known for their beautiful reminiscence of the tabernacle's form, with one notable difference: they were stationary. Throughout the history of the people who worshiped at this site, the prophets challenged the spiritual inclination of the nation to develop and blindly hold to traditions in place of a lively relationship with God.

The tabernacle had accompanied the people on the miraculous Exodus journey. The journey was not only marked by miracles but was in itself a miracle as a nation moved from one land to another, claiming its God-given place in the world. It was the focal point of a people who often followed God out of amazement, not always out of loyalty. The temple structure bore testimony from one generation to another of the struggle of a people to maintain a steadfast covenant with God in that homeland. Dwelling in the Promised Land meant learning to be a nation of rulers, rather than a ruled nation.

Remembering that dynamic image of the moving house of God, New Testament Christians described the church as a community of "living stones . . . being built into a spiritual house to be a holy priesthood, offering spiritual sacrifices acceptable to God through Jesus Christ." As Paul implies, the holy place in the church is not a part of the structure, but the essence of the relationships we have with one another in Christ, "And in him you . . . are being built together to become a dwelling in which God lives by his Spirit."

Christ calls us to a new level of authenticity in our relationship with God, with ourselves, and with others. What follows is a movement toward community, toward relating to other believers. I believe dazzlement is a vital place for communities of faith to cultivate. All too often, the enthralled believers are subtly encouraged to tone down their awe and conform to the less enthusiastic norms of the group. Congregations do well to maintain a well-cultivated garden of dazzlement in their midst.

The Need for Immediacy

My growing up in a Baptist tradition was influenced by a high value for "clean living" as expressed in strong prohibitions against smoking or other uses of tobacco, drinking, cussing, dancing, and worldly music. Symbolism was discouraged in church buildings, which tended to have auditoriums (not sanctuaries) that were plain and devoid of religious symbols except for civil religion, such as the U.S. and Christian flags. This blandness was partly due to the relative poverty of the congregation and partly due to our identification with poor, blue collar people, and partly as a carryover of Puritan starkness. There was a strong suspiciousness of symbol, analogy, metaphor, and allegory.

The vestiges of this plain board literalism were apparent during my seminary education. An ornate addition had been donated to the campus to house a wax Lord's Supper, based on the famous painting by Leonardo da Vinci. The gallery was abandoned by the benefactor when a missionary complained because of his struggle to convert Catholic Brazilians from their worship of icons. The structure has since been dedicated to the missiology department and the wax sculptures relocated to another site off campus.

At the same time, my religious heritage was strongly flavored with the Baptist respect for individual conscience and "soul competency." In this stark religious environment, which provided little beauty, symbol, or sensuality, I experienced a rich inner life of color, imagery, and ethereal euphoria. The placid and reserved cadence of worship was punctuated by the emotional release of the altar call response where my inner neurotic struggles could be voiced in the preacher's ear while the congregation sang an additional verse of the invitation hymn in accommodation to the seeker's need.

As a high schooler I presented an Easter program in my little church. I combined original compositions with the music of my favorite rock artists against the backdrop of a slide show of various historical stained-glass windows from churches I had recently visited in England. It was for me analogous to Luther's nailing his ninety-five theses on the Wittenberg church door, using the church as a communal structure for one's declaration of individualism. My congregation afforded me such a place of self-expression.

One way to cultivate dazzlement in community is by honoring the need for immediacy in life and worship. By immediacy I mean a sense that God is present here and now and can be interacted with. This is one of the basics of Christian mysticism: the belief that a person can have an experience of the presence of God. In my research on congregational cohesiveness, I discovered that the frustrated "quest for experiential Christianity" is a major reason why some church members drop out. In *Reclaiming Inactive Church Members,* I wrote: "The underlying question behind . . . these pilgrimage stories is whether or not a reconciling God is active in the lives of persons to lead them to wholeness. Otherwise, the Christian faith is merely the upholding of ancient rules in a mechanistic life of meaninglessness. These inactive members are looking for a life of purposeful religious experience."[18]

An emphasis on signs and wonders is one expression of the quest for a meaningful and immediate experience of God. Many of the mystics throughout history reported visions, locutions [the word sounds less psychotic than "hearing voices"] and other forms of intense experiences of the presence of God. Our need for a sense of connection with God and a confirmation of God's presence is a powerful one. Jung noted this need in spiritual development as a signal of moving into psychological maturity.[19]

A signal of deepening maturity is illustrated in Peter's vision of the ceremonially unclean creatures in Acts 10. Three times Peter saw a vision of animals, reptiles, and birds which were prohibited as food by Mosaic law. Accompanying the vision was the locution to "kill and eat . . . do not call anything impure that God has made clean."

The vision marked a turning point in Peter's spirituality, when he would begin to relate with openness to non-Jewish persons. Even while Peter was considering the meaning of his vision, messengers arrived from Cornelius, an Italian centurion, seeking Peter's ministry. In response, Peter did something he would normally not do: enter the home of a Gentile.

Peter was at a crisis point. Christianity was beginning to spread outside of Jewish circles. The Spirit of Christ was calling the disciples into the shadow lands of Gentile territory. This new freedom in Christ from ceremonial law was a lively struggle for Peter and a controversy in the church. Paul later reported that he confronted Peter for vacillating on his freedom and capitulating to the old Mosaic taboos on occasion.

Peter needed his faith community to help him find the meaning of his vision or, in the case of Cornelius, to *be* the meaning. This fresh emergence of Christ in his life threw all his theology on its head. What was wrong, under the old system, is now rightly pursued. Without the interpretation of our experiences by our community, we may be hard pressed to keep our bearings doctrinally.

Dazzlement is crisis: an emergence of Christ that brings new meaning to our lives. In crisis, when we are "flat on our back" with awe, we need the community of faith to interpret the crisis event for us and hold us as we reckon with the experience of God.

An Environment of Dazzlement

A second way to cultivate dazzlement is to foster a dazzling environment for community. Dazzlement gives us a new way of looking at God that fits with our experience. Community gives us relationships with sojourners who are likewise discovering God in new ways. In community we not only have a story to tell, but a place to tell it.

Worship services are worthy of our best planning and preparation, not just in the logistics of the order of worship but in intentionally creating an environment in which we recount the stories of faith. The use of well-chosen words and application of relevant theology, time for reflection, stirring music, arousing art, and architecture can all serve as precursors to a meaningful spiritual experience.

The environment of dazzlement includes the social setting. Occasions for having and sharing experiences of the presence of God in concert with another person or small group is vital. Participation in groups for prayer or spiritual direction where fresh experiences and new images of God are welcomed is also key.

The dazzling environment also entails the dynamics of the community's social system. The call of the renewing Spirit may come from a variety of sources, both from inside and outside the community.

Communities all have their Historians who know the community's stories, Innovators who press for change, and Peacemakers who seek to maintain the status quo. The Historian may actually serve as a mouthpiece for renewal by calling the community to reflect on how God has been revealed throughout the community's journey, and on occasion by reminding the community of their identity in the context of God's faithfulness. Innovators see new possibilities and Peacemakers often serve to manage the tension between memory and vision so that relationships in the community are enhanced. The depth of the community's soul can be seen in how it values the call of God and affirms those who are instruments of that call, even when this emergence creates tension.

Contemplation

A third way to deepen community-in-dazzlement is not only to create and recognize occasions of dazzlement, but also provide for contemplation. The tension must be maintained between our experience of God in community with others and our own sense of personal journey. The contemplative journey may lead us to the edge of community, seeking the solitary life, or to the center of society as prophets and social activists. A healthful community blesses both these traditions and supports persons as they seek either solitude or fellowship.

Another aspect of this tension of solitude and social involvement for a community of faith is in the maintenance of its own sense of journey. Many faith communities maintain this tension through their buildings. A contemplative spirit might lead a church to be thoughtful in attending to the congregation's history and how to memorialize the past foundations on the property. At the same time, the contemplative church is always observant of the dynamic nature of its own growth and development. It is all too easy for churches to either hang on to outmoded floor plans and useless stuff, or too quickly renovate and discard.

The first church I pastored many years ago was a small open country church in northeast Texas. One vestige of the church's distant past was a bell mounted on a stand outside the front entrance of the sanctuary. Pictures of the church building decades ago show that a primitive tower once housed the bell, which was used to summon local residents to meetings. Legends were extant about the demise of the bell tower—tornado, fire, deterioration—but the bell remained as a symbol of the church's presence and mission in the small farming community. At sunrise on Easter Sunday each year, the bell is rung, sending out its reflective signal that the church is both deeply rooted in past generations as well as grounded in the constant resurrection renewal of the living Christ. Ironically, that church, with its old-fashioned persona, was probably more open to innovation than any other church I've known. Perhaps the faith community that treasures the roots of its identity, perceptively distinguishing the significant from the insignificant, is most free to develop new perspectives for its own growth.

Discerning what in our past to hold onto, and what to let go of as we fashion our stories of community, is one aspect of contemplation. Another aspect of community and individual contemplation is historically known as the "examen of consciousness," or the "examen of conscience." It is a process of discerning the presence and will of God by looking deliberately at one's way of living.

At the outset of his ministry, Jesus engaged in such a self-examination. He was led by the Spirit into the desert to be tempted by the devil. After a forty-day fast, Satan tempted the famished Jesus to turn stones into bread, leap from the pinnacle of the temple and bow down and worship him. Jesus was confronted with the foundational temptations of his ministry, and all three involved dazzlement. Should he be a bread Messiah, garnering a following of astonished hungry masses? Should he be a sensational Messiah, amazing the crowds with superhuman feats such as jumping off tall buildings? Or, should he be astonished at the power of Satan rather than in his own identity?

Dazzlement is a place of temptation as well as closeness to God. Temptation comes in times of strength as well as weakness. As with Jesus' temptation to feed himself with loaves made from rock, our temptations of astonishment at our own powers includes the deception that we shouldn't use our powers for ourselves. They are only for others, we may conclude. The struggle is to know the difference between when we are serving others or ourselves; the temptation is to split the two. It becomes an either/or: to serve God by serving others or not serve God by serving ourselves. The basis of the temptation is in our construing God as only external—out in the world—and to detach from our interior self.

This is a lively temptation for those of us in the helping professions who typically struggle with unconsciously meeting our own needs by helping others. Helping others can be a temptation if we impose our need-to-be-needed on others, casting them in the role of the needy. The evil in this is twofold. One evil is the disabling of others so that we can employ our gifts in a way that serves our needs, not theirs. Another evil is our self-neglect, leading to burnout, as we cut ourselves off from the creative energy that arises from a faithful use of our gifts and giftedness. This form of service becomes a discipleship that leads to disillusionment rather than new levels of distraction and dazzlement.

Contemplation gives communities the ability to reflect on the nature of service: is it a ritualized behavior or a creative energy? A story from Matthew 17 illustrates the difference between ritual and revelation. Peter was told by Jesus to go catch a fish, get a coin out of its mouth and pay the tax for them both. Since ancient times, Israelites were required to pay an annual half-shekel tax for the support of the temple. Even after the destruction of the temple, the Romans continued to collect the tax for the temple of Jupiter.[20] Jesus instructed Peter in an innovative means of fulfilling this ritual requirement to maintain an institution that had lost its relevance. Soon Jesus would cleanse the temple by overturning the tables of money changers, highlighting its original purpose as a house of prayer. The temple tax was like "taxation without representation." Jesus knew this temple, like its predecessor, would soon be destroyed.

In dazzlement over the revelation of God, we transcend ritual. Years ago, I had a fishing experience analogous to Peter's. On a deep-sea fishing trip one summer, our boat's captain spent hours ritually taking us to all his favorite fishing spots. There were no fish. Finally, he used the sonar to locate the fish, and we all caught plenty!

Jesus, who knows what is down in the shadowy sea of our soul, emerges with treasures. Discerning communities wait for the revelation of Christ, with its power to transform.

The story of Jonah and the sea serves as another good biblical analogy of the revelation of God to a discerning community and how patterns of behavior are often hard to change. When the revelation came to Jonah to go preach to the Ninevites, he resisted. Apparently, Jonah valued the comfortable categories of his faith, which freed him from any responsibility for the spiritual welfare of his enemies. From the standpoint of ritual, revelation seems dark and evil, so Jonah rejected it and took a boat for Tarsus. En route, Jonah's boat was caught in a fierce storm. Hell-bent on not going to Nineveh, Jonah sensed the relationship between the storm and his alienation from God. He instructed the crew to save themselves by throwing him overboard into the sea, the abode of evil and death. With the humorous twist of the great fish that swallowed him, Jonah was delivered, and three days later was spat upon the shore with a new sense of mission, to his chagrin. Through his preaching the city repented and was spared the judgment of God. Bitter at the salvation of his enemies, Jonah sulked outside the city walls. Jonah was willing to use his redemptive gifts for everyone but himself!

Dazzlement is recognizing the treasures that emerge among us. Though tempted to reject the revelation, we soon realize the treasure that has emerged from the shadowy and lowly places. By embracing the emerging revelation of Christ, we are then empowered to use our gifts in redemptive and wonderful ways.

In first-century Palestine, shepherds were not considered the most respectable characters. Yet to a group of shepherds appeared angels announcing the birth of the Christ child. The incarnation is shrouded in mundane and humble trappings: conceived "out of wedlock" to displaced parents, the Christ was born in a stable and heralded to shepherds. The Christmas narrative teaches us much about cultivating dazzlement in community and recapturing the awesome mystery of God in our midst. Suddenly, Christ lights up our night sky with song and, before we know it, we are on a pilgrimage seeking Christ in the most unexpected of places!

Prayer of Dazzlement

For the birth of new hopes,
  I give thanks, O God.

In the hope of new beginnings,
  I wait for what emerges.

In the hope of deeper insight,
  I reflect on where I've been.

In the hope of life more simple,
  I say No to all but Your best for me.

In the hope of overcoming the snare of sin,
next time,
  I seek to be honest with myself, this time.

In the hope of You, and only You,
  I open my arms for embrace.

May I see Your face in all that rises to meet me today,
  Your path in all my journeys,
  Your light in all my decisions,
  Your grace in all my shadows;
  Your eyes, beholding me in love.

                                        Amen.

Reflection

What would it take for Christ to sweep you off your feet?

When do you feel most child-like?

On what are you focused that is not Christ, but could be of Christ and lead you to Christ?

Reflect on an "Aha!" moment when reading the Scripture, or a "Wow!" experience in life. What emerged and why was it a treasure?

Drive out into the country on a moonless, starlit evening and look up. Journey to a breath-taking vista and take it all in. Peer into the eyes of a newborn child. Observe the heroic courage of a person living creatively with a chronic illness or disability. Journal your reflections.What masks do you wear now? What mask are you attempting to wear when speaking to God?

What do you have a tendency to judge most harshly? Is Christ revealing to you some treasure from your "shadowy depths?"

What is your spontaneous reaction to exposure to the light of Christ's penetrating and illuminating gaze? How do you arrive at a balance between honesty regarding your inner darkness and acceptance of Christ's acceptance?

Reflect on what new name Christ may want to give you to reflect a change in your direction, focus or self-awareness.

In your religious community is there anything that before was wrong, but is now "rightly pursued?" What further changes might be "in the wind" of the Spirit's breath?

Endnotes

1 *Castle* (Van de Weyer), pp. 22-23.

2 Teresa, Vol. 3, p. 377.

3 *Interpreter's Dictionary*

4 Bly, Robert. *Iron John* (New York: Addison-Wesley Publishing Company, Inc., 1990), pp. 5-7.

5 *Pilgrim's Progress*, p. 65.

6 Donald Capps, *Deadly Sins and Saving Virtues* (Philadelphia: Fortress Press, 1987), p. 74.

7 Capps, pp. 91-92.

8 Abraham Maslow, "Neurosis as a Failure of Personal Growth," *Humanitas*, 1967, 3:163, quoted in Becker, p. 48.

9 Jung, Carl G. *Modern Man in Search of a Soul* (New York: Harcourt, Brace and Company, 1933), pp. 236-237.

10 Ibid.

11 Ibid.

12 Matthew Fox, *Meditations with Meister Eckhart*, (Sante Fe: Bear and Company, Inc., 1982), pp. 71, 74, 80.

13 *Interpreter's One Volume Commentary*

14 James William McClendon, Jr., "Toward a Conversionist Spirituality," *Ties That Bind: Life Together in the Baptist Vision* (Macon: Smyth & Helwys Publishing, Inc.), p. 23.

15 Ibid, pp. 23-24.

16 Teresa, Vol. 2, pp. 300-301.

17 Broughton, p. 33.

18 Jones, Mark. *Reclaiming Inactive Church Members* (Nashville: Broadman Press), 1988, p. 59.

19 Kelsey, Morton Kelsey. *Encounter with God* (Bethany Fellowship), reviewed in *Catalyst*, Vol. VI, No. 10, Oct. 1974 (Word, Inc.: Waco, Texas) and *Speaking in Tongues: An Experiment in Spiritual Experience* (London: The Epworth Press, 1964). Kelsey examines spiritual experience from a Jungian perspective.

20 *Interpreter's One Volume Commentary*, p. 631.

3

Discipled by Christ

The lake is immense in breadth, but lean in span. Across the nearside the traveler can see the emerging woods. A falcon resting at treetop surveys a nearby glade and then sails for the distance on huge flapping wings.

Mossy rocks protrude from the water's surface like knobby roots. Studying the slick steps, the traveler stretches out his arms for balance while making his way over the gnarled bridge.

Midway on his ethereal journey, he pauses to measure his progress on the stark surface. Phantom gray shadows dart across his vision as his eyes strain to maintain perspective in the black and white. Glancing toward shore from his pose on the cobbled bridge, the massive trees return his salute with vivid greens upon a luminous blue sky. Staring back at the rocky crags of his birth, back lit by the mid-morning sun and haloed by his filmy eyes, he pauses at his predicament. Half-way to, halfway from; nowhere to stand but on the thinning stones moistened by the ripple waves.

MSJ

Discipleship is a comfortable place on the journey of Christ. It is a place of definitions and distinctions. It is a place, for all appearances, in which we can settle into a way of life with the assurance that we are in the way of God. Yet, the comfort of assurance is mixed with the discomfort of transition. In Charles Dickens terms, it is the best and worst of times. We may someday look back on our first days of discipleship as idyllic and naive, perhaps with a bit of embarrassment for how we took the journey so simplistically and compulsively. Upon arrival, however, discipleship can appear as an august place of true significance for we have important work to do here.

Dazzled by Christ, we naturally seek a way to maintain the glory of our new discoveries. On the Mount of Transfiguration, Peter was likewise dazzled by the sight of Jesus in shining appearance speaking with Moses and Elijah and the sound of the thunderous voice of God. He blurted out a disciple's request to build a tabernacle for the three celestial personages, as if to capture the moment and relish it. That is discipleship: committing ourselves to the new way of life God has opened up for us.

Jesus amplified the noble character of discipleship in the manner of his calling. Like King Arthur gathering knights for his Round Table, Jesus invoked a traditional summons for his inner circle. It was a show-stopping moment. *Come, follow me.*

Symbols of Discipleship

Typical of any teacher or rabbi, Jesus' disciples bore distinctive signs of their class. The knights of Jesus' Round Table had their own equivalent of an identifying coat of arms, shield, crest, flag, vow, and probably even a secret handshake. Only, the marks of Jesus' disciples were in their character and behavior.

Discipleship is about having a visible method of living out the principles of the teacher. Disciples can be distinguished by their appearance, methodology, vocabulary, devotion, character qualities, and mind-set. Jesus calls persons to be disciples, to recruit disciples, and to assume the distinguishing characteristics of Christian discipleship.

A Name and a Prayer

In the Bible, a person's name may have special spiritual significance. This can also be true today in that our names often reflect some family lineage or a feeling our parents wished to convey by the sound of our name. Perhaps names were chosen for us because of their biblical or religious symbolism.

Adam's name, meaning "red man" or "earth man," is possibly derived from the earth from which he was formed. The meaning of Eve is stated outright in Genesis 3:20 as reflecting her motherhood of "all the living." Adam's blessing and curse both relate to his working the land for sustenance: the bounty of the Garden of Eden and the toil of the thistle-infested barren soil. Eve's blessing and curse both inhere in her relationships: motherhood, but with the increased pain of childbearing; partnership, but with the domination of her husband.

In following the call of God, many biblical characters received a name change reflecting their pilgrimage. Abram, who became a "stranger in a strange land" in his obedience to God, had his name changed to Abraham when God formed a covenant relationship with him. Abram, meaning "noble father," was changed to Abraham, "father of nations," indicating God's plan for him as the source of a new covenant community. Abraham's wife, Sarai, also underwent a name change. Sarai, or "princess," was changed to Sarah, a similar and newer form of Sarai. The exact difference in meaning between Sarai and Sarah is unknown but apparently marks her co-participation in the covenant.

One of the most remarkable accounts of a person's spiritual journey is the life of Jacob. Second born as a twin of his brother Esau, Jacob's name has the somewhat stigmatized connotation of "supplanter," or "deceiver," but may have a root meaning of "follow." His name was given as a depiction of his birth, holding the heel of his brother.

In his younger years, Jacob lived out the shadowy meaning of his name by supplanting his brother of both his birthright and patriarchal blessing. In fleeing his brother's wrath, Jacob had his first personal encounter, or distraction, with God at Bethel. Years later, fleeing his uncle Laban (who proved to be quite a match for Jacob's deceptive character), he again encountered God, this time in the form of a wrestling angel. The night Jacob spent striving with God bore Jacob a spiritual breakthrough, a blessing, and a new name: Israel, "one who struggles with God." As Israel, Jacob was able to reconcile with his brother Esau and become the father of the twelve tribes.

The narrative of Jacob reveals the deep significance of name changes. In following God, our identity finds its true center. Only as our journey is defined by our discipleship of God can we find the meaning—and true destiny—of our lives.

In the New Testament era, name changes reflected the rich mixture of culture and language as well as some form of personal conversion. Simon Peter is a good example. *Simon* is from the Hebrew, "God has heard." *Peter* is the Greek equivalent of the Aramaic *Cephas,* "rock." Aramaic was the Hebrew-derived language common to Palestine; the language of Jesus. "You are Simon son of John," Jesus told Peter, "You will be called Cephas." Building upon this meaning, Jesus blessed Peter's insight into His messianic nature, "you are Peter, and on this rock I will build my church." Apparently, Peter had "heard" God in his discernment that Jesus was the Christ. Flesh and blood had not revealed it to him.

"Simon" could have been a typical ancient mother's thanksgiving that God had heard her prayers for a son; "God has heard" *my* prayer. Perhaps it was his father's prayer reflecting the nation's longing for deliverance; "God has heard" *our* prayer. In light of all these possibilities, Jesus dared to suggest that impulsive, volatile Simon embodied the character of a foundational, rock-like faith.

Refreshingly, when God looks upon us, God sees not so much who we are, but who we can become. The divine Jeweler's eye sees the diamond in the rough, the potential that may be revealed through grace. Salvation is not only what we are saved *from*, but what we are saved *to*. We are not only persons who pray, but we become the answer to prayer.

The jewel that lay in the heart of Mary Magdalene was perhaps only seen by Jesus. As far as we know, Mary's name was never changed, but the connotation of her name changed as her life was changed. Tradition associates Mary Magdalene with the "sinful woman" of Luke 7 who anointed Jesus feet. However, the only clear references to Mary's previous character is the statement that Jesus had cast seven demons from her and the implication of her name. Magdala was known as a licentious town.

Whatever Mary's past, she became a woman most revered. She was a financial supporter of Jesus' ministry and was present at his crucifixion. She visited the tomb of Jesus after his death and was greeted by angels and by Jesus himself with the message of his resurrection, which she reported to the eleven remaining apostles.

The apostle Paul is most commonly known by this Greek form of his name. The Hebrew version is *Saul.* His adaptation of his name grows from his conversion experience and commissioning by Christ as a missionary. It was one way for Paul to distinguish the nature of his ministry as primarily to the Greek-speaking Gentiles.

For centuries, the members of certain religious orders have taken the name of a venerated character as a form of devotion, such as Sister Mary Magdalene or Brother John. Some later became venerated in their own right: John of the Cross; Mother Teresa. The decision of a name was made with much thought and prayer and reflected some major element of the person's faith journey and calling. Perhaps we would do well to adopt a not-so-literal version of this renaming and seek to discern the unique nature of our spiritual identity and name it.

My own journey toward self-awareness has taken me into the origins and meanings of my name. Mark is from the author of the New Testament Gospel and stands in complement to my older brother's Old Testament given name: David. As a means of carrying on her family linage, my mother gave me the middle name Sibley to provide some distinction to my common surname. Genealogy has revealed much concerning my Sibley roots. Tracing the Jones line, however, has proven more difficult because of its commonality and my grandfather's reticence to discuss family history. Mark is from the Latin for hammer, while Sibley is a contraction of sib, or kinsman, and lea, meaning land or field: *kinsman land* or *peaceful land.*

Reflecting on my name has helped me to get in touch with the paradoxes in my personality. I seek peace in relationships and struggle with the use of my personal authority, but the peaceful places I seek are often created when I employ my power authentically. In this light, I've had many rich meditations on Psalm 16:5-6:

> Lord, you have assigned me my portion and my
> cup; you have made my lot secure.
> The boundary lines have fallen for me in pleasant
> places; surely I have a delightful inheritance.

Discipleship is a place of name-taking; a time to
reflect on our identity and the form of our devotion.
Perhaps your name holds some meaning for you, or a
meaning to redefine in light of God's grace. What identity is Christ giving you?

* * *

Along with a disciple's name, pupils of the teacher
are given a disciple's prayer. "Teach us to pray, just as
John taught his disciples," requested Jesus' disciples.
Jesus' response was to give them what is now referred to
as the Lord's Prayer or the Our Father.

> Our Father which art in heaven, Hallowed be thy
> name. Thy kingdom come. Thy will be done in earth, as
> it is in heaven. Give us this day our daily bread. And
> forgive us our debts, as we forgive our debtors. And
> lead us not into temptation, but deliver us from evil:
> For thine is the kingdom, and the power, and the glory,
> for ever. Amen. (Matt. 6:9-13 KJV).

Another example of a disciple's prayer is the Seren-
ity Prayer quoted often in twelve step recovery programs, such as Alcoholics Anonymous.

> God, grant me the serenity
> to accept the things I cannot change,
> Courage to change the things I can, and
> Wisdom to know the difference.

Prayers of discipleship are often heard subtly in the
phrases and images of spontaneous prayers, as in some
of the prayers I remember from throughout my life. My
father's favorite address for God is as "dear and most
gracious." The image of a "lighthouse on a hill" was

common in a deacon's offertory prayer, which always included a call to mission. Images of children pervaded the prayers of an elderly woman. Prayer requests for rain characterized a young boy and intercessions for pets, a young girl. A farmer's rote prayer ended each time with a benediction for God's perpetual presence "from time to time."

Crosses and Chains: Counting the Cost

> And anyone who does not carry his cross and follow me cannot be my disciple . . . in the same way, any of you who does not give up everything he has cannot be my disciple. (Luke 14:27,33)

The disciple's life is a committed life. The cross, for Jesus, was the ultimate symbol of commitment to his mission. For his followers, there were also crosses to bear and chains to wear because their mission and message set them at odds with political and religious institutions. Any discipleship that eschews the cross is false discipleship, said Bunyan. The Christian life is by definition counter-cultural in that it always seems to challenge the values of any system in which it is expressed. Paul and the Christians of the first centuries of the church were so much as resigned to this inevitable certainty. "In fact, everyone who wants to live a godly life in Christ Jesus will be persecuted," Paul concluded.

One temptation is to resolve the tension between gospel and culture by creating a Christian society. Augustine had his vision of the City of God, and Calvin, among others, sought to make it a reality by establishing a social order that was thoroughly Christian. But, history has recorded countless failures of any society that sought to impose the Christian ideal: the Spanish Inquisition, witch hunts, and countless other examples of the torturous failings of a "state church." It is as if the two— Christianity and Christian government—are immutably incompatible. Religion and government bring out the worst in each other when fused; the best when kept separate. The most heroic of religious martyrs and victims were those who were persecuted by religious powers using state sanction, Jesus being the archetype.

For New Testament Christians, crosses and chains were symbols of their submission to a higher order. In accepting a status of servant of Christ, they transcended any earthly authority. One of Paul's designations of himself was as a "prisoner of Jesus Christ." It was "for the hope of Israel" that he was chained. The usual Roman custom was to chain a prisoner to a guard, making the guard every bit as much a prisoner. For Paul, his chains symbolized his attachment to Christ and were used to take his own captives; at least one of Paul's guards converted.

The paradox of freedom is symbolized in chains. Jesus' teachings, which give us the truth that sets us free, are never more active than when we are bound. Exterior bonds only reveal interior freedom. Ancient wisdom teaches that we overcome by yielding: "Yield and overcome; bend and be straight; empty and be full; wear out and be new; have little and gain . . ."

To yield to our limits is to find true freedom to overcome all limitations. When surrendered to Christ, even death cannot hold us, as Jesus taught with a parable, "unless a kernel of wheat falls to the ground and dies, it remains only a single seed. But if it dies, it produces many seeds. The man who loves his life will lose it, while the man who hates his life in this world will keep it for eternal life (John 12:24-26)."

Discipleship is about living within our limits. Another temptation regarding cross-bearing and chain-wearing is the notion that we can become limitless. Let me be clear. There is a difference between becoming limitless and transcending limitations, just as there is a difference between becoming a god and being godly. Actually, spirituality is all about limits. The most divine act is the incarnation: God becoming human and choosing to live within the limits of human existence. The emphasis here is on choice. We may lose our sense of freedom by not recognizing our options and ability to choose. Even the most desperate of situations cannot strip us of our most human—and divine—quality: the ability to choose. Victor Frankl, in his book *Man's Search for Meaning*, documented how this most basic element can make all the difference in life—even in a Nazi concentration camp. One thing that can never be taken from us is the freedom to choose our response; in choosing how we respond we create meaning, and through finding the meaning of a limitation we thereby transcend it.

The disciples of Jesus indeed had their crosses to bear. Legends have it that Andrew, Bartholomew, Philip, Simon the Zealot, and Peter were martyred by crucifixion. Purportedly, Andrew and Peter felt unworthy to die in the same manner as their Master and asked for their crosses to be different. The Andrew Cross is traditionally in the shape of an X while Peter's cross was upside down. Likewise, New Testament writers avoided referring to their own sufferings as a metaphorical cross. Paul chose instead to use the term "thorn," which had almost identical meaning, in 2 Corinthians 12:7-10, "there was given me a thorn in my flesh, a messenger of Satan, to torment me."

Obviously not all Christians are given a cross of martyrdom to bear or chains of persecution to wear, but discipleship has its price: our crosses of self-sacrifice and chains of limitation. Discipleship is not just an inner discipline and experience. For Moltmann, the spiritual discipleship of Christ that we cultivate in the soul must also correspond to discipleship in actual human, political contexts.

There are two extremes, though, in the way we might respond to our crosses or chains. Some Christians avoid a basic level of commitment to Christ which creates any tension in their relationships, while others artificially create victim scenarios in order to "suffer for Christ." Richard Niebuhr referred to these extremes as the "Christ of Culture" and the "Christ against Culture."

In the first case, Jesus was very clear that discipleship entailed a cross. "If anyone would come after me, he must deny himself and take up his cross and follow me." Discipleship involves self-denial and surrender.

In the story of the Rich Young Ruler (Matt. 19), Jesus was approached by a man who wanted to know what good thing he must do to inherit eternal life. Ultimately, Jesus invited him to sell all his possessions for the poor and follow him. The man balked. Of course, he balked! What Jesus was in effect saying to him was that God didn't want part of what he had, but *all* of it!

By surrendering all that we are and possess to Christ, we transcend the limitations of our attachments. Those who waver at such a ponderous commitment see only too clearly the breadth of it. A surrender to leave all, as Christ left all, requires what John Mogabgab terms "participation in the heart of Christ" which "draws us into the same relationship that Jesus enjoyed with his Father."

* * *

In the temptation to create our own victimization, it is important to note that not every hardship is a cross. In fact, not every hardship is for us to bear. But, if our belief system requires that we endure hardship as a means of spiritual growth or reward, then we will likely create persecution for ourselves where none may exist. We may do this by taking such a caustic approach in living our faith that others are bound to reject us or protect themselves from us. Their is a difference between righteousness and obnoxiousness.

We may also invite victimization by acting so powerless that others are invited to take advantage of us. There is a difference between persecution and victimization. Persecution arises extrinsically out of our identification with an ideology or community whereas victimization is intrinsic to our self-perception of powerlessness.

Flora Slosson Wuellner provides some advice for discerning the difference between a cross, on the one hand, and not living out of our personal power, on the other hand:

> Only rarely are we asked by God to stay in a destructive situation. We are to preserve ourselves in wholeness and to release ourselves from injustice and danger unless we feel especially called to a particular cross. And then we will know it to be our cross by the strength, peace, and authenticity we feel . . . A cross to which God calls us is the choice we make in freedom to reach out to lift a burden or share suffering with another . . . a true cross is offered in freedom and includes something of God's passion of compassion.[6]

The Yoke of Loyalty

> Take my yoke upon you and learn from me, for I am gentle and humble in heart, and you will find rest for your souls. For my yoke is easy and my burden is light. (Matt. 11:29-30).

Jesus knew about yoke-making and yoke-taking. Working with his stepfather Joseph, Jesus no doubt learned to fashion yokes and plows, which were typical fare for first-century carpenters. Yokes enabled two animals to be harnessed together and connected to a plow. More sophisticated yokes were tailored to the form of the specific animals in order to increase comfort and minimize chaffing. Yokes of this sort that I have seen are works of art.

Yokes were also worn by prisoners and slaves, and the term became synonymous with subjection and servitude. For example, Paul instructs servants who "are under the yoke" to "count their own masters worthy of honor." More broadly, being yoked had the connotation of working together with a "yokefellow."

Biblically, the yoke was a spiritual symbol. Paul encouraged the Galatians to stand firm in their grace-ful freedom in Christ and not to "be burdened again by a yoke of slavery," referring to the Mosaic law. The Corinthians were warned to maintain their Christian distinctiveness and not "be yoked together with unbelievers."

Jesus' use of the term grew out of the rabbinical tradition. To take the yoke of a teacher was to become a pupil or disciple and submit to the "Master's" instruction and lifestyle. Jesus contrasts his yoke of grace with the heavy burdens of legalistic teachers, namely the Pharisees. Theirs was a bondage to an impossible task. The law is like a Sisyphus hill: all work, no reward.

The grace of Christ not only fits us perfectly, but it wears well. It is the difference between the curse of work and the blessing of work.

Love fulfills the law and transforms a yoke of bondage into a yoke of freedom.

To serve Christ is to love Christ, for Christ sets us free. On occasion, slaves in the ancient world who had been granted their freedom continued to serve their former masters out of loyalty. Discipleship is a yoke of loyalty and love: fragile, but stronger than iron. It is a yoke to be desired.

The best case for discipleship, according to Dallas Willard, is not in the costs of discipleship, but in the costs of nondiscipleship.

> Nondiscipleship costs abiding peace, a life penetrated throughout by love, faith that sees everything in the light of God's overriding governance for good, hopefulness that stands firm in the most discouraging

of circumstances, power to do what is right and withstand the forces of evil. In short, it costs exactly that
abundance of life Jesus said he came to bring. The cross-
shaped yoke of Christ is after all an instrument of
liberation and power to those who live in it with him
and learn the meekness and lowliness of heart that
brings rest to the soul.[8]

Yoke-bearing is finding comfort in the disciplines of
faith. In discipleship, we develop what has historically
been called a "rule of life," a pattern or habit of devotion,
that produces in us the desired results of piety. As Peter
said to Jesus, "To whom [else] shall we go? You have the
words of eternal life."

The yoke of discipleship provides a safe place to get
to know ourselves. There is something about submission that creates boundaries within which we may feel
secure, much as a child needs security to develop competency and self-esteem. We will eventually grow beyond the stage of living by mere rules. Paul referred to
the law as a "schoolmaster" we outgrow in faith. But,
there are some rules we never outgrow, such as "look
both ways before crossing the street," or "serve your
guests first."

As yokes need disciples, so disciples need yokes.
Discipleship is a place on the journey of Christ where we
need boundaries, strong charismatic leadership, and
established order. It is with the yoke of discipleship that
we harness the dazzling breakthroughs in our faith
journey and milk them of their meaning.

Cloak and Book: Mastering the Methods

To continue with Jesus' earthy metaphors of Discipleship, the cloak and book are to the disciple as a
stool and stall are to a dairy farm. Milking the meaning
of Dazzlement—the work of the disciple—requires devotional disciplines.

Historically, disciples have attired themselves in a way that identified them with their teacher. Nurses' caps were not long ago a symbol of the school from which the nurse graduated but have since been laid aside for "scrubs" and more fashionable uniforms. Professors still carry on this tradition by donning their academic garb for graduation ceremonies, with stoles and caps from their alma maters.

At the hospital where I once worked, I would often see a particular nursing instructor who still wears her cap and white uniform. In addition, a few Catholic nuns make daily rounds in their habits, although it is sometimes a mind bender to see these elderly sisters walking along in their tennis shoes.

The history of religious "habits" is illustrative of the disciple's cloak. "Habit" comes from the Latin for "condition" or "dress" and carries a double meaning. The ancient clothing of a particular profession conveyed the meaning of a lifestyle or pattern of life, as it still does in certain professions today. A friend, and former nun, once told me how the nuns' habit originated as the dress of the common milkmaid: it was an attempt to identify the order with a most common and humble lifestyle. It did not have the unconventional appearance that it does today. Now in our society, a religious habit has the opposite effect, setting a person apart. Habits can long outlive their meaning.

The professional habit, or uniform, indicates to society that a person has gained mastery and has developed reliable patterns of competency or is an apprentice to a master. The physician's lab coat, the police uniform; a judge's robe. Whether Jesus' disciples wore distinctive clothing is unknown, but their apprenticeship role was clear. The "school" of Rabbi Jesus was his presence; his disciples followed him to observe his behavior, listen to his teaching, and imitate his values. Paul was interested that Christians "put on" the garment of Christ-like living, ". . . put off your old self, which is being corrupted by its deceitful desires; to be made new in the attitude of your minds; and to put on the new self, created to be like God in true righteousness and holiness (Eph. 4:22-24)."

Scripture depicts believers in heaven clothed with white robes, symbolic of the righteousness of Christ. Christian in *Pilgrim's Progress* received a disciple's raiment on his journey which set him apart from the townspeople.

Disciples still follow and observe Jesus, only now the observable Christ is in the books of Scripture and the lives of other disciples. Academically, the term for Bible study is exegesis, meaning "to explain," or draw the meaning *out* of (ex-) the text. I remember the first time I heard the word, it sounded something like "exe-Jesus." The word picture I had in my mind was drawing Jesus out of the text, which by the way, is a good way to define exegesis! Disciples, in their exegetical devotion, draw a picture of Jesus from their sacred texts in order to emulate him. Christians inherited a strong Hebrew exegetical devotion which centered around the books of Moses, the Psalms, and other Scriptures. Not only were the Scriptures studied thoroughly but were used in prayer. The Jewish exegetical tradition was explained to me by a Jewish friend as "read it, taste it, and be it." A Jewish mother, when her son began to read the Torah, would place a drop of honey in his mouth, reminiscent of Psalm 119:103, "How sweet are your promises to my taste, sweeter than honey to my mouth!" Ezekiel's call symbolizes being the word of God, as he was given a scroll by God with a message and then told to eat it and go proclaim the message. "And it tasted as sweet as honey in my mouth," Ezekiel reflected (Ez. 3:3).

Lectio Divina, or "divine reading," is a very old form of prayer that utilizes a biblical passage in a series of four steps. *Lectio,* or reading, involves reading a brief Scripture. *Meditatio* is a meditation on the text in an attempt to make it personally relevant. The third step, *oratio*, is prayer: responding to God from the message of the text. *Contemplatio* is a contemplation on the experience of God in the prayer. A twelfth-century monk described the four steps of the *Lectio Divina* as: reading seeks, meditation finds, prayer demands, and contemplation tastes.

The disciple's book becomes a part of the disciple, and the disciple in turn becomes the book. Anton Boisen, the founder of clinical pastoral education, used the phrase, "living human documents," to emphasize the true nature of theology. Boisen wanted his students to know that beyond the sacred texts they studied in seminary were the texts, just as sacred, of the lives of their patients and peers. It is from these living human documents that they would perhaps learn the most about the ways of God.

The Fruit of the Vine: Spiritual Growth

As disciples taste "that the Lord is good" through the methods of discipleship, they then begin to embody the milk and honey of the spiritual life. It is this incarnation of the gospel that is most evident in the way people conduct themselves, displaying deep values and investing in relationships.

Teresa could not say enough good about disciples:

> We may call these souls blessed . . . I am convinced that our Lord will henceforth never cease to keep them in security of conscience . . . God has shown them no small favor . . . They are very desirous not to offend [God]... [Devoted Christians who] spend hours in meditation, they employ their time well, exercise themselves in works of charity to their neighbours, are well-ordered in their conversation and dress, and those who own a household govern it well.[10]

Those who followed Jesus, seeking to learn his methods and uncover his secrets, soon learned that what governed Jesus' actions was not a code of rules, but a heart of love. Jesus lived a radical love.

The classic parable of Jesus, which forges the distinction between discipleship piety and godly love, is the Good Samaritan in Luke 10. The story is told in response to a canon lawyer's quandary over Jesus' teaching on neighborly love and responsibility.

The lawyer's question was a narrow one: how to be justified before God.

Jesus' response: love.

The lawyer retorts with a self-revealing request for clarification: Who is my neighbor?

A man is mugged at the outskirts of Jerusalem and lay in shambles on the side of the road, Jesus hypothesized. Though the religious types left him to his misery, a foreigner came to his rescue.

The story teaches that radical love prompts us to cross all manner of boundaries and conventions in our care for others. This is the true fruit of discipleship. Love is demonstrated in our instinctive willingness to let another's crisis be our crisis.

In essence, discipleship goes far beyond the disciplines of a pious life. As I once heard a friend put it, discipleship is not so much about mastering disciplines as having the discipline to be mastered.

Discipleship is not the mastery of a method, but a constant relearning. We never outgrow the need for a Good Samaritan to come along after us and point out our blind spots.

The Way

> I admit that I worship the God of our fathers, as a follower of the Way.
>
> Paul before Felix (Acts 24:14)

Discipleship is the highway of life's journey. The real traveling is done on the highway. Discipleship is a mode of spiritual growth that gives us the sense of "getting somewhere." We can mark our progress with attainment of piety and knowledge.

A highway has distinct boundaries; it is best to stay on the road, within the stripes, and to obey the traffic laws. Discipleship, perhaps more than any other place on the spiritual journey, is a shared experience. The conventionality of discipleship requires that we adopt certain norms of behavior and belief in order to function in the society of fellow pilgrims.

A highway is paved by others beforehand at great expense of time, energy and resources. The community of discipleship is not only a geographical network of relationships, but a historical one. From the canonization of Scripture to the development of denominations, the trail has already been blazed. Discipleship is not about cutting new paths through uncharted lands; it is about following the map, adhering to the tenants, obeying the rules, and respecting the wisdom of those who have gone before us and borne witness to the guidance of God, generation after generation.

Highway travel requires occasional stops for rest and refueling. In their jealousy of the fast lane, disciples often lament the waning of their energy. Alas, the power is not of ourselves, but of the Spirit. Our vessels run empty. Layovers at the journey's roadside offer an opportunity to once again be distracted by Christ into a dazzling renewal. As Elijah was fed by an angel so he could journey on to Horeb, we continue on for the next leg of our journey in the strength of God's rejuvenation.

And finally, a journey does not merely consist of highway travel. The road is a means of reaching a destination. On a larger scale, our life's journey will entail numerous arrivals and departures, exchanging one vehicle for another, and sharing the journey with various traveling companions. Ultimately, discipleship as a methodology cannot carry us to the higher and deeper paths of spiritual experience. These paths must be created in our own unique search for intimacy with God. Along that path we will discover and discard images of God. Each will offer limited light. Like Christian and Christiana in *Pilgrim's Progress*, we will find new companions to accompany us for parts of the journey, but the paths we traverse will be of our choosing.

With Christ on the journey, the way leads to change and growth. Whatever the road, when journeyed with Christ, the route leads to revolution.

As Jesus made his way to Jerusalem for the last time, he foretold an incredible story. Many parables broke open the imagination of his hearers about the nature of the Kingdom of God. The first shall be last and the last first. In a world that often excluded children, Jesus bid them come to him as honored guests. He turned the established concepts of faith upside down.

After his resurrection, Jesus met two disciples on the road to Emmaus. There he revealed the hope of a new order. Their hearts burned within them, warmed by the transformation of bewilderment into dazzling imagination. Over five hundred disciples received such visits by the resurrected Christ. The movement metamorphosized from a rabbinical school to a transformative journey.

A chief persecutor of the church, Saul was met en route to Damascus by a brilliant Christ. Blinded by the vision and cast from his mount, Saul's whole ideological world crumbled in the presence of undeniable experience. Casting down what opposes the truth, Jesus saved Saul from his own bitterness and Fundamentalism.

The End of the Way

For the disciples, the last journey with Jesus to Jerusalem ended not in victory, but dismay. The oven of Jesus' confrontation with world power was heating up. He left off the cryptic paradoxical language and began to speak more clearly, more audaciously, about his mission, his identity, and his fate at the hands of the political machine. When Peter objected, Jesus scolded, "Out of my sight, Satan!"

Disciples like the predictable, the knowable, the sure bet. Jesus turned the tables. Disciple prayers are polite, correct, externalized . . . and manipulative. Jesus was on a mission and he had no stomach for political correctness or comfortable staidness. The fire of his destiny scorched all dross from his engagements with others. Soon after Jesus' death, this fire would light on the heads of his disciples in a Pentecostal explosion of power. It is a fire of giftedness, not methods. It is a fire that torches our illusions of the way we believe God "should" behave. This fire purifies our souls and refines our gifts for creativity.

Discipleship is not necessarily a creative place. Disciples love the tried and true, the same old stories; the conventional form.

But, sooner or later, Jesus will take his disciples to the brink of destruction and invite them to leave behind their security blankets. Leave behind the method and fly with me, bids God. The discipline comes from the relationship, not vice versa.

The gospel story includes one sad soul who couldn't let go; one disciple who valued the method more than the relationship. Judas was the Patron Saint of Blind Faith. When he saw that Jesus was breaking the mold and moving beyond the popular notions of a military Messiah, Judas had to make his play. This Christ he saw emerging was either the salvation of the world or its destruction. He knew he had to either kill Jesus or be killed by him; betray or be betrayed.

Jesus called his disciples to betray their holy objects and images and follow him. Leave your riches for the poverty of God and be rich in spirit. Leave your families and be my brothers and sisters. Leave your books and be my flesh and blood.

Like Captain Ahab pursuing his Moby Dick shadow, Judas had been captured by what he pursued. Like Jonah, fleeing from the love of God in his hatred and bitterness, Judas found himself in a deep abyss. Unlike Jonah, however, Judas would not allow himself to be spit out in liberating transformation.

Peter, too, was consumed by his shadow as the climax of the drama approached. Carrying a knife to Gethsemane, he was prepared to kill for Jesus, but before the night was through he had used the sword of his tongue to deny him three times.

Judas and Peter both teach us something about faith and discipleship.

Following Christ eventually brings us to a point where we must betray and deny any ideal of Christ that doesn't embody the Spirit of God. We will have to kill him or be killed by him. We will have to either turn from the Real Christ in order to preserve our own illusory kingdoms, or allow the Real Christ to reveal to us our True Self, surrendering our self-illusions in a painful transformation.

With Judas and Peter we may discover the grandiosity of our compulsiveness.

For many, this is why the journey does not proceed beyond Discipleship. Disciples hold their masters to the discipline they are learning. We want to hold the moment, to capture it and bind it fast so that we may maintain our compulsive control.

In this grandiosity, we are unwilling to relinquish control. Jesus says to us "I am the way and the truth and the life," but our lives may be focused on our way and our truth and our life rather than on Christ. We become caught in our own web of illusion.

In Luke 10, Jesus was hosted by two sisters, Mary and Martha. As Jesus taught, Mary sat and listened while Martha prepared hors d'oeuvres. Frustrated with her sister's disinterest in being the perfect hostess, Martha asked Jesus to straighten Mary out, "Tell her to help me!"

"Martha, Martha," Jesus consoled, "you are worried and upset about many things, but only one thing is needed. Mary has chosen what is better."

Mary and Martha have long served as symbols for different ways of relating to Christ. I think of Martha as the epitome of Discipleship—minding her manners, filling her socially-expected role, while Mary gives herself to transformation.

To progress in the journey and to follow Christ in His own transformations, we must be willing to be transformed. As Jesus was willing to die to his life and method, so must we. Without death there can be no resurrection.

Teresa uses the analogy of a silkworm to convey this truth. The little silkworm spins its coffin-cocoon and there dies, only to emerge a new creature with wings.

The lives of a snake and caterpillar are similar in many respects. Both crawl and both shed their skin. The difference is that after emerging from its old skin the snake is still a snake, but the caterpillar is a butterfly. The snake is still crawling; the butterfly soars.

Discipleship and Community

Picturing Judas alone cutting his deal with the religious leaders—or Peter alone outside the Sanhedrin courts denying knowledge of Jesus to strangers—is a graphic view of Discipleship at its weakest. Yet, these scenes are re-enacted daily by disciples who find themselves alone in their disillusionment. What breaks down for these souls who are adrift?

Discipleship is by nature a community spirit. It is in the conventionality of faith and methodology for growing

in faith that disciples thrive and green their budding
spiritual powers. But, it is this conventionality that can
become dogma. Deviate from it and you are threatening
the status quo. Question it and you speak heresy.

It is no accident that Jesus died as both a heretic and
insurrectionist. He was a radical in the most profound
senses of the word. Eugene Peterson describes Jesus'
parables as time bombs that have a delayed reaction in
subverting the world view of those who ponder them.

As disciples, we are not here to conventionalize the
world but to undermine it.

The church is not a factory for indoctrination, but a
staging area for revolution.

Listen to Annie Dillard's aghast bemusement at the
irony of spiritual community:

> Why do people in churches seem like cheerful,
> brainless tourists on a packaged tour of the Absolute?
> ...On the whole, I do not find Christians, outside of the
> catacombs, sufficiently sensible of conditions. Does
> anyone have the foggiest idea what sort of power we so
> blithely invoke? Or, as I suspect, does no one believe a
> word of it? The churches are children playing on the
> floor with their chemistry sets, mixing up a batch of
> TNT to kill a Sunday morning. It is madness to wear
> ladies' straw hats and velvet hats to church; we should
> all be wearing crash helmets. Ushers should issue life
> preservers and signal flares; they should lash us to our
> pews. For the sleeping god may wake someday and
> take offense, or the waking god may draw us out to
> where we can never return.[11]

Safety is found in numbers, but the Great Insurrectionist's community is not about safety. It is about daredevil, death-defying danger. I have not come to bring
peace on earth, Jesus announced, but a sword.

The threat to our community is not individualism; it
is apathy and laziness.

Apathy, in the sense of having buried our anger and
woundedness so deeply that it has sapped all motiva-

tion for connecting. Laziness, in that we become drowsy in the warm bed of country club luxury or town hall fellowship. If God calls, take a message.

The key to the engine room of our community ship is another sort of indifference. Ironically, this indifference to all but God's desire has come to be known as interior freedom. It is an indifference, the spiritual masters insist, to all but the will of God. Such an indifference frees us from all "inordinate attachments." Otherwise, we are bound to the harbor of our traditions and safe methods.

If Discipleship is about knowing and doing the will of God, then interior freedom is the prerequisite course. Too many Christians have flunked out.

Imagine what church business would be like if all decision making was based on a communal discernment of God's will that demanded a relinquishment of all claims on the outcome. It would force us to listen to one another as a way of listening for the voice of God. It would entail scrapping some very logical plans for some rather outrageous notions. It might involve waiting when we would like to be acting; and acting when we'd rather be waiting. It might mean a conversion to the position of the minority. Find the edge, find the fringe; find the least considered, and there you will likely find Christ. Rather than brick and mortar, church buildings should be inflatable castles like children jump in at birthday parties. They would expand and contract with the movement of the body. They could be relocated at a moment's notice. And they would require the Spirit-wind to keep them inflated else they lose their shape altogether.

Prayer of Discipleship

Take, Lord, all my liberty,
   my memory, my understanding
      and my whole will.

You have given me all that I have,
   all that I am,
      and I surrender all to Your Divine will.

Give me only Your love and Your grace.
   With this I am rich enough,
      and I have no more to ask.

                                                    Amen.
                              Ignatius of Loyola

Reflection

When do you feel most you?

Why do you avoid solitude? What do you find in solitude? In what ways do you discover yourself to be a gift that enriches community? . . . that threatens it?

Is your weariness related to operating out of weakness or an overextended strength?

Are you a religious person or a spiritual person?

When you get in trouble, is it for being a Mary or a Martha?

Do you consider yourself problem centered or God centered?

At what edge, on what fringe, have you found Christ?

In what way is taking upon yourself the "Yoke of Jesus" a freeing experience for you?

As a Christian, you have "put on Christ." Has the original garment you put on outlived its meaning, or changed to continue to speak its meaning to current society?

Have you ever felt that participating in church put you in daredevil, death-defying danger? Would this be possible? Desirable? True to Jesus' example?

Endnotes

1   Lao Tsu, *Tao te ching,* trans. Gia-fu Feng and Jane English (New York: Random House, Inc., 1972), chapter 22.

2   Moltmann, *Experiences of God*, p. 73.

3   Niebuhr, H.R., *Christ and Culture* (New York: Harper & Brothers, 1951), pp. 40-41.

4   Mogabgab, John S., "Courage," *Weavings,* Vol. XII, No. 3, May/June 1997, pp. 2-3.

5   Jones, Mark. "Anger and Personality Disorders," *The Journal of Pastoral Care.*

6   Wuellner, Flora Slosson. *Prayer, Fear, and Our Powers.* Nashville: Upper Room Books, 1992, pp. 85-86.

7   Willard, Dallas. *The Spirit of The Disciplines.*

8   Ibid.

9   Morello, Sam Anthony. *Lectio Divina and the Practice of Teresian Prayer,* 1995: ICS Publications, Institute of Carmelite Studies, Washington, D.C., p. 23.

10 *Castle* (Van de Weyer), pp. 31-33.

11 Annie Dillard, *Teaching a Stone to Talk: Expeditions and Encounters* (New York: Harper & Row, Publishers, 1982), pp. 40-41.

12 From Richard J. Foster, *Prayers From the Heart,* p. 27.

DISILLUSIONMENT:
A TURNING POINT

4

DISILLUSIONED BY CHRIST

The moon casts no light but has turned its face to the depths. Forsaken of all starlight, the night sky is obscured by a pallor gray cloudiness. Sandstone boulders glow strangely in a darkness so dense that only the images of his mind's eye can be seen dancing like stalking demons on his vision's periphery.

A howling silence, a cold dry wind that roars like distant sea waves through the cliffs; a white noise pervading a dark conspiracy of stillness. It is here in the secrecy of this placelessness and aloneness and nothingness that the traveler finds what cannot be found anywhere or from anyone or in anything.

MSJ

Powerfully brilliant images of Messiah blazed in the minds of the disciples as they traveled with Jesus. The Mosaic prophet, the psalterian priest, the prophetic judge, the Maccabean king—historical lenses through which they viewed him—electrified their expectancy and solidified the boundaries of their understanding of his essence. Iconoclastically Jesus assaulted these motifs with increasing clarity as his ministry progressed. In Caesarean Philippi, he confronted his disciples' images by asking, "Who do people say the Son of Man is?" and most poignantly, "Who do you say I am?" After hearing Peter's confession of Jesus as the Christ, Jesus described the upcoming sufferings he was prepared to face. Peter was dumbfounded and his protest earned him an even more shocking rebuke from Jesus, "Out of my sight, Satan! You are a stumbling block to me; you do not have in mind the things of God, but the things of men."

On the road to Jerusalem for what he knew was the last time, Jesus pulled no punches in striking at the Messianic illusions of his followers:

> "We are going up to Jerusalem, and the Son of Man will be betrayed to the chief priests and the teachers of the law. They will condemn him to death and will turn him over to the Gentiles to be mocked and flogged and crucified. On the third day he will be raised to life!" (Matt. 20:18-19)

And Jesus proceeded to do just that. By week's end his followers were scattered, scared, stunned, and hopeless. Their theologies held no room for the concept of a crucified God. With their images of Jesus dashed, they hid in secret meeting places and some even reverted to their former vocation of fishing. There was no longer anyone to follow, since they had been disciples of their illusions, not Christ.

* * *

I approach this chapter with a reverence akin to what I feel when I hear a person sharing their innermost painful thoughts and feelings. In such a holy moment there is a vulnerability that lays open the heart to the gaze of others. What I seek to describe here is for me the most significant place of conversion in my spiritual journey. If my description has a familiar sense for you, I pray that I enunciate its meaning in a way that creates a more profound awareness of the sacredness of your own story. On the other hand, if my representation of this spiritual locality bears no resemblance to any spot on your spiritual map, I pray that you may gain a sense of awe at the dark night others have beheld, perhaps with thankfulness for your own faith and perhaps with a reverence for a relationship with God so vastly foreign to your own, but nonetheless holy.

At one level, there is admittedly no way to elucidate this darkness. I struggle here to present the experience in some systematic form, but find this an unwieldy challenge since the experience of disillusionment is in itself formless. John of the Cross's poetry proclaims the babbling sound of those who seek to speak words of faith to a disillusioned soul:

> All who are free,
> tell me a thousand graceful things of you;
> all wound me more
> and leave me dying
> of, ah, I-don't-know-what behind their
>   stammering.[1]

John's reproduction of the stammering "babbling bits" can be heard more clearly in the onomatopoeia of the original Spanish, *un no sé qué que quedan balbuciendo.* In his commentary on the stanza, John invites us to consider that for those who travel in the darkness of an obscure faith with hearts that beat for union with God,

... there is a certain "I-don't-know-what" that one feels
is yet to be said, something unknown still to be spoken,
and a sublime trace of God as yet uninvestigated but
revealed to the soul, a lofty understanding of God that
cannot be put into words . . . since it is not understandable, it is indescribable, as a result, [the soul] says the
creatures are stammering, for they do not make it
completely known.[2]

Disillusionment is a turning point that leads from
the most conventional of faith experiences to a solitary
walk with God; a walk so solitary that it may feel like a
walk without God.

Losing Our Illusions

As Henry Sloan Coffin once said, we would not be
disillusioned were it not that we had illusions. Disillusionment is a place where we lose our illusions. It is the
soul's deep work of outgrowing images of God and
preparing the winter's soil of a barren soul to receive
new images.

Images of Faith

Faith creates images. We project into the air of our
imaginations what we believe. We image God, and then
relate to God, ourselves, and others out of that image.
As our image of God develops, so our faith develops.

When disillusionment comes, we often look for a
culprit, a crisis to blame for the unseating of our comfortable images of God and self. Disillusionment is born
of crisis in the truest sense. A crisis is when we no longer
have the option of continuing as usual; the bridge is
washed out. Disillusionment is when our working image of God no longer works. God as a benevolent grand-
fatherly figure, God as warm fuzzy maternal nurture,
God as a cosmic AAA towing and repair service, the all-
ears God, the Perry Mason God with an eternal database

of all human actions and thoughts, the thunder bolt wielding Zeus God, the cut-you-some-slack generous God, the Creative Inventor and Celestial Mechanic God—none of these fit any longer. God has somehow become unfamiliar to us, and we are left gazing at God as if standing on a precipice staring blindly into a dark, misty abyss. No recognizable form meets our eyes.

> I said to my soul, be still, and let the dark come upon
> you
> Which shall be the darkness of God. As, in a theatre,
> The lights are extinguished, for the scene to be changed
> With a hollow rumble of wings, with a movement of
> darkness on darkness...
>
> T.S. Eliot, *Four Quartets*[3]

In her poignant self-portrait, Kristen, age eleven, submitted a photo of her own shadow framed by the shade of trees for a *Life* magazine cover story on "Kid's Pictures of God." Her caption: "This is a picture of shadows. God is like a shadow—blurry—because nobody has a clear image of Him."[4]

With a formless God who seems absent to us, we are faced with the temptation to either form our own image of God or to forsake the belief that a relational God exists at all. In either case we have come to confuse the image with the ineffable reality behind the image, what John terms the "I-don't-know-what" God.

The second commandment forbids the making of "graven images," as if God reserves the exclusive rights in creating our images of the divine. In disillusionment we grieve the loss of our extinct image with which we have grown accustomed and can do little more, in faith, than wait upon the emergence of a new image which re-presents God to us in ways that exceed our wildest creative imagination. After all, no image, whether of our creation or not, can contain the mystery of God's essence. In our spiritual journey we range from one image to another, outgrowing one and then another as we move along in our growing awareness of "the multifaceted grace of God."

For Abraham and Sarah, a singular image was that of a great nation of descendants more numerous than the stars of the sky, stars placed in the heavens by God, like a child throwing sand into the sea. Emerging long past his mother's child-bearing age, Isaac's birth represented the fulfillment of this dream. Then came disillusionment. In asking Abraham and Sarah to sacrifice Isaac, God was doing more than testing their faith. God was revealing God's nature as transcending any image, no matter how miraculously conceived.

In discipleship, we operate out of our primary image of God brought along from our early formative years, which has both conscious and unconscious levels. For example, consciously we may be most aware of our fatherly image of God as a benevolent deity who watches over us. We may be unaware, however, of the potent judgmental connotations this image holds for us from long-forgotten connections with a critical parent figure who watched over us with punitive injustice.

In disillusionment, we are called to sacrifice our images on the altar of faith, trusting in the God we cannot comprehend. We experience the despairing loss of our illusory notions of God as a deity we have fashioned to represent some aspect of our expectations. In discovering the illusion of our outmoded image, we may feel duped and mistreated that God would have continued the charade: "Thou hast deceived me and I am deceived," (Jeremiah 20:7 KJV).

The Dark Night of the Soul

Disillusionment, in my use of the term, refers to the classical meaning of John's Dark Night of the Soul, which is to come to a state in faith of "unknowing" and union with God in that unknowing. John's classic works,

The Ascent of Mount Carmel and *The Dark Night of the Soul,* spell out systematically the soul's progress through detachment from the world and attachment to God. The first of the three phases of the dark night is the *twilight* of *purgation* when the soul breaks free of its denial and illusions. This dusk phase of the night is when we experience a stripping away of our attachments to any objects of desire or even the methods we use to reach God. We are like a vine pruned by the careful husbandry of God, an image based on John 15.

Helplessly we watch the night deepen to *midnight,* the second phase. In this darkness, as painful as it is, we discover what we would never see in the light: the illumination that faith is the only way to God. Drawing from the biblical theme that the righteous live by faith, John details the transformation that occurs in the soul as we reach the bottom ground of our faith.

Our faith enables us to wait in the darkness for what no physical eye can behold: the dawn of God's arrival. This third phase is a transformation of the night from a disillusioning wilderness to a romantic garden grotto where we rendezvous with our divine Lover. The Song of Solomon provides the imagery for John's love poem upon which his books comment: *The Dark Night of the Soul* is really a celebration of John's passion for God. In the divine romance, Lover and beloved become one in spiritual union.

Coming to the End of the Road

Midway in our life's journey, I went astray from the straight road and woke to find myself alone in a dark wood.

Dante

More often than not, when a person shows up at my counseling office it is a dark night that has brought them there, not just the "dark night" of a problem, as the term is typically used, but the dark night of disillusionment. They do not come for creative ideas in living the holy life. They do not come to celebrate their intense love for Jesus.

They come because they have secretly harbored in their souls the darkness of a faith that no longer gives them a sense of consolation, and they are hesitant to reveal this to even their closest friends. They come, like Dante, midway on life's journey, having lost their way and awakened in a dark wood of angst. They come because they feel they have lost the edge in their spiritual life. They come because their discipleship has run dry. They come because they are angry at God. They come because the discrepancy between doctrine and faith has become unbearable. They come because they are restless. They come because they feel something is terribly wrong. They no longer want to live by their parents' values. They are bored with church. They are at the end of a job or career or relationship. They come because they are depressed or anxious or having thoughts that disturb them. Sometimes they are not sure why they come.

When they come, telling me their stories of light turning into darkness and faith fading into doubt, my ears perk up. The story takes on a familiar tenor. I feel a holiness settle into the room. Sometimes I imagine myself as a midwife seeking to discern whether the labor pains signal an impending birth. I wait in attentiveness, for I know that often the person in front of me is about to make a significant recapitulation in their discipleship and once again find themselves distracted by God into a wonderful excursion of dazzlement and renewed discipleship. Or, I know that we may wait in vain for a distraction. The night of disillusionment may only grow darker. Either way, I know they are on a journey that God will honor.

The Nada Point

Disillusionment can be seen as a transition to a deeper spiritual life. Our disillusionment breaks us from the cycle of distraction-dazzlement-discipleship and into a new level of the journey. John of the Cross portrayed the new level as a coming to the end of the paved road on the journey up Mount Carmel, beyond which is "Nada, nada, nada," or nothing, nothing, nothing. "Here there is no longer any way because for the just man there is no law."[5]

This nada point begins what Scott Peck calls "the road less traveled." "Each one of us must make his own path through life," he says, ". . . the journey through life is not paved in black top."[6] Accordingly, Peck asserts that much of our emotional and spiritual crises arise because we deny the complexity and non-directedness of life.

Seeking an image that gets at the spiritual crisis we often refer to as depression, Thomas Moore opts for the Renaissance imagery of Saturn, the Roman god of the harvest. A Saturnine phase, says Moore, may usher in a sense that life is over. To apply this mythopoetic image to the end of the road experience, persons "in Saturn,"

> are disillusioned because the values and understandings by which they have lived for years suddenly make no sense . . . the emptiness and dissolution of meaning that are often present in depression show how attached we can become to our ways of understanding and explaining our lives. Often our personal philosophies and our values seem to be all too neatly wrapped, leaving little room for mystery.[7]

As a natural aspect of life, the spiritual darkness of "depression," according to Moore, brings gifts to the soul and is "an initiation, a rite of passage" into a more imaginative life. Rather than seeing this place of darkness as a pathology, an "alternative would be to invite Saturn in, when he comes knocking, and give him an appropriate place to stay." Moore's point is well made. We best make a place for disillusionment, or Saturn may have "no place to go except into abnormal behavior and acting out."[8]

The Great Divide:
Discursive and Contemplative Spirituality

> I shall be telling this with a sigh
> Somewhere ages and ages hence:
> Two roads diverged in a wood, and I —
> I took the one less traveled by,
> And that has made all the difference.
>
> Robert Frost

Disillusionment signals a Great Divide in the spiritual journey. Two distinct modes of prayer flow from the watershed of disillusionment: what John of the Cross characterizes as the *discursive* and *contemplative*. The discursive life can be seen as the cycle of distraction-dazzlement-discipleship. It is a mode of prayer marked by discourse, action, and structure.

On the other side is contemplation. The contemplative life is a life of being with Christ, not just talking to Christ or obeying Christ or even following Christ. Contemplative terminology may include strange and suspicious words to a disciple. For what purpose would one want to just be with Christ without any notion or intention of accomplishing something by that being? It is precisely this sense of uselessness that hems in the disciple from stepping off the pavement and into the journey of his or her true self in Christ. As Lao Tzu said centuries ago:

> When they lose their sense of awe,
>   people turn to religion.
> When they no longer trust themselves,
>   they begin to depend upon authority.[9]

This distinction between awe and religion captures eloquently the difference between discursive and contemplative spirituality. Awe is the result of trusting what is emerging from the interior sources of the self. Religion and authority depend on exterior sources.

I started college on a music scholarship as a theory and composition major. Though my quest was to be a composer rather than a performer, the curriculum required the mastery of an instrument. Fairly proficient on the piano and seeing the keyboard as a superior medium for composition, I dutifully signed up for piano lessons. My professor considered it his cross to bear to sit with me that one painful hour each week as I struggled with my "inability" to play music as written, with classical interpretation.

One day my professor was late for our lesson. Bored sitting in his studio, I hated to let a nice grand piano go to waste, so I started playing some of my favorite jazzy improvisations. My astonished mentor listened behind the door for a few moments before entering. Hearing me play evoked a memory of his early days as an aspiring pianist. In the second world war he was an enlisted soldier whose talents were known but misunderstood by his commanding officer. With morale low, the colonel wanted him and a few others to entertain the troops with some popular jazz numbers. He protested that he could not improvise.

Decades later, my professor was trying to shape students in his own style when he heard me jamming away in his studio. That day was a turning point in our relationship. Rather than continuing with his poorly-disguised frustration, he recommended that I find a good jazz piano teacher and develop my talent. In one lesson I went from being his worst student to one with a promising future. His style was playing what is written; mine was writing what is played.

Two Trees

Belden Lane offers a fitting analogy for contrasting discursive and contemplative spiritualities in recounting two tree stories: Shel Silverstein's modern classic, *The Giving Tree*, and the 2400-year-old tale of the Taoist philosopher, Chuang Tzu, the "useless tree."[10] Silverstein describes the saga of a boy and a tree. The boy is perpetually unhappy and the codependent tree happily gives of itself to satisfy the boy: apples for money, branches for a house, trunk for a boat, and finally a stump for the old "boy" to sit on at the end of his life.

The Taoist tree story, by contrast, is about the contemplations of an ancient sage on the uselessness of a large tree whose branches were so twisted as to be unfit for lumber, its sap too bitter for tapping, its leaves too malodorous and fragile for weaving or mulch. Even its roots where too gnarled and knotty for carving. From the tree the sage learned "the subtle use of the useless."

I like to think that there is a place on the spiritual journey at the pavement's end where these two trees stand. One is continually cut to a stump by those wishing to harvest its benefits. The choppers use its wood to finance some excursion back into their distraction. The other tree stands tall and large, barely blemished by the passing traffic. Those who pause beneath this tree are often never seen on the pavement again.

There was once such a tree on the earth in an ancient garden. The inhabitants of that garden were so fascinated by its forbiddenness that they defied its uselessness and ate of that fruit. It was a tree not to be eaten from or chopped or woven or tapped, but a tree only to be contemplated.

In this garden the two special trees were known as The Tree of Life (or Contemplation) and the Tree of Knowledge (or Power). The gardeners were not able to eat from both, for to eat from one disallowed the other.

The Tree of Life bore a soulful fruit that granted continued life to the person who ate from it. The Tree of Knowledge, however, bore a forbidden and irresistible fruit, that once eaten, transformed the fruit from the Tree of Life into a curse.

So it is with this juncture in the spiritual path. The pilgrim must choose between life and knowledge: the path of being or the path of doing. To continue in the path of life, we must choose the way of unknowing. To choose the pursuit of knowledge is to block our experience of the God who is hidden, for God cannot be fully known.

Our relationship to God is like a tree, ever growing and changing, yet remaining rooted in the nurturing soil of the ageless Spirit. In disillusionment, it is our reflection on God's past faithfulness and our trust that goodness is God's essence that gives us the fortitude to weather the darkness. As Jürgen Moltmann expressed this tension, "Hope without remembrance leads to illusion, just as, conversely, remembrance without hope can result in resignation."[11]

The True God and the True Self

The patient was a man in his eighties, restrained to his bed because of delirium. I could hear him screaming from down the hall, screams which instantly subsided to encouraged pleas as I darkened the door of his room. Forewarned by the nurses that he was out of control, I politely greeted him. Frantic, he shook his pointed hand toward the wall and begged me, with a persona of all good sense, to help his son. "What's the matter with your son?" Pointing more strenuously, "He's tied up over there. Somebody help him! Look! Look!"

Pity flooded into my chest and throat at the sight of this poor hallucinating man. Looking again at his intent stare to the side, I was pulled, inexplicably, into his delusion. *Folie à Deux*. Bending down with my face only inches from his, I turned and looked at both our reflections in a mirror on the wall. There he was, restrained and horror-stricken. There I was, dumbfounded: "You're seeing yourself in the mirror!"

After a somewhat lucid conversation—a chair strategically placed to obscure the mirror—we prayed together. And I didn't forget to pray for the father's son, wherever he may be.

The Christ event is God's way of bending down and looking at our world from our perspective so that we may see ourselves from God's perspective.

Disillusionment removes the facade of false images and allows for the emergence of the True Self—the selfhood that rises from the grave of our death with Christ, not from the idolatrous creation of our false self. There comes a point in which the window of the soul becomes also the mirror of the soul; when what is seen internally reflects more of the divine presence than that which is seen externally. The frame of reference for our self-perception shifts from outside to inside. We move from being the seen to the seer, from an absorbing self-consciousness to a freeing self-transcendence.

Stuckness and Recapitulation

He discovereth deep things out of darkness
                                    John Bunyan

The nada point is a point of departure in many possible ways. Some sojourners retreat from the dryness of disillusionment, retracing their steps back to green pastures where their faith is renewed and their inspiration is energized. A brick wall awaits other travelers, who hit disillusionment like a golf ball pits a sand trap. But, some tenacious souls learn to adapt to the arid climate, developing new and creative ways of living.

Recapitulation

The nada point may be a place to recognize the dryness of our discipleship and, like Elijah, to receive a fresh distraction from God. Elijah prayed that it would stop raining so that people would realize their need of God. Settling down by the Brook Cherith, Elijah waited for the drought to have its effect. God sent the ravens to feed him. But before long the brook dried up, and Elijah had to change his plans of riding out the famine in style. Soon, he was finding that God had other ways of caring for him.

We experience the same kind of recapitulation when we are swept off our feet by some new discovery about God or ourselves. Growing stale with the same old religious activities, we attend a workshop and suddenly find ourselves engrossed in a new paradigm. A whole new world opens before us and before long we are dazzled by the awesomeness of God in new ways.

Stuckness

The nada point may be a bog of stuckness where the traveler is paralyzed in cynicism. Jonah was such a person. God called him to preach to the Ninevites; he refused and took a ship to Tarsus. God sent a storm; Jonah tried to commit suicide in the sea. God sent a big fish to swallow him and spit him out on the beach. After the old enemies of Jonah repented at his preaching and were spared the judgment of God, Jonah camped outside the city, sulking. The story ends in an impasse.

As for Jonah, disillusionment is the end of the story for many disciples. They become inactive church members, agnostics, antagonists, perennial mourners, victims; lost searchers in a plethora of religions or philosophies.

There are many causes of stuckness. We may run aground upon illusions of ourselves of which we are unaware or unwilling to let go of. Exemption from aging. Being the smartest guy in the department. Not being capable of certain sins. Self-sufficiency, self-confidence, self-awareness.

We may also find disappointment in our illusions of others. Pastors are perfect. Love means never arguing. The company has your best interests in mind. Our illusions of others may include the illusion that someone knows the answers or the way out of the darkness.

Not knowing our own story can be a source of stuckness. Not knowing the real story of family dynamics and events that our parents felt were too shame-laden to reveal. Hidden alcoholism, hidden abuse; hidden unfaithfulness.

Entering the Darkness

Our point of departure may be to press forward into the darkness. "To enter the road is to leave the road," says John. Some pilgrims, like Job, remain undaunted in their faith and give themselves in total self-abandonment to the darkness. Facing all manner of adversity, they continue to look to God for strength and guidance. By some unknown grace they respond to the darkness, "Though he slay me, yet will I hope in him" (Job 13:15).

As Hemingway observed vicariously, "The world breaks everyone, and afterwards many are strong in the broken places." There is a faith that shines brightest in the darkest moments. It is the faith of Paul, who experienced a power "made perfect in weakness." It is not so much a faith in an ultimate rescue, but a faith that gives the soul to God in pure trust. It is a faith that is willing to come to the end of itself until nothing remains but love. It is an aching love which John laments:

> Where have you hidden,
> Beloved, and left me moaning?
> You fled like the stag
> After wounding me;
> I went out calling you, but you were gone.[12]

An elderly friend of mine once remarked from his west Texas hospital bed about coming to a place in his walk with Christ, "when faith turns to love." Then he just nodded, smiled, and said, "Whew!" Those words burned into my mind with an intensity I still cannot describe since I heard them over fifteen years ago. I remember pondering them in my study and thinking that someday I would grasp his meaning. I believe now that my friend had come to a point where he loved God, not for what he knew about God, but for what he didn't know. The author of *The Cloud of Unknowing,* an anonymous fourteenth-century English mystic, phrased it this way: "Thought cannot comprehend God. And so, I prefer to abandon all I can know, choosing rather to love him whom I cannot know. Though we cannot know him we can love him."[13] Love transcends unknowing. It is the same type of experience John described:

> . . . never seek satisfaction in what you understand about God, but in what you do not understand about him. Never pause to love and delight in your understanding and experience of God, but love and delight in what you cannot understand or experience of him. Such is the way . . . of seeking him in faith. However surely it may seem that you find, experience, and understand God, because he is inaccessible and concealed you must always regard him as hidden, and serve him who is hidden in a secret way.[14]

God has "made darkness his covering" (Ps. 18:11). In seeking to love and please God in our unknowing, we pray with Thomas Merton:

> My Lord God, I have no idea where I am going. I do not see the road ahead of me. I cannot know for certain where it will end. Nor do I really know myself, and the fact that I think I am following your will does not mean that I am actually doing so. But I believe that the desire to please you does in fact please you. And I hope I have that desire in all that I am doing. I hope that I will never

do anything apart from that desire. And I know that if I do this you will lead me by the right road though I may know nothing about it. Therefore will I trust you always though I may seem to be lost and in the shadow of death. I will not fear, for you are ever with me, and you will never leave me to face my perils alone.

Discursive and Contemplative Spirituality

Dark faith is deep faith. It is faith that perseveres into the darkness and dryness of disillusionment and transforms the soul. Remember, Teresa advises, that in the driest desert of prayer our will grows in its capacity to love God all the more. When we feel that we are accomplishing nothing is when we are in fact accomplishing the most.[15] The prayer of dark faith has a Spartan spirit. As Dom John Chapman depicts it:

> Prayer, in the sense of union with God, is the most crucifying thing there is. One must do it for God's sake; but one will not get any satisfaction out of it, in the sense of feeling "I am good at prayer. I have an infallible method." That would be disastrous, since what we want to learn is precisely our own weakness, powerlessness, unworthiness. Nor ought one to expect "a sense of the reality of the supernatural" of which I speak. And one should wish for no prayer, except precisely the prayer that God gives us—probably very distracted and unsatisfactory in every way.[16]

What occurs in this dark night and arid desert is a profound shift in our spirituality. So radical is this change that John compares it to the difference between walking and flying, in the language of Isaiah 40:31, "but those who hope in the Lord will renew their strength. They will soar on wings like eagles; they will run and not grow weary, they will walk and not be faint." The soul, John says, "runs without fainting by reason of its hope. The love that has invigorated it makes it fly swiftly."

By holding so tightly to our neat and clean images of God, we may eventually close ourselves off from other ways of relating to God that transcend our current imagination. Margaret Mead once remarked that the technology of automobiles is still locked into the image of the horse-drawn carriage. The early automobiles were called horseless carriages. The technology is based on walking. Today, the engine is still generally placed where the horses used to be, and we still rate engines in terms of horsepower! The Wright brothers were able to step out of this paradigm and use the internal combustion engine to power a totally different kind of vehicle: one that flies. Perhaps this is why the road runs out at the nada point: God wants us to fly the rest of the way.

For Teresa, the difference between discursive and contemplative spirituality is like a butterfly that has emerged from its cocoon spun while a caterpillar. "It no longer has any esteem for the works it did while a worm, which was to weave the cocoon little by little; it now has wings. How can it be happy walking step by step when it can fly?"[17]

Discursive and contemplative spirituality, to use other Teresian images, are as different as watering a garden with a bucket filled from a well and the watering a garden receives from a good soaking rain.[18] Or again, it is the difference between two types of Moorish fountains found in Spain which "are filled with water in different ways," says Teresa. "With one the water comes from far away through many aqueducts and the use of much ingenuity; with the other the source of the water is right there . . . there is no need of any skill, nor does the building of aqueducts have to continue; but water is always flowing from the spring."[19] As Jesus said to the Samaritan woman at the well, "Everyone who drinks this water will be thirsty again, but whoever drinks the water I give him will never thirst. Indeed, the water I give him will become in him a spring of water welling up to eternal life" (John 4:13-14).

The author of *The Cloud of Unknowing* described the difference between discursive, or "active," and contemplative spirituality as illustrated by the personalities of Mary and Martha. In Luke 10 when the sisters hosted Jesus in their home, Mary was apparently enthralled with the great teacher and sat at his feet hanging on every word. Her desire was to simply be with Jesus. Martha, on the other hand, was burdened about her responsibilities as a host and her sister's mindlessness of her household duties. Her focus was on doing. Martha was an active; Mary a contemplative. "Martha, Martha," Jesus winsomely chided, "you are worried and upset about many things, but only one thing is needed. Mary has chosen was is better" (41-42).

The author's advice for those entering dark faith's cloud of unknowing is to place a "cloud of forgetting" between themselves and the world, "Forget that kind of everywhere and the world's all. It pales in richness beside this blessed nothingness and nowhere."[20]

> If you came this way,
> Taking any route, starting from anywhere,
> At any time or at any season,
> It would always be the same: you would have to
> put off
> Sense and notion. You are not here to verify,
> Instruct yourself, or inform curiosity
> Or carry report. You are here to kneel . . .[21]
>
> T.S. Eliot

Dark faith is indeed deep faith. It is faith that, in the darkness, experiences a metamorphosis and develops wings. It is faith that finds the source of life in an inner spring, not in external ingenuity. It is faith that finds God, not in spite of darkness, but because of darkness, for only in darkness do we lose the capacity for illusion. As John of the Cross says,

> Seek him in faith and love, without desiring to find satisfaction in anything, or delight, or desiring to understand anything other than what you ought to know. Faith and love are like the blind person's guides. They will lead you along a path unknown to you, to the place where God is hidden."[22]

The Root of Bitterness

I am the man who has seen affliction
    by the rod of his wrath.
He has driven me away and made me walk
    in darkness rather than light;
Even when I call out or cry for help,
    he shuts out my prayer.
He has filled me with bitter herbs
    and sated me with gall.
You have covered yourself with a cloud
    so that no prayer can get through.
Yet this I call to mind
    and therefore I have hope:
Because of the Lord's great love
    we are not consumed,
    for his compassions never fail.
They are new every morning;
    great is your faithfulness.

                              Lamentations 3

Disillusionment may entail a bitter response but does not end there. Bitterness, on the other hand, can be a spiritual black hole that devours the soul and consumes faith. The writer of Hebrews urges us to give special care to those who, in their pain, turn a hard face against God: "See to it that no one misses the grace of God and that no bitter root grows up to cause trouble and defile many" (Hebrews 12:15). Rather, we are to consider Christ's suffering so that we do "not grow weary and lose heart." This was Teresa's advice to those who encounter difficulties in prayer: embrace the cross.

In my conversations with disillusioned persons, I perhaps err at times on the side of encouragement and confrontation. When I see bitter herbs growing in the garden of a person's spirit, I want to reach down and pluck them out. My mentors have cautioned me about this tendency, but I know what devastation a root of bitterness can wreak.

For five long years I was not on speaking terms with God because I was so bitter. I didn't recognize it as bitterness at first, but I thought of my dryness in prayer as a grief reaction to what I perceived as mistreatment. Although I told myself that others have had far worse experiences than mine and have emerged with faith intact, in honest moments I held God responsible for this injustice and felt betrayed. It was an arduous journey for me, including therapy for depression and panic attacks, before I was able to connect this experience with my childhood and see a pattern of revictimization in my life.

Eventually, I instinctively did what Teresa advised: I embraced the cross. When there were no satisfactory answers to my angry "why" questions, the incarnation and death of Christ took on a new meaning.

> Embracing the cross,
> Let us follow Jesus,
> He is our way and light
> Abounding in consolations . . .
>   Teresa

God did not help me to make sense of my world but entered into its senselessness with me. While I could no longer trust in the theologically tidy God of my discipleship, I could trust this God who entered fully into the messy quandary of human existence and death. God has never looked the same since, and I never want to go back to that black hole again.

Rescuing others from their bitterness can be like helping a butterfly out of its cocoon. The results can be harmful, if not disastrous. I'm learning to face this propensity to rescue others for what it is: a lack of faith that God is present and active even in the darkness and an idolatry of my own need to be needed. Nothing gets me into my own shadow like being with people in their darkness.

What, then, are we to make of experiences that defy any semblance of divine order? What about tragedy? What about oppressive, diabolical abuse? Dark faith makes no excuses for God; dark faith holds nothing back from God. The danger lies not in our anger over our victimization, but rather in allowing the victimization to become our identity. By taking on the identity of a victim, we unconsciously destine ourselves to experience the victimization over and over in order to confirm who we are as a victim. Victimization becomes revictimization: an insidious root of bitterness.

Naomi, in the book of Ruth, lost not only her husband but her sons as well. Left in dire poverty, she changed her name from Naomi, or "pleasant," to Mara, which means "bitter." "The Almighty has made my life very bitter," she lamented. "I went away full, but the Lord has brought me back empty. Why call me Naomi? The Lord has afflicted me; the Almighty has brought misfortune upon me" (Ruth 1:20-22).

Thérèse of Lisieux struggled her life long with victimization and a pervasive feeling of being unloved and abandoned. Having lost her mother at the age of four, she was extremely insecure and hypersensitive to any slight. She transformed her own sense of victimization through her faith in the merciful love of God and her desire "to be His victim of love," perhaps reminiscent of

Job's statement of faith, "though he slay me, yet will I hope in him" (Job 13:15). Like Job, and in spite of her own persistent dark night and a religious climate that emphasized the punitive nature of God, Thérèse asserted that "God knows only how to love and be loved."

Some persons have the depth of spirit to find a piton of faith on the sheer cliffs of despair. Like Bunyan's pilgrim, faced with death in the dark dungeon of Doubting Castle, they find within themselves the key to their own release. It is at such times, that the faith gifts we've received along the way become golden.

A Bitter and Stormy Night

And the ragged rock in the restless waters,
Waves wash over it, fogs conceal it;
On a halcyon day it is merely a monument,
In navigable weather it is always a seamark
To lay a course by: but in the sombre season
Or the sudden fury, is what it always was.[23]

T.S. Eliot

Jesus invited his disciples to sail the lake for the far shore. Mid-journey, a "furious squall came up, and the waves broke over the boat" (Mark 4). They were afraid the boat would swamp, while their oblivious master slept in the stern. "Don't you care if we drown?"

Rebuking the wind, Jesus calmed the storm. Now, they were terrified of *Him*. "Who is this? Even the wind and the waves obey him?"

Jesus leads us into the stormy night where only he can rest. And rest he does: silent, passive, and unaffected. Like Job, we complain to our silent God only to receive silence. But, when God eventually awakens and speaks, we terrifyingly long for the silence.

After making their way across the lake, the storm-weary sailors encountered another storm: a man full of demons (Mark 5). Jesus' exorcism sent the spirits into a herd of pigs who stampeded into the lake and drowned. At that, the native Gaderenes had had enough and asked Jesus to leave.

Going through disillusionment we meet our demons. Jesus creates chaos as well as stillness. The price of healing our sick souls may be higher than we anticipated. What began as a jaunt of merry men turned out to be a dark, stormy night of abandonment and ghosts. Teresa recounted, "I spent nearly twenty years on that stormy sea."

The dark night is essentially a way of defining God by negation—by what God is not. God is not definable. There is a difference, however, between saying that God cannot be defined and that God does not exist or that God is not good. It is important to contrast disillusionment with other experiences of disenchantment that have neither the characteristics nor redeeming qualities of the dark night. "Dark night" is a common term in our vernacular and has come to mean a difficult or profoundly dispiriting experience. Giving the term this connotation removes it from John's mystical meaning and equates the dark night with resentment and hopelessness. The persistent, ingrained bitterness that many persons feel in the aftermath of a traumatizing event, or as the result of unresolved grief, is not synonymous with what I am describing as disillusionment.

Martin Luther was plagued throughout his life by his *anfechtungen,* or spiritual trials, that were so great and so much like hell that no tongue could adequately express them . . . At such a time, God seems so terribly angry, and with him the whole creation. At such a time, there is no flight, no comfort, within or without."[24]

Teresa gives a candid description of her own stormy seasons:

> It happens to me on some days—although not often, and the experience lasts about three, four, or five days—that it seems to me that all the good things,

fervor, and visions have been taken away; and even taken from my memory, for I don't know, although I may want to, what good there has been in me . . . All my bodily ills together afflict me. My intellect disturbs me because I cannot think anything about God, nor do I know what state I'm in. If I read, I don't understand. It seems to me I am full of faults, without any courage for virtue, and that great courage I usually have dwindles to this: that I'd be unable to resist the least temptation or criticism from the world. It occurs to me then that I'm good for nothing, that no one could force me to do more than what is ordinary; I feel sad; I feel I've deceived all those who have given me some credit. I should like to hide some place where no one would see me; not solitude for virtue's sake, but out of [cowardice].[25]

John describes three storms of the dark night that are "burdensome trials and sensory temptations that last a long time, and with some longer than with others."[26] Seekers experiencing these storms often seek spiritual direction or counseling to deal with the religious, psychological, or spiritual issues related to these trials. What John describes as storms in the dark night might be referred to today as doubts, temptations, depression, or anxiety attacks.

Erotic Storms

John refers to a "spirit of fornication," a spirit of desire that arises from the dryness we begin to experience in prayer as we enter the dark night. The sense of aridity compounds our desire, and we are tempted to inordinate means of satisfying ourselves, such as Jesus was tempted to make bread from stones or Esau to sell his birthright for a bowl of pottage. A heightened eroticism emerges that draws us to attachment and indulgence just when we are beginning to master ourselves. These "foul thoughts and very vivid images," as John calls them, break into our consciousness uninvited and in full force. Probably the best modern term to define what John was describing is addiction. In this storm our compulsions arise with virtual irresistibility.

The Greeks well knew the line that separates attraction from addiction and depicted these overwhelming forces of human nature in their mythology. The goddess Artemis was a great huntress, vowed to chastity, who slew any unwary man who happened to catch a glimpse of her bathing. A cold-hearted goddess, she was associated with the moonlit night in which she hunted in her untamable wildness. The Romans likewise named the bright morning star after their fair goddess of love and desire, Venus-based on the same Greek counterpart. We now know this planet to be a swirling hotbed of corrosive gases. The storm of desire tempts us to come near, but it burns us when we do.

Working as a therapist in a downtown center not far from a large seminary campus gave me a perspective on erotic storms. This innovative center had begun the first sexual addiction treatment program in town and most of our clients were from the nearby seminary. These erotic storms signaled an extreme imbalance of compulsiveness regarding sexuality.

Listening to the stories of these tormented seminarians and their families, it became clear that a driving force in their religiosity was their sexual conflicts. They lived the pious life in public and pulpit, but privately their lives included pornography and, for some, prostitutes. This shadow aspect of their lives that they sought to deny came roaring back from the darkness in guilt-inducing, shame-based compulsive behaviors.

It is the detachment of body and soul that seeds the clouds of the erotic storm. Repressing our sensual drives only sets up a delayed emergence of what is repressed in a greater and more chaotic form.

The grace of this storm invites us to be more loving and to bring more of our suppressed passion and sensuality into our relationship with God. What may well be at the heart of fornication is the withholding of some aspect of ourselves from God and seeking its fulfillment elsewhere. It is no accident that the Old Testament prophets so often likened the covenant relationship of God and Israel to a marriage and idolatry as unfaithfulness.

Mary's anointing Jesus' feet with perfume portrayed the sensual possibilities of prayer: "she poured it on Jesus' feet and wiped his feet with her hair . . . the house was filled with the fragrance" (John 12:3). The prudish reaction of those present revealed how uncomfortable they were with her unabashed affection.

It is the paradox of indulgence and withholding of self that forms the nucleus of addiction—and its remedy. John provides us with a profound image of this paradox by referring to attachments as parasitic fish, which attach themselves to sharks and ships by means of suction cups on the back of their heads.

> An individual's appetite and attachment resemble the remora, which, if successful in clinging to a ship, will hold it back and prevent it from reaching port . . . it is regrettable, then, to behold some souls, laden as rich vessels with wealth, deeds, spiritual exercises, virtues, and favors from God, who never advance because they lack the courage to make a complete break . . . .[27]

The remedy is in the paradox itself. The anatomy of a remora allows it to remain passively attached by the force of water against its head. The faster the shark swims, the more fast the remora attaches. When a remora wishes to detach itself from a host, it simply swims forward. When a shark feels the remora attached to its underside, however, it instinctively tries to dislodge it by lurching forward, which only seals the attachment more firmly. If the shark had the awareness of the physics of this attachment, it would swim backwards with the force of the attachment—against its instincts—and free itself.

The key to detachment for John and Teresa, however, is not fortitude. It is courage. We don't free ourselves by working harder but by the courage to go with what makes no sense: to break the cycles of compulsive behavior by first breaking out of the mindset that holds us. John bemoans those poor souls who "never advance because they lack the courage." "Therefore, courage my daughters!" Teresa encouraged her sisters in their detachment from self-will and earthly things that they may see God. Courage is what we need to enter the marriage chamber of our God.

Our erotic storms invite us to bring our desire to God rather than to worldly attachments. In this regard, John was an extremist. His devotion took the form of asceticism: living an austere life of self-denial. Though John's asceticism may be repugnant to us, it had a purpose.

John was an ascetic, but he was also a lover. The more dispassionate he became of anything worldly, the more voluptuously passionate he became in his relationship with God.

Angry Storms

This storm arises from a "spirit of blasphemy," the temptation to say something untrue about God: God does not exist, God hates me; God is unloving. Blasphemy is often equated with acting out angrily in disobedience against God, such as Moses striking the stone with his rod in frustration.

In the dark night, there is plenty to be frustrated about. We grow frustrated with the dryness of our prayer. We grow frustrated with the barrenness of our relationship with God, John says, as a baby experiences the frustration of weaning.

> It should be known, then, that God nurtures and caresses the soul, after it has been resolutely converted to his service, like a loving mother who warms her child

with the heat of her bosom, nurses it with good milk and tender food, and carries and caresses it in her arms. But as the child grows older, the mother withholds her caresses and hides her tender love; she rubs bitter aloes on her sweet breast and sets the child down from her arms, letting it walk on its own feet so that it may put aside the habits of childhood and grow accustomed to greater and more important things.[28]

In this storm of anger, an irascibility grows, and we may become irritable and disconsolate. Blasphemy may not literally be as much a problem—spouting off some sacrilege—as our reticence to voice what we truly feel. For pious disciples, this may be the worst temptation of all: to express anger at God.

That anger surfaces in our spirituality at all may be a storm in itself, for no emotion is as loaded with meaning as anger. Surveying the Christian literature on anger, or how to deal with the anger of others, reveals volumes of research, advice, and warning. Theologically, most disciples view anger as incompatible with their Christian faith. This dogmatic banishment of the irascible emotions only dooms us to act out our anger in more destructive ways: spiritualizing and polarizing differences of opinion, depression, manipulation and judgmentalism.

One of the most angry persons I've ever known once shared with me an article he had written on how to deal with anger, which really was about how to not be angry. Unfortunately, though I never saw him "lose his cool," he had a distinct way of creating chaos in office politics by pitting people against each other.

I must confess that I've made quite a study of anger myself and have contributed my share to the literature. *Reclaiming Inactive Church Members* turned out to be a guide for creating inclusiveness in the faith community for angry people. A journal article entitled "Anger and Personality Disorders" was a model for identifying the various styles of anger as a diagnostic tool for helping congregants (and their congregation) deal more redemptively with their unhealthy ways of expressing anger.

The temptation of anger is a fight or flight reaction: wanting to fight and take a stand but being too afraid; wanting to flee but being too ashamed. It is not knowing when it is time to stand firm and work through an issue or when standing is re-victimization. Codependency, after all, is little more than taking responsibility for changing someone only to be victimized by them.

The gift of anger is in its demand for honest full disclosure and the grace of this storm lies in its invitation to be more honest and authentic in our relationship with God, ourselves, and others.

Storms of Confusion

Our demon in this storm is a vertiginous spirit, or spirit of vertigo and dizziness, that arises with our sense of powerlessness to pray. John draws the image from Isaiah 19:14, "The Lord has poured into them a spirit of dizziness." Full of scruples, perplexities, obsessions, and compulsions, we are overcome with self-doubt. We don't know what is right, and what we think is right doesn't feel right. We struggle to even explain our predicament to others. As disciples, we became so compulsive about our knowing and doing God's will; now we are uncertain and full of second guessing: I seek to be a loyal servant of God, but am I doing this service out of pure motives?

Early in my pastoral career I remained after services with the senior pastor to counsel a young man with persistent doubts. He had tried to be saved but couldn't shake the lingering doubts that perhaps he was not truly sincere and, therefore, was still destined for hell. A very religious person, he attended church faithfully and maintained a rigorous devotional life. My colleague took the straightforward tack of leading him in prayer to give his life to Christ. After the final amen of a heartwarming prayer on our knees, our counselee would tearfully confess that he still felt unsure. With some exhortation and scripture quotes, we would repeat the process again and again. It soon became obvious to me that our supplicant was not the only one confused.

As Merton explains, vertigo is a natural by-product of our faith in the unseen reality of God:

> The [person] who feels the attraction of the Divine Truth and who realizes that he [or she] is being drawn out of this visible world into an unknown realm of cloud and darkness, stands like one whose head spins at the edge of a precipice. This intellectual dizziness, *spiritus vertiginis,* is the concrete experience of [one's] interior division against himself by virtue of the fact that his mind, made for the invisible God, is nevertheless dependent for all its clear knowledge on the appearances of exterior things.[29]

This whirlwind's grace leads us to be more trusting. In our confusion we are taught to rest in God rather than our efforts to achieve righteousness.

* * *

Our reaction to the storms of the dark night may result in assuming a stance that is opposite to the temptation of the storm—sometimes referred to as *reaction formation.* When repressed, the storms emerge in a disguised form. The erotic storm of fornication may be repressed by reacting to sensuality with anhedonia, the absence of pleasure. Puritanism, a way of life that guards against anything sensual, is the result. The storm of anger may be repressed as victimization, by unconsciously setting ourselves up to be hurt by the anger of others. As Karpman has pointed out, victimization eventually emerges as persecution—victimizing others. And finally, the storm of confusion stirs up all manner of doubts. A reaction formation against doubt is dogmatism: an ardent championing of hard-and-fast beliefs.

What causes these storms? A way of understanding the origin of these spiritual tumults—one that may have been familiar to John of the Cross—is in the Platonic concept of the soul. Plato, in *Phaedrus*, pictured the soul as a chariot pulled by two horses. The charioteer is reason, or the divine element in the soul. The horses *Thymos* and *Epithymia* are the dynamics of spiritedness and appetite. Not only do the horses pull in different directions, but they have lost their wings: their means of sharing in the divine nature. It is this inherent tension of fleshly drives bridled by reason and the fallen state of the soul that accounts for the tempests of the spirit.

Another way to conceptualize the nature of these storms is in the Saturnine mythology referred to above by Thomas Moore. Storms result when Saturn, a morose spirit, comes knocking and we resist giving him a place to stay. Just as the Romans celebrated the Saturnalia festival each December to mark the winter sowing season, so we should allow our mood to have its rhythm. To deny ourselves these dark periods of languor and lassitude is to shut ourselves off from important soul work, which will culminate in a harvest of rejuvenated creativity. The expense of maintaining a pious facade or a persona of smiley triumphal faith will eventually deplete our spiritual reserves, resulting in the outbursts of a languishing soul.

While Greek and Roman mythology grants us some powerful metaphors for our spiritual struggles, Nemeck and Coombs provide a more biblically-based explanation for the origin of these storms. Storms are the result of sanctification, the process of gradually being formed into the likeness of Christ:

> Both Christ and sin live simultaneously in us (Gal. 2:19-20; Rm. 7:17). However, there is no peaceful coexistence between the two. As Christ increases within us, he purges us of the sin to which we cling. In Christ, we thus experience the depths of our inner poverty.

A basic law of psychology predicates that we facilitate the release of something deep within us by allowing it to pass through consciousness. Thus also, we facilitate God's transformation of our deepest inner poverty by allowing ourselves to experience that poverty on a conscious level.

. . . These storms are the result of two clashing forces: God directly transforming us and our own inner poverty—specifically, selfishness—resisting his loving activity. Thus, God has to purge us of our egocentrism so that we can be free to respond in love to his initiative. In this sense, God is the cause of our night. But we, together with our innate weaknesses, are the cause of the pain suffered during the night. Our natural limitations are immeasurably compounded by our personal sinfulness as well as by our incorporation in the sin of the world. Furthermore, God's own transcendence and the transforming union which he is so intent upon effecting for us add an increased intensity to our darkness.[30]

What we learn in dazzlement about our shadow side comes to bear in disillusionment in a sobering way. The principle stated in chapter two was that the light reveals our shadow, with accompanying feelings of awe, guilt, and shame. In the stormy dark night, however, we may see nothing but our shadow! The storms of the night bring us face-to-face with the inescapable reality of our dark side.

Nemeck and Coombs: the storms "are sometimes violent and wreak havoc. While we are in the midst of them, they seem interminable. They uproot and tear down. They destroy and overthrow so that something new can spring forth."[31] For Teresa, "there is no remedy in this tempest but to wait for the mercy of God."[32]

There are many types of spiritual storms, and we may personally be prone to certain ones. Just as some areas of the country are prone to tornados and others to hurricanes and still others to earthquakes or mudslides, so it is with individual souls and the storms of the dark night.

What the lightning reveals in our stormy darkness is to be faced, not shunned. Thomas Keating describes contemplation as taking the cover off the sewer hole of our inner self and taking a long, loving look inside. It is time to name our demons and, in grace, to befriend them. What may appear as foe may be in truth our friend. The shadow is that part of ourselves that is neglected and rejected—coming forth in the darkness of Teresa's castle as creepy, crawly serpents. The stormy night confronts us with our utter humanity in all its expressions.

Possibilities for redemption lie in the eye of each storm. By embracing our shadow, we are able to redeem these storms by connecting them to their underlying virtues and turn to the Christ who comes to us from the shadow with a grace for a greater integration of our being. In so doing, we may learn to accept God as God is (transcendent) and ourselves as we are (needing redemption).

The storms manifest our struggle to accept our humanness and relinquish our illusions about ourselves. As we accept our humanity, we then become more integrated, whole, and healed. Christ is our model who, though divine, sought full humanity. In contrast, it seems that we humans historically have a hard time accepting our humanness. After all, the original temptation was to eat of the Tree of Knowledge in order to be like God.

Likewise, Christians throughout the ages have wrestled with the humanity of Christ, finding it much easier to affirm Christ's divinity. The Docetists taught that, when Jesus walked on the beach, he left no footprints—but only appeared to be human. One notable fourth-century church leader, Apollinarius, Bishop of Laodicea, taught that Jesus was fully human except for his mind, which was divine. Gregory of Nazianzus led the church's refutation of Apollianarius' teaching:

> We do not separate the Man from the Deity . . . at once earthly and heavenly, tangible and intangible, comprehensible and incomprehensible; that by one and the same person, perfect man and perfect God, the whole humanity, fallen through sin, might be created anew . . . For what he has not assumed he has not healed.[33]

Jesus' journey was about fully assuming human nature so that he might fully heal human nature. Our journeys, then, are about becoming fully human and fully healed through faith in Christ. The storms of our spirit erupt as part of this healing process.

A Night of Suffering with False Gods

Thus far I have made distinctions between the dark night of disillusionment and two psychological states that are commonly equated with it: a root of bitterness and depression. Bitterness and depression are both pathological to the soul and, if not remedied, may lead to grave harm to a person's well-being and relationships. While there are storms in the dark night, bitterness is a malignancy of resentment and cynicism that chokes out the possibility of faith. Depression may indicate a medical condition requiring professional treatment. Sometimes it is hard to discern the difference between depression—or what Teresa often referred to as "melancholy"—and a spiritual dark night. Because of the body-mind-spirit unity, depression may be either a cause of spiritual darkness or the result of it. For this and many other reasons, when Saturnine depression makes a call, it is wise to seek the companionship of a spiritual friend who is familiar with the ways of the soul. While it may be good spiritual form to give Saturn a room in our interior castle, we need not give up the whole house!

In order to further clarify the nature of disillusionment, I will contrast it with three interpretations of suffering: punishment, temptation and grief, which are easily misidentified as disillusionment. Our interpretations of suffering are just that: interpretations that offer only a limited perspective. Eventually, any image of God or interpretation of God's actions will come up short in explaining our experience of God. For example, if our darkness is God's punishment, then we must have done something to deserve it, or else God is unjust for punishing us without cause. If temptation is the purpose of the dark night, then we are being tested by God—or else we are an unwilling player in a sadistic cosmic comedy.

If the dark night is the result of losing something or someone dear to us, then we must come to terms with the God who gives and takes—or else we should never allow ourselves to become attached or connected to anything or anyone. But, the dark night is none of these. If we construe the dark night as revealing anything about God, then it is not the dark night. The dark night does not reveal; it conceals. In the dark night, God is nothing: neither a punisher, a tempter, nor a grim reaper. These ways of imagining God, as all others, are only partial at best in conveying the divine nature in relation to the human predicament. What the darkness of disillusionment reveals, it reveals about us.

The issue here is idolatry. In biblical terms, idols are false representations of God. False representations of God have power over us because we venerate them as if they were truly God. Idolatry creates what Merton described as the "web of illusion," when a person "spins a whole net of falsities around his [or her] spirit by the repeated consecration of his [or her] whole self to values that do not exist."[34]

Punishment from an Angry God

One biblical image of God is a loving parent who chastises God's children:

> Endure hardship as discipline; God is treating you as sons. For what son is not disciplined by his father? If you are not disciplined (and everyone undergoes discipline), then you are illegitimate children and not true sons. Moreover, we have all had human fathers who disciplined us and we respected them for it. How much more should we submit to the Father of our spirits and live! . . . No discipline seems pleasant at the time, but painful. Later on, however, it produces a harvest of righteousness and peace for those who have been trained by it. (Heb. 12:7-11)

I suggest that one way to think of chastisement is in terms of limit setting and limit experiencing. To be human is to bump up against our limitations and experience the pain of that awareness. God, like a celestial referee throwing a providential penalty flag, points out when we've stepped out of bounds. For some this boundary line is primarily a limitation in what they can comprehend; for others, it is the limitation of what they can accomplish, or accumulate, or create, or control. The classical writers often referred to the dark night or aridity of the soul as something we may bring on ourselves by not honoring our limitations—and thus our humanity. It is our illusions about ourselves that set the stage of disillusionment, not just our illusions about God. John makes a careful distinction between the dark night and spiritual dryness brought on by our own fault: "These aridities may not proceed from the sensory night and purgation, but from sin and imperfection, or weakness and lukewarmness, or some bad humor or bodily indisposition."[35]

Our tendency to harbor illusions about our limits, or lack of them, is historically referred to as pride. The best cure for pride, and illusion, is self-knowledge. As the author of *The Cloud of Unknowing* explained, "People are humble when they stand in the truth with a knowledge and appreciation for themselves as they really are." Anyone seeing themselves as they truly are, the author continued, would be aware of two realities: the "weakness of the human condition," and the "transcendent goodness of God."[36]

Discipline, then, is learning to live within our limitations. As we submit ourselves to the regimens of diet, exercise, work, recreation, sleep, or devotion, we experience the freedom of revitalized energies and creativity. The more we come to peace with our limits, the more we are able to get in touch with the transcendence of God.

Yet, there is no value in sugar coating the dark night of disillusionment with theological language that leaves God smelling good while mortals bear all the fault. Sometimes, the darkness of suffering *feels* like punishment. Images arise in our minds of an angry God hurling Zeus-like thunderbolts down upon the objects of God's scorn. The same psalms that offer the most comforting jewels also contain caustic images of divine retribution. The God of the Bible is sometimes depicted as an avenger, a destroyer, a terror; a sulphurous consuming fire raining down on the wicked. Psychologically, these biblical images may become fused with childhood experiences of parental punishment, producing a toxic potion. Deep in our minds, we come to believe in a force in the universe that is out to get us. But, ultimately even these powerful images fail in the dark night of disillusionment; they cannot hold the meaning of our experience of the transcendent God.

Temptation from an Uncaring God

As John of the Cross points out, the dark night contains storms of temptation: spirits of blasphemy, fornication, and confusion to tempt us into disbelief and sinful action. In dark faith, we are greeted by false gods who vie for our loyalty. When we have no sense of God's presence, we may succumb to images and interpretations of God that ease our pain, make sense of the chaos or allow us to maintain our self-image or current patterns of behavior. As Jacob discovered when he began to come to terms with himself, the dark night is a time of intense struggle with the forces within us.

I laid on the couch in the den and watched daytime television during a long illness. It had been weeks since I was able to work, and I was not improving. One program I tuned into was a local televangelist who offered prayer for persons such as I who were discouraged. He believed I would be healed instantly. I felt compelled to pick up the phone and dial the number on the screen, hoping to hear the voice of someone who appreciated my plight. But then I heard the preacher's offer for a tape series of his teachings for a mere one hundred dollars with the promise that it would turn my life around. The health-wealth-and-success theology of the program was alluring but empty.

Looking back on that experience, I realize now that I was in the process of coming to terms with a stressful situation. My illness was somehow related to that stress and my inability to deal with it. I'm glad I didn't opt out for an easy answer and instead chose to remain in the darkness and struggle with my issues. As a result I had to face my limitations and learn some new ways of relating, changes I might not have made if I had embraced the idols of my temptation. I came to the hard truth that my image of God as a fix-it man was no longer working for me.

Some Christians feel that the experience of temptation itself is somehow indicative of a failure on their part or a mysterious absence on God's part. Because of these beliefs, temptation may be a precursor of the dark night since it challenges our illusions about God and self and invites us into the tensions of spiritual growth. Anyone who believes they have transcended the struggles and tension of temptation is deluded.

Rather than viewing temptation as an indicator that we are on the wrong path, temptation may be an essential element in growth. Paul encouraged his readers to rely on God in the midst of temptation, knowing that God will not allow us to be tempted beyond what we are able—with God's help—to bear (I Cor. 10:13).

As in Jesus' temptation experience in the wilderness, laces of spiritual aridity can be proving grounds for the mettle of our souls. The greater the aridity, the greater the dangers. The dark night is fraught with temptation, and it seems the darker the night the more profuse the temptations that accompany it.

Temptations reveal most acutely the way we respond to crises and the level of responsibility we are willing to assume over our own lives. It has to do with our locus of control: internal or external. Those with an external locus of control tend to believe that others or outside influences govern their lives. They relate to others in a dependent, perhaps complaining fashion. Persons with an internal locus of control believe that they have a profound impact in the events of their lives and chose to live in self-determining, self-defining ways.

A drought lingered one summer and the black north Texas dirt cracked open. My yard looked like the epicenter of an earthquake with gaping crevices crisscrossing the property. A farmer friend found it hard one day to keep count of his piglets. Searching through the barnyard, he discovered several forlorn piglets crying out from down inside wide cracks in the ground!

Some people seem to be crack fallers—prone to victimization—who respond to disruptions with a chaotic helplessness. Or, they may be so vigilant of danger that they choke the spontaneity out of life, lest they be caught defenseless.

Victor Frankl, Nazi concentration camp survivor and author of *Man's Search for Meaning,* recounted the dramatic difference in persons' response to crises. Frankl observed how some prisoners would give up and die while others persisted and survived the cruelest and most inhumane treatment. The crucial factor in survival, Frankl noted, is in one's response or the willfulness of one's response. Circumstances and institutions may strip us of every conceivable shred of self-control, but no one can take from us our control over how we respond.

Perhaps one of the roots of addiction is the belief that a temptation does not contain a choice. Temptation may be intense. We may be caught at the weakest possible moment, for temptation tends to arise when we are most vulnerable. But temptation, for all its danger and seduction, is really about how we define ourselves in a trying moment and the choices we make in responding to that trial.

There comes a point in the dark night when we must decide whether to shake our fists into the bleakness of the obscurity and fret over why God has forsaken us or whether we will define the moment for ourselves, abandoning ourselves to the darkness with a dignity that comes only from within.

Grief from a Depriving God

Since disillusionment entails the loss of previously held images of God, self, and the world, it would be appropriate to refer to the dark night as a place of loss and grief. Such a ubiquitous experience in life, grief is a process of letting go. It is in these experiences of loss that we may most keenly experience life as a *journey.* We move on from one experience of loss to another. Nothing in this life is really permanent; nothing lasts forever.

Deciding that an old car has outlived its usefulness. Discovering that a pet has died. Taking a new job and leaving an old one. Coming home to a burglarized house. Adjusting to a new neighborhood.

One illusion of grief is that God sadistically deprives us of what makes life meaningful. God is a taker.

John and Teresa spoke much of detachment as an essential part of the process of letting go. "Let's be quick to do this work," Teresa urged her sisters, ". . . by getting rid of . . . our attachment to any earthly thing . . ." It is our attachments that keep us from spiritual freedom, she continues, "How can [the soul] be happy walking step by step when it can fly?" For John, "It makes little difference whether a bird is tied by a thin thread or by a cord," either way it cannot fly.[37] If John were alive today, he might observe how only a few small wheel blocks keep a huge jetliner from flying.

I believe that what Teresa and John are saying to us is that God is not found in our attachments to anything or anyone. Our attachments may in fact obscure a sense of God's presence and inhibit the "freedom of the divine union." The dark night is a place of total abandonment, of letting go of all things, even our cherished images of God. Only as we let go of the old, can we take hold of the new. Until we break free of our illusions, we are bound by them.

William Bridges, in *Transitions*, delineated a four-fold process we often go through during a significant life transition and grief experience. *Disengagement* signals the beginning of a transition, when we are separated from activities, relationships, or environments that were important to us, such as moving to a different city because of a job transfer. *Disidentification* is the change in our self-perception that results from the loss of role we experience in a transition or when a new situation doesn't have the same familiarity. A widow, for example, not only loses a husband, but the lifestyle of being that man's wife.

Disenchantment is moving on to deeper levels of understanding and letting go of previously held perspectives.

> The lesson of disenchantment begins with the discovery that in order to change—really change, and not just to switch positions—you must realize that some significant part of your old reality was in your head, not out there. The flawless parent, the noble leader, the perfect wife, the utterly trustworthy friend are an inner cast of characters looking for actors to play the parts... that reality has many layers, each appropriate to a phase of intellectual and spiritual development. The disenchantment experience is the signal that the time has come to look below the surface of what has been thought to be so.[38]

Bridges contrasts disenchantment with an experience he calls disillusionment, when a person is stuck in their old patterns and beliefs and cannot move on to new realities. Actually, the concept of disenchantment fits nicely with my definition of disillusionment. At the root of the word disenchantment is the meaning of being freed from a spell or charm that controlled us. Illusions may have much the same effect on us: spellbinding us to the view of life they present. Disillusionment, though often painful, is a breaking of the spells that bind us.

Bridges' later writings on job transitions encourages his readers to give up the illusion of a job—work hard and they'll keep you—and move on to the more autonomous perspective of self-employment. Once the illusion is abandoned, we are free to define our way and find our path—analogous to the nada point in dark night of disillusionment.

A final descriptor of the experience of transition is what Bridges refers to as *disorientation*, the feeling of losing one's bearings and moving out into uncharted and empty territory without a sense of direction.

The dark night of disillusionment entails all of these aspects of transition. Disillusionment teaches us that we cannot take our familiar environment for granted, and we certainly cannot derive our identity from it. Life's landscape encompasses hilltop vistas and cool valleys, river rapids and steep cliffs; wide oceans and expansive deserts. But, we are not hillside inhabitants or valley people, riverbank residents or cliff dwellers; sea creatures or desert denizens. We are sojourners—mountaineers and explorers, river rapid runners and sky divers; sailors and nomads.

Grief may usher in one or more of the spiritual storms of the dark night. An erotic storm of grief may take the form of addictive or compulsive behaviors, clinging to objects or persons who symbolize our loss: the widower who lapses into promiscuity or the young widow who becomes overprotective of her children.

Feeling that our anger is unholy signals a blasphemous storm. We fear to express our grief to God lest we offend the divine. If I blame God for the flood that ruined my home, will I be punished with a flood of worse crises?

The storm of confusion in grief leaves us not knowing what to believe anymore. How could a loving, all-powerful God allow such a violent act? If a respected spiritual leader fails our moral expectations, how can we believe in the transforming power of faith?

When we worship our suffering, we allow it to control, consume, and define us. Let go of the illusions.

Losing My Faith or Losing My Mind?

> For in this state grace is so hidden that not even a very tiny spark is visible. The soul doesn't think that it has any love of God or that it ever had any . . . all of this seems to have been dreamed up or fancied . . . our great

God wants us to know our own misery and that He is
king; and this is very important for what lies ahead . . .
provided one doesn't lose one's mind . . .. [39]

Teresa

When in the dark night of disillusionment, we may
feel that we are losing our faith, or our mind—or both.
The experience feels foreign to us, so foreign that we
may not even recognize our disillusionment for what it
is. We may assume some kind of depression has apprehended us—or grief, or temptation, or that God is punishing us for some terrible sin we've committed. The
Land of Disillusionment has no familiar landmarks or
direction signs. We feel lost and confused.

Looking back on when I first became aware of my
sense of disillusionment, I'm now a bit surprised that I
was taken so off guard. After all, the more I listen to the
stories of others, the more common this experience
seems to be. Why wasn't I more aware of this collective
phenomenon?

Now that I've had some time to reflect, I believe my
bewilderment was largely the result of not having
learned the language of disillusionment. My faith community, like most, did little to teach me this language. It
was there all along but not emphasized in the core
curriculum. Discipleship was emphasized: knowing the
Scriptures, personal devotion, evangelism, and mis-
sions—but not the dark night. In the University of Discursive Spirituality, Disillusionment 101 was offered
only rarely and at odd hours. And this is why I've
written this book: so others may know the language, or
at least know that such a language exists. As strange a
place as disillusionment is, there is a language spoken
here. It is a very old tongue and many classic works are
written in it. Unless you know the language, you may
have missed the message of these trailblazers who preceded us on the journey.

The terminology of disillusionment can provide a way to describe our experience of the dark night and enable us to converse with others of dark faith. Disillusionment to a spiritual pilgrim is akin to writer's block to an author: having a term for it helps one to cope with it. Knowing that writer's block is a common experience for authors helps one to retain some hope during those dry spells when inspiration is as scarce as rain in a west Texas summer.

The language of dark faith is a rich language, what Teresa termed the "language of the spirit." Any primer on disillusionment should contain chapters on metaphor, paradox, mysticism, faith development theory, and culture. The more I become conversant with my own processes of disillusionment, the more I see how each of these elements are crucial in my navigation. With these tools, I have learned to unearth the markings left by others who have preceded me on the trails of this dark wood. Somehow, just knowing that others were here before me gives a great comfort. It helps me to remember that I am not losing my faith—or my mind—after all.

Speaking in an Unknown Tongue: Metaphor and Paradox

A patient had just that morning received the dreaded word: cancer. After explaining the diagnosis and prognosis to the patient and his wife, the doctor asked me to check in with the couple to provide some support. Upon entering, I first thought I was in the wrong room. The couple was sitting on opposite sides of a bed stand playing cards. They greeted me pleasantly and showed no signs of grief or stress whatsoever. The conversation was boringly benign, even in response to my pointed questions about the doctor's report. "Fine," they said, "we're just fine." Abandoning my tack and deciding to go with the flow of the polite and shallow dialog, I asked, "Whatcha playing?" "Solitaire," said the wife.

There are many levels to a conversation: the surface meanings and the deeper symbolic meanings. The language of disillusionment is a language of metaphor and paradox. Any linguist of the dark night knows that truth can be expressed at more than one level and learns to listen for the deeper meanings. A couple playing at a game-of-one is a scene both metaphorical and paradoxical.

The deepest level of community is often metaphorical or symbolic. Baptism and the Lord's Supper are significant meeting points between an individual and the faith community. They connect our stories with the Christ story. They speak at deep levels about conversion and renewal, death and resurrection; grief and celebration. The gospel gives us a repertoire of symbols, similes and metaphors with which to share our own unique experiences. The conventions of faith provide a palette of colors with which to paint the scenes of our interior world for others to see; portraits that bear witness to the presence of God within and among us.

Some faith communities, however, have a suspicious view of anything non-literal, such as those who used the story of the four rabbis to teach the dangers of mysticism and its proclivity for the metaphorical and allegorical. Look what happened to the great rabbis, they warn: either they died, went crazy, or lost their faith. Stick with what is known, don't be led astray into alternative ways. There's danger when you leave the beaten path.

Obviously there are dangers on the spiritual journey, and sound doctrine is a basis for any true spiritual growth. But limiting ourselves to the literal and eschewing the symbolic is like teaching a course on agriculture and emphasizing the toxicity of certain plants while instructing students to stick with growing green beans and potatoes. With such narrow focus, albeit safe, we miss out on the wondrous assortment of edible and nutritious foods. Another approach would be to teach students how to discern the life-giving foods from the poisonous. Spiritual sojourners become botanists of the garden of life, identifying grace plants along the way and utilizing them for their nutritional, medicinal, and aesthetic gifts.

One such spiritual botanist was Carl Gustav Jung, who provided a pivotal integration of psychology and spirituality. Jung saw the themes of unconscious imagery, or archetypes, in the major religions of the world and postulated that this connection transcended ego and time—what he called the *Collective Unconscious.* Jung believed the ego to have a "transcendent function," or ability to produce symbols that allowed for the resolution of conflicts between the conscious and unconscious.

Paul Tillich, in *Dynamics of Faith,* drew heavily from Jung in reflecting on the symbolic nature of faith. Tillich noted that symbols "grow out of the individual or collective unconscious" and form the language of faith, which "has no language other than symbols." Faith symbols are used in "myths" or stories that depict "divine-human encounters." In outlining three ways of relating to the symbols of faith and myths that employ them, Tillich first described *natural literalism,* which makes no distinction between the symbolic and literal: all things are taken literally. The Genesis account of creation, for example, is taken to mean that the earth was created in six twenty-four-hour days. Simple enough.

Conscious literalism often occurs when a person is faced with evidence that contradicts the literal interpretation of a symbol. The study of geological findings may have the effect of "breaking the myth" by showing that it contains symbolic meanings beyond the literal. How do I reconcile the Genesis account with geological science and its theories that the earth is millions of years old? A literalist must disprove the opposing view so that the myth remains unbroken, the symbols remain literal, and the anxiety evoked by this disparity is soothed. Religious authorities may be consulted to fortify one's literalism. The alterative for others is to embrace the scientific explanation. Science, though, has its own form of literalism.

Like the body of Christ symbolized in the Lord's supper, a symbol contains no power unless it is broken. "Christianity denies by its very nature any unbroken myth," says Tillich:

> because its presupposition is the first commandment: the affirmation of the ultimate as ultimate and the rejection of any kind of idolatry. All mythological elements in the Bible, and doctrine and liturgy should be recognized as mythological, but they should be maintained in their symbolic form and not be replaced by scientific substitutes. For there is no substitute for the use of symbols and myths: they are the language of faith.

Broken symbolism, or what Tillich refers to as "broken myth," is an awareness that the symbol "points beyond itself" but also "participates in that to which it points." As such, the symbol "opens up levels of reality which otherwise are closed" and "unlocks dimensions and elements of our soul." Symbolic faith sees meaning in the creation account that goes far beyond the literal.

Allowing symbols to be broken and spill their perfume can be unnerving. It takes courage to doubt the literalism of a belief and face realities that exceed human comprehension, Tillich explains:

> Doubt is overcome not by repression, but by courage. Courage does not deny that there is doubt, but it takes the doubt into itself as an expression of its own finitude . . . courage does not need the safety of an

unquestionable conviction. It includes the risk without which no creative life is possible.[40]

Disillusionment brings us face-to-face with the limitations of literal faith. The methodology of our discipleship proves no match for the challenges of the dark night and its imagery. We may long to go home again to where we could take things at face value and believe that our acts of faith produced predictable and controllable results. But home will never be the same once we've entered the dark night, not because the world has changed; we have. Here none of our methods work, none of our theories hold up; none of our expectations can measure the experience. We are left only with love.

The Language of Love: Mysticism

In dazzlement we learn the language of infatuation. In disillusionment we begin to learn the language of intimacy. We speak the language of infatuation when we are taken with someone. Their presence evokes our passion. But the language of intimacy is required when we experience the longings of being *without* someone. The absence and longing we feel creates the "wound of love," to which Teresa and John so often referred:

Since I die of love,

Living apart from love,
. . . I die because I do not die.[41]

This language of love Teresa was speaking is historically known as mysticism. Just the mention of the term is enough to start the *Twilight Zone* theme song to playing in most people's minds. The origin of the word is the Greek *mysterion,* or "secret rite," and referred to the mystery religions. Most folks today are not interested in religious experiences "for members only," requiring a secret password and handshake for admission.

Lest we assume that mysticism is a foreign devil for Christians, or at least non-Catholics, Roman Catholic scholar Donald Christopher Nugent has noted the striking mystical and theological similarities between Teresa, John, and Martin Luther. All reported dramatic conversion experiences replete with mystical trappings. All were Christ-centered, Scripture-based, and grace-oriented in their theology. All had a faith passage comparable to the dark night of the soul

Mysticism has gotten a bad rap historically, according to Nugent's sources, as a "sophisticated spiritual narcissism lacking in a proper sense of sin." Seen to be the child of Neoplatonism and knowing no doctrinal boundaries, mysticism is portrayed as incompatible with Paul's theology of justification by faith and Christianity in general.

From my perspective, the mystical element of Christian experience has obviously been confused with the spiritual metaphysics of the New Age and the magical aspect of virtually all folk religions of all ages. We might as well say that since the vast majority of non-Christian religions have sacred texts and buildings, we should throw out the Bible and tear down all church buildings.

If anyone thinks John to sound strangely eastern, Nugent invites them to compare his koanistic verses with Luther's well-known paradoxes:

> A Christian is a perfectly free lord of all, subject to none.
> A Christian is a perfectly dutiful servant of all, subject to all.

> Sin boldly, but believe firmly.

> God's faithfulness and truth always must become a great lie before it becomes truth.

> God cannot be God unless he first becomes a
> devil.
> We cannot go to heaven unless we first go to
> hell.
> We cannot become God's children until we
> first become children of the devil.

Nugent argues that for John and Teresa, as Luther, Scripture was the ultimate test of truth, not mystical or subjective experience. The Bible was the only book in John's study. His knowledge of and reference to Scripture was second nature: "Taking Scripture as our guide we do not err." Against the biblical standard, Teresa gauged any spiritual impression, knowing that it only "bears the credentials of being from God if it is in conformity with Sacred Scripture...and if it should deviate from Scripture just a little, I would have incomparably greater assurance that it comes from the devil...."[42]

Deriving from Luther a solemn debt, Protestants and free church evangelicals are heirs of his mysticism as well as his evangelical doctrine. His famous tower experience was the pivot point for both: when he envisioned justification by faith alone and ecstatically "entered through open doors into paradise itself."[43]

In Teresa's Spain, as in any society that restrictively defines the scope of religious experience, there were excesses. Some groups reacted to the oppressive authoritarianism of the state church by pushing the margins of worship to ecstatic experiences characterized by trances, locutions (voices), visions, and even levitation. The culture was highly charged with suspicion and fear. The Moors and Jews, forced into conversion by the Inquisition, were held suspect of secretly carrying on their religious practices. Luther's Protestantism loomed as a heretical and revolutionary cloud from the north.

Whether out of naiveté, lack of education, political cleverness, or fear of the Inquisition, Teresa located herself squarely in the midstream of her Church. She concluded *The Interior Castle* with a prayer for the Lutherans, which to her misinformed mind was a "miserable sect," and submitted herself "in everything to what the holy Roman Catholic Church holds, for in the Church," she professed, "I live, declare my faith, and promise to live and die."[44]

Apart from some notable aberrations, however, mysticism is wildly mundane. For Teresa, mysticism is simply experiencing God. Her mystical doctrine of trusting one's inner experience is remarkably similar to the Baptist doctrine of soul competency: that each soul—in congruence with the community of faith and Scripture—is competent to have a personal relationship with Christ without the agency of any person or institution.

Sounding like a Masters and Johnson description of human sexuality, Bernard McGinn gives an encompassing definition of mysticism: "the preparation for, the consciousness of, and the reaction to what can be described as the immediate or direct presence of God." McGinn's view of mysticism is admittedly colored by Teresa's emphasis on "consciousness of the divine presence."[45]

One does not experience the wound of love from studying theology, but from the kiss of God.

Teresa dispels any illusions that mystical experience is reserved for the elite cadre of saints who rarely dot the map of history. Nor is it a paranormal phenomenon known first hand only by clairvoyants and alien abductees. Mysticism is the experience of all seekers of God. Perhaps if Teresa were alive today she would clarify for us that the problem is not that we fail to have mystical experiences of God, but that we wouldn't recognize a mystical experience if it ran up and grabbed us.

I'm convinced that mystical experiences are a wide-spread and universal phenomenon. We either don't recognize them, are uncomfortable sharing them, or repress them from memory. Like many children who don't know better, at about age eight I was walked home by an angel from church one Sunday night. Looking back, that period in my life was particularly trying, and my guardian angel was a welcome assurance.

The spirituality I most retain from my growing-up years is from Wednesday night prayer meetings. There were times during congregational prayer, or prayer groups, that I was caught up in rapture. But, did I dare to tell anyone? As my pastors talked to me in rational terms about prayer as "adoration," "supplication," or "intercession," I was regularly experiencing God's presence in far more personal ways.

While it is as natural as can be that we have mystical experiences, we do not instinctively know the language. Most of us are like young Samuel who heard God's voice but didn't recognize it. His mentor Eli finally realized what was going on and schooled the boy in how to converse with God: "say, 'Speak, Lord, for your servant is listening'" (I Sam. 3:9).

To admit to hearing the voice of God these days would buy you a one-way ticket to the psychiatric lockup. But not only does Teresa mention such locutions, she systematically describes them. The emphasis I am making here is not so much on her treatment of mystical experiences, but that she had a language with which to treat the subject. She was fluent in the language of encounter.

Actually, Teresa downplayed the importance of visions, locutions and other supernatural phenomena. I fantasize that if Teresa were to witness a prayerful sister levitating in the chapel, she would probably have thrown her a cloth and asked her to clean the ceiling. For Teresa, the significance of mystical experiences lies in the effect they have on our lives: "virtue, peace, calm, and improvement in the soul." These "jewels the Spouse begins to give the betrothed," include a sense of God's greatness, our self-knowledge, and humility in seeing ourselves in relation to God, and detachment from earthly things, except for the service of God.[46]

"So you are to begin with that first form of contemplation which the old mystics sometimes called the 'discovery of God in His creatures,'" counsels Evelyn Underhill. The experience of God begins in the mundane: "not with some ecstatic adventure in super-sensuous regions, but with the loving and patient exploration of the world that lies at your gates." With our feet planted in "common life" and our spirits "stayed upon eternal realities," Underhill insists, we are "better able to discern the real from the illusory issues" leading to our "own gradual upgrowth to the full stature of humanity."[47]

The Christian life is inherently mystical, and as Underhill points out:

> Christian literature begins with a handful of letters written by a mystic: that is to say, with the epistles of St. Paul . . . this means that the earliest documentary witness to Jesus Christ which we posses is the witness of mysticism; and it tells us, not about His earthly life, but about the intense and transfiguring experience of His continued presence, enjoyed by one who had never known Him in the flesh.[48]

The mystical vernacular is the language of "intense and transfiguring" encounters with God. "One must have been in love one's self to understand a lover's state of mind," said William James.[49]

The particular kind of mysticism that is perhaps most powerful in effecting the treasured results in the soul that Teresa and Underhill commend is apophatic mysticism, or the dark night of disillusionment. Apophatic mystics, such as John of the Cross, believe that God is most keenly experienced in negation, "with no other light or guide" than the one that burns in our heart.

> This guided me
> more surely than the light of noon
> to where he was awaiting me . . .[50]

"Contact with human creatures is given us through the sense of presence. Contact with God is given us through the sense of absence," explains Simone Weil, elucidating John's paradox. "Compared with this absence, presence becomes more absent than absence."[51]

The essence of the dark night is the paradox that God is as much hidden as revealed. Indeed, it is the revelation of God that most obscures, for every understanding of God creates a thousand misunderstandings.

In discipleship we bask in the glow of God's revelation: in the Bible, the doctrines of our church; the answers to our prayers. Continuing the journey, we come to a place of total darkness where God is hidden. Only as we experience the hiddenness of God as well as the revelation of God may we experience the paradox that is God.

In dazzlement, it is the unknowable nature of God in creation that overwhelms us with a sense of finitude. The ensuing desire to avoid this sense of being overwhelmed and to achieve some sense of control in life is the precursor of discipleship, where our methodology grants the illusion of control and mastery. Dazzlement, then, is the cornerstone of religion.

For McGinn, apophatic mysticism is poignantly relevant today with its emphasis on the perceived absence of God:

> If the modern consciousness of God is often of an absent God (absent though not forgotten for the religious person), many mystics seem almost to have been prophets of this in their intense realization that the "real God" becomes a possibility only when the many

false gods (even the God of religion) have vanished and the frightening abyss of total nothingness is confronted. If everything we experience as real is in some way present to us, is not a "present" God just one more *thing?* This is why many mystics from Dionysius on have insisted that it is the consciousness of God as negation, which is a form of the absence of God, that is the core of the mystic's journey.[52]

Charles Wesley said, "God does nothing but in answer to prayer." Apophatic mystics might say it differently: God does no thing—for God is no thing.

In this regard, the virtues of apophatic mysticism compare with the "jewels" of Teresa's raptures. The dark night teaches us about God's transcendent greatness, for God cannot ultimately be experienced in any thing or defined by any concept. As we accept the transcendence of God, so we come to a more humble view of ourselves as finite creatures. The outcome is detachment from earthly things in order to accentuate the experience of God. The darker our world, the more shimmering the divine.

> O guiding night!
> O night more lovely than the dawn!
> O night that has united
> the Lover with his beloved,
> transforming the beloved in her Lover.[53]

I sometimes wonder how I might have been aided in my first experiences of disillusionment if my faith community had provided me a thoroughgoing presentation of the spirituality of the dark night. Perhaps my confusion would not have been so bitter or my pain so sharp if I had known my experience was so classic and archetypal. I remember sharing with a group of fellow ministers how my journey with God had "come to the end of the pavement," and the astonishment I felt years later when I read John's description of the nada point in the Ascent of Mount Carmel: "here there is no longer any way . . . nothing, nothing, nothing . . . and even on the Mount nothing." I have spent many a night in Bunyan's Slough of Despond without knowing that it even had a name or that so many had fallen into it before me. So dry has my prayer life been on occasion that I would have no doubt gained comfort from John's and Teresa's descriptions of aridity. Would I have weathered with less injury some of the frightening tempests of faith if I had been taught about the storms and trials which John and Teresa describe?

On the contrary, perhaps I was exposed to this theology more than I recall but was unable to grasp it. The dark night of disillusionment is a developmental process and typically a phenomenon of midlife. In childhood, adolescence, and young adulthood, I was so much on the road that I rarely thought that the road might end. I was comfortable with my proficiency in reading the signs along the road and the drawings on my map. I never imagined that the highway was just one mode of travel among others and that my journey of individuation would require me to cut my own path through uncharted territory—and even learn to fly.

The Language of Faith Development

In the 1971 screenplay *The Horsemen*, Uraz (Omar Sharif) is the son of the greatest horseman in Afghanistan. Striving to live up to his father's reputation, he competes in a raucous tournament of Buzkashi and breaks his leg. Waking in a hospital, he realizes the depth of his crisis. Not only has he failed to match his father's reputation as a horseman, but he has been subjected to western medicine as well. Leaving the moral perils of city life, Uraz heads for home on a mountain trail where he rips the cast from his leg and binds up his wounds with pages of Mohammed's writings. Soon gangrene sets in and his leg must be amputated. Crippled, but not defeated, he embarks on a quest to prove his worth as a horseman.

For Uraz, the power of the prophet's words were in the pages. He was a man in the natural literalism stage of Tillich's paradigm. Losing his leg in spite of replacing the cast with Mohammed's writings brought him to the brink of conscious literalism. Does he make it to the stage of broken myth?

One of the most fortified of all illusions is the belief that the faith life is static rather than dynamic. It was the illusion of Israelite priests who for centuries kept Moses' bronze serpent in the temple, as if to preserve the power of a special moment for all time, even at the risk of worshiping a bygone relic rather than the living God. It was the illusion of Peter on the Mount of Transfiguration, daunting him to freeze the extraordinary experience in time rather than face the real struggles of life. It is the illusion of anyone with scrapbook religion, collecting snapshots of divine encounters and pressing them between faded papers. It is the illusion that motivates a modern Uraz to produce cabalistic code books of hidden meanings in the biblical text like children's word search puzzles. It is the illusion of midlife. It is the illusion that keeps brokers of spiritual real estate in business, selling what people believe to be permanent addresses at which to build enduring structures of dogma. But soon those structures begin to show signs of age and deterioration, for no structure can house for long the experience of God.

Eventually we come to see that our faith experience cannot be captured like a genie in a bottle and summoned on demand to grant meaning to life. More likely, it is we who are captivated. As Paul says, "I press on to take hold of that for which Christ Jesus took hold of me" (Phil. 3:12).

Why is disillusionment such a disheartening surprise? One reason may be a lack of fluency in the language of faith development. At the outset, like Christian in *Pilgrim's Progress*, we have no way of knowing that our journey will not always be straightforward and plainly marked. Neither can we traverse summits for which we are not prepared. It is a matter of faith development that we do not see disillusionment as a matter of faith development. Seeing faith as developing is a lesson of disillusionment. In the journey of faith we progress in the Spirit's time. We do not experience the dark night until it is time.

In the terminology of my old trusty Greek grammar, the New Testament language of salvation is both punctiliar and progressive. Punctiliar faith refers to a decisive moment of conversion while progressive faith is an ensuing process. I have been saved and I am being saved. One sense conveys that salvation happens to me; the other that salvation is a process in which I am very much involved. A dyad of Jesus' parables in Matthew 13 illustrates the distinction. Punctiliar faith is analogous to a treasure hidden in a field and found by a man. Serendipity! He then gave all that he owned to possess the field and, thereby, the treasure. Progressive faith is seen in the merchant who sought for a pearl of great price. The serendipitous moment culminated a search. He then gave all that he owned and thus was possessed by the treasure.[54]

A treasure possessed; a treasure possessing. A treasure found; a treasure sought. In relation to the reign of God, one was a treasure finder; the other a treasure seeker. Treasure finders discover the creative work of God in the world and treasure it. They make a place to call their own where they can have their treasure. Treasure seekers have a treasure in mind and create opportunities for finding it. The treasure is within them. Life, for treasure seekers, is about the quest, of "being sure of what we hope for and certain of what we do not see" (Heb. 11:1).

The shift from finder to seeker marks the beginning of contemplative spirituality. As the author of *The Cloud of Unknowing* delineated it, one level of faith is lived outside ourselves while the other "becomes increasingly interior, living more from the depths of oneself and becoming, therefore, more fully human."[55]

Other writers define this shift in similar ways. John Westerhoff describes the journey proceeding through *Searching Faith* to *Owned Faith*. *Mystics* were previously *Skeptics* in Scott Peck's paradigm of spiritual growth. Deepak Chopra's steps of transformation depict this development as a shift from *Seeker* to *Seer*, from an outward to an inward frame of reference.

The fundamental breakthrough of punctiliar faith opens up a process of spiritualization, as well as being the birth of a process that has always been ongoing. In my faith tradition, this birth is celebrated and acknowledged with believer's baptism by immersion. Hearkening back to the murky waters of distraction, we recognize with this symbol that life has reached a crisis. Something is sinking and something is emerging, but the process is ongoing. The early Christians of Easter sunrise faith turned their faces from the darkness of sin and embraced the rising sun of grace, passing through the baptismal water of public profession donned in white robes of sainthood gleaming in the dawn. Baptism expresses the critical mass of transformation in one brilliant flash.

But, what then? How are we to construe a next step, another day? For many of conversionist faith, there remains an illusion—an illusion that calls us back time and time again to the flash point, to passive punctiliar experience. When the faith journey grows wearisome and dry, we hanker back to the exciting and refreshing day of our conversion. We keep starting the car and thinking it will drive itself. Some even literally return to the baptistry, reckoning that their punctiliar experience didn't take.

The sacramental tradition approaches the punctiliar / progressive paradox in a different way, but often with similar results. Baptized in infancy, children are welcomed into the family of faith. Then at Confirmation they consciously and intentionally claim what they had previously received unconsciously and passively at baptism. Confirmation marks a point-in-time affirmation of a process which is lifelong.

Nemeck and Coombs, coming from the Roman Catholic tradition with a sanjuanist (John of the Cross) spirituality, refer to the passage of conversion as the "threshold of immersion," the awakening of a person to the mystery of God's immersion in creation. This mystery, they point out, is "something unmistakably personal."

> . . . somewhere along the line something happens. It may be a chance encounter or a traumatic event, like a death in the family. It may be a gradual awakening or a sudden turnaround. Whatever the catalyst and however long it takes to effect, we come to a new realization. Our attitudes start changing and we begin to encounter Christ as person. Moreover, we become aware of a desire to foster an intimate, loving relationship with him. A genuine friendship with God is engendered . . . Christ not only died for all. He died specifically for me. The course of our lives is forever changed by this realization.[56]

Ideally, say Nemeck and Coombs, Confirmation coincides with this threshold. Sacrament and experience do not always coincide, however.

> To confer the sacrament of Confirmation prior to the passage of immersion is to cheat the young Christian of a very important dimension of this threshold and of his/her voluntary incorporation in Christ...if Confirmation has already been administered at an

earlier, less meaningful stage of development, some substitute has to be found to mark this passage. In our day, practices like Baptism in the Spirit often serve this purpose.[57]

I tend to believe that believer's baptism more accurately reflects the interior and unique process of a person's conversion experience—theoretically, that is. In reality, a significant percentage of baptisms in the evangelical tradition are re-baptisms. In light of the Anabaptist (literally, "re-baptist") influences of my faith, I see this as the strangest of ironies. These sixteenth-century Anabaptists were persecuted for their stance that baptism was appropriate only for those who have made a conscious, willful commitment to Christ. Their baptism as believing adults was a renunciation of their baptism as unknowing infants. Now, as if coming full circle, many evangelicals return to the baptistry not able to make a connection between their initial conversion experience as children or youth and their adult life.

Some would say the imagery of baptism is outmoded and obsolete, a symbol which is no longer able to carry the meanings of individual and corporate faith experience. For me, however, it would be more accurate to say that we typically endue baptism—along with any other symbol of faith—with our illusions as well as deep meanings. For example, the belief that baptismal waters have salvific power to literally wash away our sins may foster the illusion that all vestiges of faith struggle are also rinsed away in the process. We may need to "baptize" our symbols from time to time: acknowledging our rites of passage developmentally and our need for renewed symbols to express our dynamic faith. Baptism as a disillusioned symbol may come to express other, more timely, meanings for us. As we reflect on our baptism, we may find it now holds different and deeper meanings of our very unique experience of grace, which is otherwise inexpressible—meanings that are just beginning to surface in our awareness.

In the same way, communion is a compelling symbol of disillusionment. "This do in remembrance of me"—the litany of the Lord's Supper—expresses our thankful gift of remembering Christ's sacrifice. But, in disillusionment it is we who feel forgotten. For those interior pilgrims who make their way through the many dwelling places of the soul, we need the reassurance that we are not lost or forgotten in God's house.

This rejoining of disillusioned symbols with new meaning is what James Fowler calls "conjunctive faith." It is when we "come to terms with the fact that [our] confidence is based in part at least on illusion or upon seriously incomplete self-knowledge." When we lose our illusions about our symbols—when they lose meaning for us and begin to represent new perspectives—we then change from being the finder to the seeker. We no longer hold the meaning of our treasured symbols; they hold us. In this paradox of dynamic conversion, it is we who are redefined, as Fowler observes:

> The reality our symbols and metaphors seek to bring to expression both spills over them in excess and recedes behind them in a simultaneous disclosure and concealment of the holy . . . instead of "reading" and analyzing the symbols and metaphors, [we] learn to submit to the "reading" and illumination of [our] situations which these and other elements of tradition offer . . . faith learns in this stage to be receptive.[58]

The symbols of our faith and of our faith journey are not created by us as much as they are given to us by our culture. Culture, which T.S. Eliot described as "that which makes life worth living," forms us in its matrix of meanings. As we develop and mature in our faith, we find that our symbols hold deeper meanings that have formed us in ways we could not previously appreciate. Baptism, for example, holds meanings not only of rebirth and new life but of death as well. Until we are ready for the deep water of the symbol's meaning, the shallow connotations remain. Thus, the language of faith development is an ever-evolving language and—like growing beyond baby talk to the conversation of the elders—we learn to recognize and cherish the mother tongue of the old country.

The Language of Culture

I suspect that for most Americans, the language of dark faith is a foreign tongue and the experience of disillusionment a foreign devil. To relate John's ascetical dark night to this culture is pretty much like hosting a close encounter with an extraterrestrial life-form. It is a strange being that deserves our curiosity for the bizarre but otherwise would be relegated to psychiatry or some secret office in the Pentagon.

We are not an ascetical people. We are a sensuous people. We entertain and amuse our senses with a gamut of ongoing experiences ranging from Nintendo to fast food to rather nice sound systems in our cars. Provocative images grab our attention from billboards, television, and magazines. We go to movie theaters where we see special effects, smell pungent popcorn, drink caffeine, feel the thunder, and view spectator sex. We fill our attics and garages and rented storage space with our stuff. We buy lots of gadgets and appliances. We have garage sales and swap meets. We buy motor oil at the grocery store and groceries at the service station. We burn scented candles.

Americans, observes Steven Payne:

> ... are typically portrayed ... as the antithesis of John's doctrines ... slaves of inordinate attachments to wealth and power ... the virtual embodiment of everything in modern society that John would have opposed: prag- matic materialism, consumerism, sensualism, milita-

rism, racism, and whatever other isms you want to add.[59]

Even our churches are increasingly multimedia with spotlights, taped sound tracks for vocalists, gorgeous robes, preachers who are gifted communicators, and MIDI pipe organs. The theology typically is conservative and success oriented; the economics market driven. We have a program, a building fund, and an advertising budget. God is a sure bet.

Now enter Teresa and John with arid prayer, meditation on the suffering of Christ, detachment, purgation, and negation. Somebody call security.

Dark night theology for many of us is indecipherable in part due to its Platonic roots. The dualism of matter and spirit, body and soul that permeated Christian spirituality for centuries is now being superseded by spiritualities that are more wholistic, creation centered, and unitive. It is not the material world or our bodies that are evil, but the distortions and dualisms that result from our attachments to them. These postmodern spiritual models accentuate the good, the divine light within and an environmental—if not cosmic—consciousness. They speak to the American soul, not in support of its hedonism or what Howard E. Butts calls "our chutzpah civilization," but to its alienation from what is ultimately and originally good in it.

It is not John's asceticism that I espouse and endorse, but his passion. His flame of love for God burned so ardently that all physical attachments were consumed. No act of human will can subdue this passion, for it is ignited by the Spirit. It is this divine passion, born in the dark night, that can burn away the vestments of the false self created in our alienation from the *imago dei* and attachment to things. The dark night evacuates the heart's throne room of this false self and prepares the way for loving transformation and union with God—in whom we find our true self. The dark night is not the annihilation of the self, but the salvation of it. It is the false self and its structures that must be stripped away so the true self may re-emerge. It is precisely at this point that John's message sounds so foreign to our ears. Because, as Edward Ruscil explains, the false self protects itself by fooling us into believing that true selfhood comes with the addition of status or even spiritual qualities. As Ruscil points out, "John of the Cross suggests that true self-actualization entails a subtraction, a stripping or self-emptying that aims at ridding us of this false self and its illusions. Thus the negative aspect of self-emptying is for the positive goal of finding our true selves, and thereby becoming more authentically human . . ."[60]

As Steere puts it, asceticism is only a means to an end. Mysticism and asceticism form a balance of spiritual development. We only deny ourselves in order to fully possess.

In his sketch of Mount Carmel, John wrote at the bottom the following verses which express this irony of the dark night:

> To reach satisfaction in all
> desire satisfaction in nothing.
> To come to possess all
> desire the possession of nothing.
> To arrive at being all
> desire to be nothing.
> To come to the knowledge of all
> desire the knowledge of nothing.
> To come to enjoy what you have not
> you must go by a way in which you enjoy not.
> To come to the knowledge you have not
> you must go by a way in which you know not.
> To come to the possession you have not
> you must go by a way in which you possess not.
> To come to be what you are not
> you must go by a way in which you are not.[61]

In John's theology, the spiritual life is about *todo y nada*, all and nothing. To experience God, who is all, we let go of everything else. This is the heart of his asceticism, his passion for God in keeping with the Great Commandment to "Love the Lord you God with all your heart and with all your soul and with all your strength" (Deut. 6:5). "But be careful!" Merton cautions:

> the key word in each of [John's] rules for entering into the ascetic night is the word "desire" . . . it is not pleasure, knowledge, possession or being as such that must be "darkened" and "mortified," but on the passion of desire for these things . . . far from seeking to deprive the soul of pleasure, knowledge, and the rest, [he] wants us to arrive at the purest of pleasure and the highest knowledge . . .[62]

What John offers us is a view that suffering is not necessarily an alien invasion into our world, but a dynamic part of it, and results in large part from our attachments. "Life's inseparable companion" is Sufi master Vilayat's title for suffering. Coming to terms with suffering is intrinsic to Buddhism's four noble truths. More than just the experience of pain, suffering is a heightened consciousness. In suffering we are most fully aware of our separation form God, self, and the world. We are aware of our fragmentation and disconnection. We are more acutely aware of our longing for wholeness.

Many in our culture, though, would make Christianity a religion of non-suffering, even to the extent of teaching that Christian faith and personal suffering are incompatible. In true Western pragmatism, religion's primary purpose is to provide fixes and remedies for all of life's problems: "whatever the question, Jesus is the answer!" This is why I believe if spiritual development proceeds beyond discipleship, it must enter disillusionment. In disillusionment we discover that the method of our religiosity no longer works for us, and we are left to face the emptiness of our attachments.

If John's asceticism feels foreign to us, it might be that our culture is so foreign to New Testament Christianity and its culture. It is easy to overlook the obvious asceticism of Jesus until we begin to differentiate the message of the Gospels from the messages of our culture. Niebuhr's "Christ above culture" calls us to transcend our culture and embrace the mystery of Christ's *kenosis:* "Who, being in very nature God, did not consider equality with God something to be grasped, but made himself nothing . . ." (Phil. 2:6-7).

Navigating the Nada

Wherefore Christian was left to tumble in the Slough of Despond alone: but still he endeavored to struggle to that side of the slough that was further from his own house, and next to the Wicket-gate; the which he did, but could not get out because of the burden that was upon his back: but I beheld in my dream, that a man came to him, whose name was Help, and asked him, What he did there?

Sir, said Christian, I was bid to go this way by a man called Evangelist, who directed me also to yonder gate, that I might escape the wrath to come. And as I was going thither, I fell in here.

But why did not you look for the steps?

Fear followed me so hard, that I fled the next way, and fell in.

Then said he, Give me thy hand: so he gave him his hand, and he drew him out, and set him upon sound ground, and bid him go on his way.[63]

The Pilgrim's Progress

Being up to your armpits in the miry struggles of faith may not be the best place to consider friendly advice, as Bunyan illustrates. What might be more comforting is a helping hand. While no one can literally pull us out of our spiritual bogs, there are some matters of practicality that deserve mentioning.

The dark night of disillusionment is a scary place indeed, but often it is our run from fear itself that lands us headlong into the most frightening of abysses. One such abyss is the "mire of our miseries" Teresa describes, which results from being overly scrupulous and compulsive:

> If we are always fixed on our earthly misery, the stream will never flow free from the mud of fears, faintheartedness, and cowardice. I would be looking to see if I'm being watched or not; if by taking this path things will turn out badly for me; whether it might be pride to dare begin a certain work; whether it would be good for a person so miserable to engage in something as lofty as prayer . . . the fears come from our not understanding ourselves completely. They distort self-knowledge; and I'm not surprised if we never get free from ourselves . . .[64]

This bit of Teresian wisdom speaks volumes to me about my own struggles in my "mud of fears" and the self-consciousness that arises from my distorted self-knowledge. In these distortions I misperceive that disillusionment is a problem to be solved, rather than an invitation to journey with God more faithfully. When navigating Nadaland, consider some time-tested principles of disillusionment passed down through the ages by those, like John and Teresa, who were well seasoned in dark night excursions.

Take no gear

Jesus once sent his disciples out on a mission trip (Luke 9 & 10). Obviously wanting them to learn something about the faith journey, he instructed them to take along nothing: no walking staff, no purse, no bag, no bread, no money, no sandals or extra clothes. Later, at the Last Supper, Jesus stated cryptically:

> When I sent you without purse, bag or sandals, did
> you lack anything? . . . But now if you have a purse, take
> it, and also a bag; and if you don't have a sword, sell
> your cloak and buy one.

Still holding fast to their illusions about Jesus being
an earthly messiah, the disciples declared that the group
had two swords in their arsenal. Jesus responded that
two was enough—two metaphorical swords, that is.
Speaking in dark irony, Jesus was emphasizing that no
amount of preparation would suffice for the trial they
were about to face.

In the life of prayer, there comes a point in which no
plan, no method, no form will suffice. We must continue
the journey in sheer faith alone, leaving the discursive
forms of prayer and moving into contemplative prayer.
As John of the Cross counseled, if any of these discursive methods work, use them to the hilt. Or try contemplative prayer, as the author of *The Cloud of Unknowing*
advised, and see if you miss the benefits of discursive
prayer.

Discursive prayer is a sound foundation of the spiritual disciplines. But, a house does not make a home.
Contemplation is the living out of faith in the places that
we create with God.

In leading prayer groups, I have noticed how difficult it is for some to get into contemplative prayer, or
what I call the prayer of being. When invited to just sit
quietly, attending to their breathing and gently shooing
any thoughts from their minds, they can't help but get
into some kind of wordy prayer or analytical theory
about the nature of things. They just can't leave aside
the doing in order to just be. The surest sign of contemplative prayer for me, conversely, is when I feel a bit like
I've botched it because nothing happened.

What the spiritual journey is ultimately about is
being with God, not with godly things or godly people
or doing godly deeds or thinking godly thoughts, but

just simply being with God. To remain absorbed with
the paraphernalia of prayer and discipleship to the
exclusion of contemplation is like spending a romantic
encounter with our loved one worrying about whether
the music is just right or which fork to use with our
salad. This is the behavior of people who are uncomfortable and unsure of themselves. People who are really
fond of each other just enjoy one another's company.

Can you risk letting go of your compulsions and
routines? Jesus highlighted the relational passion of
God in the way he reinterpreted the law to a pharisaical
generation, "I desire mercy, not sacrifice" (Matt. 9:13),
echoing the prophetic call to authentic living in relationship to others. Mercy, the way of relating, took prece-
dence over sacrifice, the religious ritual. Religion, for
Jesus, never took the place of relationship. Leave your
gift at the altar if you have wronged someone, "first go
and be reconciled . . . then come and offer your gift"
(Matt. 5:24). Religion could never substitute for authentic relating with others, nor with God:

> Many will say to me on that day, "Lord, Lord, did
> we not prophesy in your name, and in your name drive
> out demons and perform many miracles? Then I will
> tell them plainly, "I never knew you" (Matt. 7:22-23).

In laying aside our religious baggage, we are free to
break the routine or keep it, whichever helps us maintain relationship.

Let God Drive

Get in the back seat of your spiritual vehicle and let
God steer. Trust the process, "for it is God who works in
you to will and to act according to his good purpose"
(Phil 2:13). This is why John called it the *passive* night:

> Since this love is infused, it is more passive than
> active and thus generates in the soul a strong passion of
> love . . . these properties are actions of God more than of

the soul and they reside in it passively, although the soul does give its consent.[65]

The paradox of passive night is that one of the best ways to discern what God wants is by honoring our longings. This paradoxical conversion came to a head for me one morning during my daily devotional time. Day after day, year after year, I had faithfully met God in my private quiet time. My desire was to know and do the will of God and each day I read the Scripture and prayed. But, on this particular morning something was different. A frustration that had been subtly growing in my soul suddenly spilled over into my consciousness with fury. I was sick and tired of looking for the little pieces of bread God might leave for me in the forest so I could find my way. I was sick and tired of the game of pursuit. I gave up. God was too much of a fox for me to ever catch.

It was as if I stood there in the dark undergrowth of my spiritual jungle and screamed into the denseness, "I'm going my own way now . . . if you want to come along, that'll be just fine!" Silence. Then, from somewhere up above I swear I heard an applause.

Being the good disciple that I was, I had failed to tend to one very important part of the spiritual equation: my longings. What was I doing preparing three sermons a week and attending enumerable committee meetings when my heart was in the clinical arena? I applied for an internship in a local Clinical Pastoral Education center, resigned my church, and got my smile back.

On the surface, my experience may sound like the rebellion of a soul gone astray. Not so. Actually, I was taking one of the greatest leaps of faith in my whole life: I was trusting in the creative genius of God in making me the way I am for a reason. Until I was willing to trust God as my Creator, I would only continue to deny myself—and the world—the giftedness and joy of finding my niche. God was at work in me "to will and to act according to his good purpose."

I was entering the dark night. There were no more bread crumbs to mark my path. There was no more path—only nada, nada, nada. I was going my own way, for there was no other way to go. I lost my job security—or the illusion of it. It has been an incredible, wonderful, stressful, and peaceful journey.

Clean the Rearview Mirror

The dark night is about introspection, not destination. A clean mirror is more helpful than a windshield. Since you've lost the illusion of control, why focus on where you're going? Sometimes it is more beneficial to reflect on where you've been.

In disillusionment we begin to look back over our lives and see the journey from a totally new perspective. To see our lives as a *journey* is in itself a radically new perspective for some spiritual travelers. Our life is not a fixed point from which we watch the world go by; neither is it a potpourri of various unrelated events. Life is a fabric knit together with a divine thread. Disillusionment ushers in a sense of unraveling, an awareness of all the loose ends. But, through reflection we begin to see the patterns emerge and the texture take form in life's sacred tapestry. Our view of life transforms from a series of events to a volume of graced history. We begin to see the connections among the disparate parts. The aspects of ourselves that we have denied or ignored become acknowledged, honored, and integrated into the sum of who we are.

Make Yourself at Home on the Journey

The dark night reveals our illusion of home. "This world is not my home," says the old gospel hymn, "I'm just a passin' through." We are not away from home; we are not on our way home. Spiritual homelessness is not about being without a home, but it is about not recognizing the divine hospitality because of our illusions.

Was it any accident that the first structure of worship for ancient Israel was a tent? The Tabernacle was carefully engineered to be *portable.* Home is wherever God is, for we are in God. This transcendent presence of God was rediscovered by Israel during the Babylonian captivity when the nation once again found God in a foreign land.

Being at home on the journey enables us to "dare the dark," in the words of Matthew Fox. Unless we are willing to dare the dark, he says, we are not likely to move from "superficiality to depth." Putting down spiritual roots into the deep soil of the soul is not the work of a static spirituality, but the constant call of the Spirit forever beckoning us to conversion. We are not called out of the woods, but to become woodspeople.

Pavement Does Not a Good Road Make

Pilgrim Christian admired the By-path Meadow in Bunyan's allegory, which was easier going than the rough road by the river of God. But soon he and his companion found themselves in the clutches of Giant Despair in Doubting Castle. As Jesus said, "broad is the road that leads to destruction" (Matt. 7:13).

The dry places of the spirit have their mirages; the dark woods their ghosts. Learning to live by faith alone brings us to the very edge of our senses where we are then bidden to step beyond what we can know. Anxieties arise from unknown sources and false security accompanies real dangers. Satan comes to us in times of weakness and in times of strength. God may make "darkness his covering," (Ps. 18:11) while Satan "masquerades as an angel of light" (2 Cor. 11:14).

John speaks of these dark disturbances of the spirit as "desolations," which can be intense:

Their helplessness is even greater because of the little they can do in this situation. They resemble one who is imprisoned in a dark dungeon, bound hands and feet, and able neither to move nor see any favor from heaven or earth.[66]

Disillusionment is about desolation. Desolation is a place of no light. It is Job sitting on the ash heap scraping his boils with broken pieces of pottery while his wife—his only surviving family member—advises him to curse God and die. It is Jonah in the belly of the fish and later outside the walls of Nineveh wishing to die. It is Elijah at Horeb feeling he is the only faithful person left alive on planet earth. It is David losing his son Absalom and grieving the death of the very son who lead a rebellion against him. It is Solomon's dark wisdom that "all is vanity and vexation of spirit" and "it is better to go to a house of mourning than a house of feasting."

Consolations and desolations—spirits of peace or unrest—can originate from God or the evil one, taught Ignatius. The author of the classic *Spiritual Exercises*, Ignatius detailed a wise course of discernment of the source of consolations and desolations that included a conscious detachment from the objects of our desires in order to achieve a consciousness of God's will.

Many great spiritual writers, like Ignatius and John Wesley, have pointed out that the Christian sojourner inevitably comes to junctures in their life's path that give them pause. We should be hesitant, they caution, to believe that all our impressions are from God. Echoed in the ancient wisdom literature of the Bible is the caution of trusting too deeply in our untested conclusions:

There is a way that seems right to a man,
  but in the end it leads to death.
Even in laughter the heart may ache,
  and joy may end in grief. (Proverbs 14:12)

A pilgrim on the path of virtue may experience consolation from God and desolation from Satan, counsels Ignatius. In like manner, desolations on the road of sin may be given by God while Satan consoles. For the disciple, these discernments seem straightforward: an unsettling conviction is a sure sign that God wants them to make a course correction. In the transition from discursive to contemplative spirituality, however, we can expect disturbances in the soul, not just over sin, but over grace. The waters of discernment become darkened and confused. Like Jesus' frightened disciples seeing him walk on the stormy waters of Galilee, we may mistake the presence of God for a phantom. How can we know for sure whether a disturbance in our spirit is signaling a virtuous course or a misguided one? How can we discern the difference between the voice of temptation and the voice of God? How can we distinguish the voice of God from internalized parent messages?

Forks in the road, for the disillusioned disciple, are good places for a rest stop—to deliberately consider. We may discover that what obfuscates God's will for us is our attachment to some desired outcome. Sometimes the voice of Satan is clearer when God is silent. Through detachment we may come to greater freedom to find delight only in single-mindedly doing the will of God. When in doubt, detach.

Ultimately, we may never settle the matter with absolute certainty, for certitude is but a luxury in the dark night. It may be a storm of confusion that grips our thoughts and pesters us with unmitigated scrupulosity. Our maps are useless and our compasses give false readings. We are left then to make our resolve and trust God, as Wesley advises: "Whatever your hand finds to do, do it with all your might." The virtue is not so much in the outcome, but in the humility of a soul that longs only to please God.

Disillusionment and Community

In community life we often recapitulate the formative experiences of our family of origin, unconsciously living out the dynamics of parent-child and sibling relational patterns.

On childhood Christmas mornings I rose excitedly from my bed. It was in the same house where my folks still live today, decades later. Built before I was born, this home has remained a north star constant in my life, a symbol of stability and communal rootedness.

Living the minister's life has taken me away from my home town. A nagging guilt has plagued me for not providing my daughter this stability and rootedness. One year, early in the Christmas season I voiced my remorse to her, apologizing for always taking her away from her own bed on Christmas morning so we could be with my folks. "This year," I announced repentantly, "we're staying home for Christmas." She blurted out in disappointment, "You mean we're not going to Fort Worth?"

Recapitulation is a prime response to disillusionment—seeking a return to places we have outgrown rather than adopting new ways of being. Can I learn to bless my sojourning spirit in light of my home-bound upbringing?

Just as we re-create our family of origin, so we may seek to re-create the community of our conversion. Seeing recapitulation in psychodynamic terms, perhaps the reason we recapitulate our spirituality of distractions, dazzlement, and discipleship is that we are still maintaining an unconscious block regarding aspects of our relationship with God that are anxiety-producing. We maintain our allegiance to religious institutions and dogmas that perhaps no longer serve us well, like persons who are bound to repeat a behavior until they get insight into its unconscious meaning.

Peter, for example, tenaciously held to his Jesus-the-military-messiah illusion, to the bitter end. The futility of Peter's sword in Gethsemane is portrayed graphically by Jesus' healing the high priest's servant's ear, which Peter had just lopped off. It is no wonder that Peter—only hours later—blatantly denied three times that he knew Jesus. The truth revealed: Peter really had not known Jesus after all. Nor did he know himself apart from the straightforward force-fit customs of his fishing business.

Disillusionment is when we no longer hyphenate Jesus' name with an image. Rather than Jesus-the-military-messiah, it was simply Jesus that Peter saw led away to execution, stripped of all his illusory garb. When we are able to imagine God without so many hyphenations, we can then quit hyphenating our own name with all of the illusions we hold of ourselves. Mark-the-good-boy is one of my many hyphenations.

Reactions to the Disillusioned

Hannah longed for a son, but remained childless. In her "bitterness of soul" she "wept much and prayed" in the temple (I Sam. 1). When Eli, the high priest, observed her praying in such anguish, he thought she was drunk and confronted her. "Do not take your servant for a wicked woman," she protested, "I have been praying here out of my great anguish and grief."

The way Eli perceived Hannah was colored by his own story. The duties of the high priest included not only making atonement for the people by offering sacrifice, but the scapegoating of their sins upon the Azazel goat. In this case, Eli was scapegoating his own sins onto Hannah. His sons, we are told in I Samuel 2, treated "the Lord's offering with contempt" by bullying supplicants out of the choice portions of their meat sacrifices and "slept with the women who served at the entrance of the Tent of Meeting." Eli was less than forceful in confronting their behavior and apparently enjoyed the secondary gain of their treachery. With Hannah, however, he was vigilant in accusing a lowly woman whose woeful prayers he misinterpreted.

Since community life is typically maintained by some sense of conventionality, the reaction of the faith community to a disillusioned soul may range from empathic puzzlement to harsh ostracism. The sense that others do not understand what we are going through is part of the dark night—and only compounds its painfulness. To have someone finally hear our despair and grant us a peaceful blessing, as Eli eventually gave Hannah, is an unparalleled comfort. Disillusionment is the feeling that we don't belong. We feel on the fringe, at a different level or concentric circle of faith development. For example, persons at Peck's mystic stage want community at a deeper level than most churches and religious groups have to offer. It is what David Steere calls "spiritual homelessness."

In a concert of utter dismay, Jobs friends sat silently with him for a week. But their patient consoling eventually gave way to pious philosophizing, which only provoked Job's grief into anger.

Jeremiah became an enemy among his own people as he embodied a disillusioning message. The psalmist felt mocked in his faith trials: "people stare and gloat over me" (Ps. 22:17). Jonah, in a self-imposed banishment, camped outside the gates of the city that repented at his preaching, sulking in sad disappointment that his enemies would be spared God's punishment. Disillusionment feels like being cut off from the land of the living.

Since congregational spirituality is typically discursive, churches tend to shun disillusioned members. Well-meaning church folks point the disillusioned back to distraction, dazzlement, or discipleship:

"Get your eyes off the world."

"Look at what God is doing!"

"Try harder, get on fire for God." "Repent!"

Disciples who are beginning to experience the dark night of faith may feel that a painful transition is made only more distressing by the defensiveness of their faith community. "They all tell [you] to take another [path]," Teresa warns; "they say that the path [you are] on is very dangerous."[67] Pavement people can't imagine why someone would want to go off the road or how the pavement could possibly run out before we all reach our destination. The pavement Gospel is a message of the highway—of the thoroughfare that leads straight to heaven's gate. Just stay between the lines and observe the warning signs and you are sure to make it, guaranteed. The only destination this kind of misunderstanding of providence will get you, implied Tillich, is nadaland and disappointment:

> And such misunderstanding necessarily leads to a disillusionment which not only turns the hearts of [people] away from God, but also creates a revolt against Him, against Christianity, and against religion . . . Faith in divine Providence is the faith that nothing can prevent us from fulfilling the ultimate meaning of our existence. Providence does not mean a divine planning by which everything is predetermined, as is an efficient machine. Rather, Providence means that there is a creative and saving possibility implied in every situation, which cannot be destroyed by any event.[68]

In disillusionment, we develop a capacity—and even a preference—for mystery and tension. Disciples don't like mystery and tension. They don't want dialectical theology or the cloud of unknowing; they want answers and directions.

The defensiveness that disillusioned Christians receive may be in part due to a reaction to the irascible character of the disillusioned themselves. Both James

Fowler and John Westerhoff describe spiritual development as reaching a point of individualism, typically
beginning in young adulthood, when one becomes more
critical of conventional faith. For some, this individuation process may be evocative of the angry storm of the
dark night and take the form of a judgmentalism. Mask-
ing a deeper level of anxiety, judgmentalism may be a
projecting onto others one's own disinherited values
and beliefs. Rather than facing our own internal faith
conflict, we may relate in a critical way to others who
embody the very feelings we struggle against. As Jesus
advised, we best get the log out of our eyes before
helping others with specks in theirs.

My ophthalmologist brought home to me the reality
of projection in a graphic way. I had been seeing a spot
in the vision of one eye and consulted her about it. It
turned out to be a "floater" inside my eyeball. A natural
occurrence for a man of my age, she said. "I've given
nick names to mine," she followed, with a little more
empathy. I responded with chagrin, "You mean, those
gnats I've been swatting at are really in my eye!"

Such is the nature of projection; we "name" things
out there that really are within us. No wonder folks get
a bit defensive when we start sounding critical.

One of the supreme dangers for a disillusioned soul
is a spiritual guide who is unwilling to deal with his or
her own dark night of disillusionment. This blind guide
leading the blind can direct both into a ditch of bitterness.

A friend received a pastoral visit after the sudden
and tragic loss of a loved one. Cherishing the opportunity to share the meaning of this relationship and the
devastation of the loss, my grief-stricken friend poured
her heart out. Unfortunately, the pastor's attention was
so distracted by congregational politics that he turned
the conversation to his own anxiety.

Teresa reported a similar adulteration of ministry. Ill for months with chronic chest pains, Teresa's father moved her fifty miles to a famous doctor for a grueling three-month treatment in Becedas. The doctor turned out to be a quack and her condition worsened to a near-death coma and subsequent three-year paralysis. During her stay in Becedas, she regularly confessed to the local priest, Pedro Hernández, who turned their sessions toward his own needs.

> But I was so fascinated with God at that time that what pleased me most was to speak of the things of God. And since I was so young, it threw him into confusion to observe this; and by reason of the strong love he had for me, he began to explain to me about his bad moral state. This was no small matter, because for about seven years he had been living in a dangerous state on account of his affection and dealings with a woman in that same place; and, despite this, he was saying Mass. The association was so public that he had lost his honor and reputation, and no one dared to admonish him about this. To me it was a great pity for I loved him deeply. I was so frivolous and blind that it seemed to me a virtue to be grateful and loyal to anyone who loved me. Damned be such loyalty that goes against the law of God![69]

A sucker for a well-lettered man, Teresa apparently never fully assessed the double danger of medicinal and spiritual quackery, except that she comments wryly,

> Half-learned confessors have done my soul great harm when I have been unable to find a confessor with as much learning as I like. I have come to see by experience that it is better, if they are virtuous and observant of holy customs, that they have little learning. For then they do not trust themselves without asking someone who knows, nor do I trust them . . ."[70]

Disillusioned Communities

Not only do communities have disillusioned members, but communities can be in disillusionment as well. Scott Peck, in *The Different Drum*, describes how communities go through disillusionment as a natural part of community building. He defines four distinct stages in the process: pseudo-community, chaos, emptiness, and community. The superficial feel-good level of relating that Peck calls *pseudo-community* marks the outset of most groups. When people begin to stake their claims in the group and try to convert others to their point of view, chaos results. Group chaos arises from a number of sources, Teresa noted: trying to convert others, distress over others' failings, and relying too much on reason in the interpersonal process.[71]

Many groups come to an end at this point. For those that persevere, Peck continues, a painful phase of *emptiness* ensues wherein all conflict comes to a halt and awkward awareness sets in. We begin to actually listen to one another—not in an ain't-that-nice surface way or a competitive here's-where-you're-wrong manner. The reward for staying with this tedious process is authentic *community:* forging something new that surpasses what existed before.

Healthy communities cultivate a place for disillusionment and disillusioned folks. They do this—literally and metaphorically—by creating safe places for empty moments. Unhealthy communities crowd out the empty moments with busy-ness and programming, leaving little room for the creative expressions of darker moods and haunting images of shadow. Certitude is championed and buttressed with dogma and Positive Mental Attitude salesmanship. Of their vulnerability Teresa was well acquainted:

> I have known some souls . . . who have . . . lived
> many years in this upright and well-ordered way . . .

[and] His Majesty will try them in some minor matters, and they will go about so disturbed and afflicted that it puzzles me and even makes me fearful . . . They think . . . they are more than justified in feeling disturbed . . . For everything in their minds leads them to think they are suffering these things for God, and so, they don't come to realize that their disturbance is an imperfection.[72]

I was once a member of a church that had a penchant for denying its shadow side. The informal motto was "we have no problems here." Like the good-looking family that puts on the enviable public face and then comes into therapy with all manner of heartache and dark secrets, this church's facade contained large cracks.

One of the most protected places in the church building was a small prayer chapel, furnished by the estate of a late member. Although seldom used for prayer, the room was virtually off limits for other purposes. It was a sacred cow.

One Sunday morning, I decided to stop by the chapel and—well—pray. As I turned on the indirect lighting, I thought I was hallucinating. Blinking my eyes against the gradual illumination of the room, I thought I saw the image of a skull on the opposite wall. Having suddenly abandoned my prayerful mood, I walked over to investigate. Was it just my imagination projecting an image on the rough texture of the brick wall—like seeing figures among clouds—or did I see faint pencil marks etching out the grotesque figure?

Months later, long after forswearing further visits to the chapel for prayer, I worked up the nerve to ask one of the staff members about the haunting image. Not only was he aware of the image, but he recited to me the long sordid tale of a devout elderly woman who frequented the chapel and was found there dead of a stroke. He even knew the former staff member who had drawn the subliminal image as a twisted play on the morbid event. The story's plot thickened into a sad recounting of a career compromised by immorality and personality problems. For years the ignored image had remained, not erased or over painted, like an urban legend that captured eloquently the mystique of a community that stoutly denied its chaos and emptiness.

When illusions of community are enshrined, the truths are relegated to the basement shadows where they are walled off and protected with irrational vigor. These institutional facades become traced with gargoyles in an effort to stave off the evils of revelation while unwittingly exposing the demonic. When this happens, the repressed shadow of the community is often acted out in bizarre ways by certain individuals or subgroups.

A Ministry of Disillusionment

> Into the woods my Master went,
>   Clean forspent, forspent.
> Into the woods my Master came,
>   Forspent with love and shame.
> But the olives were not blind to him,
>   The little gray leaves were kind to him:
> The thorntree had a mind to him
>   When into the woods he came.
>
> Out of the woods my Master went,
>   And he was well content.
> Out of the woods my Master came,
>   Content with death and shame.
> When Death and Shame would woo him last,
>   From under the tree they drew him last:
> 'Twas on a tree they slew him—last
>   When out of the woods he came.
>
> Sidney Lanier[73]

Disillusioned persons can be the salvation of institutions. With their lack of attachment to the thin veneer of artificial identity, they can help an organization move toward greater authenticity. Their flair for the contemplative—and dark faith— grants them a unique capacity for opening up the shadowy places of community to the fresh light of the divine. As Teresa points out, this coming into the light is not without its struggles, for spiritual darkness lies in the eye of the beholder.

> You must note that hardly any of the light coming from the King's royal chamber reaches these first dwelling places . . . The darkness is not caused by a flaw in the room . . . but by so many bad things . . . that enter with the soul and don't allow it to be aware of the light. It's as if a person were to enter a place where the sun is shining but be hardly able to open his eyes because of the mud in them.[74]

Often contemplative Christians feel out of sync with their faith community. Like a fresh breeze disheveling a house of cards, their message of mystical subjective experience may threaten the comfortable status quo based on dogma. Some communities that are unwilling to deal with their own chaos and emptiness may scapegoat their disillusionment by focusing their shame and anger on someone who stands out.

Teresa described three trials that contemplatives are likely to experience in relationship to their faith community: gossip, praise, and inexperienced spiritual guides. Gossips accuse contemplatives of being showy and deceitful. Misintentioned supporters give a trial of praise that ignores the fact that any enlightenment is solely of God. Inexperienced leaders, fearing the unusual, are likely to play on a contemplative person's self-doubts.[75]

Both Teresa and John were scrutinized by their religious authorities and knew the fear of censorship and persecution. John bore the brunt of the Inquisition mentality, while Teresa was able to nimbly walk the thin line between suspicion and popularity in ways that were at times humorous.

> Learned and wise men know about these things very well, but everything is necessary for our womanly dullness of mind; and so perhaps the Lord wills that we get to know comparisons like these. May it please His goodness to give us grace to profit by them.[76]

John and Teresa, however, were no heretics but were steadfast in their insistence that true contemplative prayer is based not on mere subjectivity, but faith bottomed on sound doctrine. John's *The Dark Night of the Soul* provides a picture of faith in the midst of *darkness* and a redefining of darkness itself. Echoing 2 Peter 1:19, he points us to the soundness of biblically-grounded faith, our only guide:

> Behold the faith spoken of by the prophets as . . . a candle shining in a dark place . . . that we should live in darkness, with our eyes closed to all other lights, and that in this darkness faith alone—which is dark also— should be the light we use.[77]

True contemplatives value community and doctrine, for it is relationship that enlivens belief. Doctrine represents the faith community's heritage of Scriptural truth and the witness of the faithful to that truth throughout the ages.

Finding ourselves in the woods of existence, we learn the value of living in community with woods dwellers. With the collected wisdom of the community and its multidimensional presence, we may find the woods to be hospitable. Alone, we languish in ignorance and fear.

When John speaks of the faith, he is not postulating some whimsical fantasy that wishes the darkness away but the pure reality that dwells within a believer—a point where space and time intersect, where the tried and true faith of generations burns white hot in the crucible of the cloud of unknowing. Our greatest security then becomes the insecurity of dark faith: giving ourselves to that which we cannot comprehend, in simple

trust. This candle shining in the darkness, this faith—
and this faith only—is our light.

The disillusioned have glimpsed this light, which
can only be seen when illusion is stripped away. Once
so enlightened, they lose all attraction for the superficial
trappings of pseudo-community.

God called Moses to Mount Sinai where he was
given the law of God on tablets engraved by God's own
hand. When he descended from the mountain with the
sacred tablets in his arms, he saw the Israelites lost in
their frenzy of worshipping a golden calf. Furious with
his community's faithlessness, he dashed the tablets to
pieces.

Disillusioned Christians, having ascended the contemplative heights into the dark clouds of unknowing,
sometimes feel disappointed and frustrated at the per-
sistence of their faith community to remain in superficial levels of faith and relationship. Historically, many
contemplatives have sought to leave community and
reside in the desert or monastic hermitages. This, for
some, is a true calling of God to separate themselves
unto a life of prayer and simplicity. By doing so, they in
fact undergird the faith community in ways that are
most profound. Others, though, move to the edge of
community not in response to the call of God, but in
living out their disillusionment. Their images of community no longer hold meaning for them. A temptation
for them is to confuse their illusions of community with
true community. It is the disillusioned, after all, that
form the avante guarde of a community's growth from
pseudo-community to true community. The struggle
for the disillusioned, then, is to affirm their own giftedness and witness to their community—bearing the gifts
of God all the way down the mountain into the chaos
and emptiness of community-in-the-making.

True community, then, is being open to and living in
the empty moment with God and with others in their

empty moments. Though the temptation always exists to deny our emptiness, grace is found there. As Jesus moved into the emptiness of his impending trial and crucifixion, he celebrated his friendship with his disciples and invited them into his emptiness.

Greater love has no one than this, that one lay down his life for his friends. You are my friends . . . I no longer call you servants, because a servant does not know his master's business. Instead, I have called you friends, for everything that I learned from my Father I have made known to you. (John 15:13-15)

Friendship tracks with spiritual development. Jesus invited his disciples into friendship. Every true friendship goes through disillusionment. Disillusionment is friendlessness. Jesus invites every friend to die with him and to rise again into a place where nothing remains but friendship.

Prayer of Disillusionment

My God, so fair,
    that lays on my thoughts
    and the altar of my heart.
Are you truly God, my Lord?

My god, so fair
    that lays now on my thoughts
    and my heart's altar, in dust.
Where are you, my true God, my Lord?

Reflection

In your life right now, are you more a disciple of Christ or a friend of Christ?

Are you hearing the inviting sounds of Christ's party or the silence of a "gentle blowing?"

What are you tempted to believe about God and yourself that—even though they sound good—are not true for you anymore?

Have you ever felt embarrassed to share what you believe about God with someone; and embarrassed about what you do not believe?

What old image of God are you losing and what new image of God are your receiving?

In what ways have you not yet assumed your humanity?

Can psychology have the final say in our religious experience?

The struggle to find God and the struggle to find oneself are inseparable. In what ways is your self-discovery bringing you to new awarenesses of God?

"God is capable of profound passivity." Have you ever experienced this passivity of God? Describe your experience and how you integrated this into your understanding of God.

At this point in your life, is your prayer more reflective of "religion" or of "awe"? What does this mean in terms of you developing relationships with God?

What illusion about yourself do you hold onto most tightly? What would happen if you let go?

"Many are strong in broken places." What are your broken places of strength?

The distance between disillusionment and bitterness may be slight. What do you see as the key to which door a person may choose?

It is in the light that shadows are revealed. What "lights" do you experience as most revealing of your dark places—those places in need of redemption?

Endnotes

1   *Canticle*, 7, p. 472.

2   Ibid., p. 502. The Spanish text and alternate translation, "babbling bits," from Willis Barnstone, *The Poems of St. John of the Cross*, New York: New Directions Publishing Corporation, pp. 44-45.

3   T.S. Eliot, *Four Quartets*, (New York: Harcourt Brace Jovanovich, 1971), p. 127

4   "Kid's Pictures to God," *Life*, March, 1998, p. 70.

5   *Ascent*, p. 111.

6   M. Scott Peck, *Further Along the Road Less Traveled*, Simon & Schuster Audio cassette, no. 1.

7   Thomas Moore, *The Care of the Soul*, Harperperrenial, 1992, pp. 142-143.

8   Ibid, pp. 136-147.

9   Lao Tzu, *Tao te Ching*, 72, translated by Stephen Mitchell.

10 Belden C. Lane, "The Tree as Giver of Life: A Metaphor in Pastoral Care," *The Journal of Pastoral Care*, Spring 1991, Vol. XLV, No. 1, pp. 15-22.

11 Jürgen Moltmann, *The Crucified God* (New York: Harper and Row, 1974), p. ix.

12 *Canticle*, 1, p. 471.

13 *The Cloud of Unknowing*, Edited by William Johnston, New York: Doubleday, Image Books, 1973, p. 54.

14 *Canticle*, 1, p. 482.

15 *Life*, p. 115.

16 Quoted in Henri Nouwen, *The Road to Daybreak*, pp. 116-117.

17 *Castle*, 5:2:8, p. 344.

18 *Life*, pp. 113ff.

19 *Castle*, p. 323.

20 *The Cloud of Unknowing*, Edited by William Johnston, New York: Doubleday, Image Books, 1973, p. 136. Cf. "Leave aside this everywhere and this everything in exchange for this nowhere and this nothing.", *The Cloud of Unknowing*, Edited by James Walsh, S.J., New Jersey: Paulist Press, 1981, p. 252.

21 T.S. Eliot, *Four Quartets*, (New York: Harcourt Brace Jovanovich, 1971), pp. 50-51.

22 *Canticle*, 1:11, Rodriguez, p. 482.

23 T.S. Eliot, *Four Quartets*, (New York: Harcourt Brace Jovanovich, 1971), p. 40

24 *Luther's Works*, 31:129.

25 Teresa, *Spiritual Testimonies*, pp. 377-378.

26 *Night*, p. 393.

27 *Ascent*, p. 143.

28 *Night*, 1:1:2, p. 361.

29 Thomas Merton, *The Ascent to Truth* (New York: Harcourt and Brace and Company, 1981), pp. 51-52.

30 Francis Kelly Nemeck and Marie Theresa Coombs, *The Spiritual Journey*, (Collegeville, Minnesota: The Liturgical Press, 1993), pp. 108-110.

31 Nemeck and Coombs, *The Spiritual Journey*, p. 109.

32 *Castle*, p. 364.

33 Henry Bettenson, editor, *Documents of the Christian Church* (New York: Oxford University Press, 1976), p. 45.

34 Merton, *Ascent to Truth*, p. 23.

35 *Night*, p. 377.

36 *Cloud of Unknowing*, p. 65

37 *Castle*, pp. 343-344; *Ascent*, p. 143.

38 William Bridges, *Transitions: Making Sense of Life's Changes* (Menlo Park, California: Addison-Wesley Publishing Company, 1980), pp. 100-101.

39 *Castle*, pp. 364-366.

40 Paul Tillich, *Dynamics of Faith* (New York: Harper and Brothers, 1957), pp. 41-54, 101. William E. Baldridge and John J. Gleason, Jr., "A Theological Framework for Pastoral Care," *The Journal of Pastoral Care*, December 1978, Vol. XXXII, No. 4., pp. 232-238.

41 Teresa, "Aspirations toward Eternal Life," *Poetry*, Vol. 3, p. 375.

42 *Life*, p. 219

43 Donald Christopher Nugent, "What has Wittenberg to do with Avila? Martin Luther and St. Teresa," *Journal of*

Ecumenical Studies, 23:4, Fall 1986; "Mystical and Evan gelical Theology in Martin Luther and St. John of the Cross," *Journal of Ecumenical Studies*, 28:4, Fall 1991.

44 *Castle*, p. 452.

45 McGinn, *Foundations*, p. xiii-xvii.

46 *Castle*, p. 390.

47 Evelyn Underhill, *Practical Mysticism* (Columbus, Ohio: Ariel Press, 1987 [first published in 1915]), pp. 13, 116-117.

48 Evelun Underhill, *The Mystics of the Church* (New York: Schocken Books, 1964), p. 29.

49 William James, *The Varieties of Religious Experience* (New York: The Modern Library, 1902), p. 371.

50 *Night*, p. 377.

51 Simon Weil, *The Notebooks of Simone Weil*, trans. Arthur Wills, 2 vols. (London: Routledge & Kegan Paul, 1976), 1:239-40, quoted in Bernard McGinn, *The Foundations of Mysticism: Origins to the Fifth Century*, New York: Cross-road, p. xviii.

52 Bernard McGinn, *The Foundations of Mysticism: Origins to the Fifth Century*, New York: Crossroad, p. xviii.

53 *Dark Night*, p. 359.

54 I wish to thank Jeanene Atkinson for relating punctiliar and progressive faith to these two parables.

55 *Cloud*, p. 59.

56 Nemeck and Coombs, *The Spiritual Journey*, p. 56.

57 Ibid., p. 57.

58 James W. Fowler, *Faith Development and Pastoral Care* (Philadelphia: Fortress Press, 1989), pp. 71-73.

59 Steven Payne, *St. John of the Cross: His Influence on Thomas Merton and Other Americans* (ICS Publications Cassettes, undated).

60 Edward Ruscil, "'I Lost Myself, and Was Found': John of the Cross For Today" *Spiritual Life*, Spring 1991, pp. 24-25.

61 *Ascent*, p. 111.

62 *Ascent to Truth*, pp. 53-54.

63 John Bunyan, *The Pilgrim's Progress* (Grand Rapids: Fleming H. Revell, undated), pp. 7-8.

64 *Castle*, p. 292-293.

65 *Dark Night*, p. 419.

66 *Dark Night*, pp. 407-408.

67 *Castle*, p. 391.

68 Paul Tillich, *The Shaking of the Foundations* (New York: Charles Scribners' Sons, 1948), pp. 104, 106.

69 *Life*, p. 72..

70 *Life*, p. 71.

71 *Life*, p. 126.

72 *Castle*, pp. 309-310.

73 Sidney Lanier, "A Ballad of Trees and the Master," from *Poems of Sidney Lanier*, 1884.

74 *Castle*, p. 294.

75 *Castle*, pp. 360-363.

76 *Castle*, p. 290.

77 *Ascent*, p. 205.

CONTEMPLATION:
BEYOND IMAGINING

5

DWELLING IN CHRIST

***

Two yellow orbs in the darkness. No sound, no scent; no perspective. Orbs of Quartz dancing in the night. Synchronized perfectly as partners at a ball. To a rhythm hypnotic; a movement bucolic. Leading on a prey; dancing to the slaughter. A lion or a lamb.

The traveler strangles his breath. Muffled heart throbs palpate his throat. Eye to eye, soul to soul; breath to breath. The hungry beast sleuths—staring staidly—his inner hollowness. The window's eye, the crystal's portal. Death stares; life dances.

Your life is mine, I give it back to you. No reason, no rhyme; no justice in the choosing. I take with me your future, I leave with you my promise. Should we meet again on a starless night, we'll dance until the feast is mine: and the offering yours.

MSJ

After years of silence in prayer, I finally came to a point where I felt I could deal with my disillusionment. After all, my disillusionment had festered into a nasty sore of bitterness. I was hurting no one but myself. Returning to prayer was like visiting an old neighborhood. Things looked remarkably the same and strangely different. It was as if my old issue had been carefully preserved and set on a shelf awaiting further investigation, like a specimen from an autopsy.

My prayer was earnest, Why did you let me down? In the quiet of my meditation, I found myself in an old Western movie saloon. There at the table, shuffling cards, was God, a black-suited, white-bearded gambler. I pulled up a chair and continued my conversation. In response to my pointed question, my Gambler God looked at me seriously for a second and then started laughing. It was not one of those sarcastic laughs, or an Ain't-that-a-stupid-question laugh, but a deep-down-in-the-belly laugh.

One of those tension-breaking, contagious kind of laughs.

All of a sudden the absurdity of the moment gripped me, and I found myself laughing along. The whole saloon was in an uproar. God was wondering the same thing with me: Where in the world can I find what Mark is looking for? I wasn't let down after all—it was more a celestial chagrin—like asking for a filet mignon at a burger joint. My disappointment with the burger said more about my illusory perspective than God's cooking.

While leading a seminar on spiritual direction, I discussed the significance of emerging God images in our prayer life. I shared that years ago one of my images of God had been that of a gambler. I didn't elaborate. After the session one of the participants gave me a copy of "The Rowing Endeth," an Anne Sexton poem that conveyed to her a similar image. The similarity shocked me, especially in light of how the details matched so many parts of the story I *hadn't* shared.

> "On with it!" he says and thus
> we squat on the rocks by the sea
> and play—can it be true—
> a game of poker.
> He calls me.
> I win because I hold a royal straight flush.
> He wins because He holds five aces.
> A wild card had been announced
> but I had not heard it
> being in such a state of awe
> when He took out the cards and dealt.
> As He plunks down His five aces
> and I sit grinning at my royal flush,
> He starts to laugh,
> the laughter rolling like a hoop out of His mouth
> and into mine, and such laughter that He doubles
>   right over me
> laughing a Rejoice-Chorus at our two triumphs.
> Then I laugh, the fishy dock laughs,
> the sea laughs. The Island laughs. The Absurd
>   laughs.

So much like disillusionment is Sexton's experience of the Dearest Dealer. God changes the rules, or we could say, calls the wildcard out-of-hearing. Perhaps we take the game much too seriously with all our rules and expectations. No methodology or theological strong-box can hold God, especially this whimsical, mischievous God. No box.

Disillusionment creates openness for new ways of relating to God. We dislodge our methodology for success and successful religion and, as Teresa often counseled, "make a virtue of necessity"—a willingness to accept God's will. There is, in my humble opinion, no development more significant in the spiritual life than this conversion. In it, the death of Christ becomes more than a historical event that demonstrates the love of God. It is an experience in which we participate. As we empty ourselves of illusionary expectations, a death occurs.

Jürgen Moltmann described the death of Christ as the death of God and the resurrection of Christ as the death of death, "as a negation of the negation of God." In so doing, Moltmann not only refuted the "God is dead" movement of the sixties but provided a theology of hope based on the promise of God rather than the limited perspective of the present. The human story is not yet completed; the final chapter remains unwritten. The resurrection teaches us that God is capable of the unimaginable, whether it be a hand of five aces or breathing new life into dead bones.

On a personal level, we make a virtue of necessity by coming to the end of ourselves. In that emptiness the Spirit of God does something new.

The Resurrection Paradigm

After the death, resurrection, and ascension of Christ, the early disciples returned to Jerusalem and waited in prayer. For forty days they lived with the emptiness— the missing Messiah, the missing apostolate left by Judas; the missing power of Jesus' charisma. What they experienced is virtually paradigmatic for disillusioned travelers on the spiritual path. I call it the *resurrection paradigm,* with four distinct phases.

First there is *a hey day in which things are too good to be true.* For the disciples, Jesus was a visionary who attracted the populace and performed miracles. His message restored hope and a sense of self-worth to a politically-oppressed and religiously-repressed people. The temptation was to believe this was the status quo: the way it would always be. Let's pitch our tents, dig a well and build the city of God right here on earth.

Secondly, what ensues is *a crisis which is too heartbreaking to endure.* In the public eye, Jesus was a rising star at the zenith of revolutionary change. Behind the scenes, powerful political forces plotted his meteoritic demise. His trial and death culminated the power-brokering in a sudden whirlwind of execution, blasting his followers with a traumatic shockwave of grief. They saw their messianic illusions reduced to nihilistic debris. Shell-shocked minds stamped with scenes of messianic blood, they saw their risen Lord through bleary eyes: appearances which only deepened the crisis . . . and shame for having been deserters from the ranks of the Absurd Army. The temptation was to believe they were rejected and abandoned.

As the disciples watched their beloved rabbi ascend to the heavens, they were left with nothing but promise. This third stage of the resurrection paradigm is *a vacuum in which nothing can exist but hope.* It is an anticipatory emptiness in which the house is swept clean, awaiting residency. It is an empty tomb whose purpose has been transformed from container to proclaimer.

The temptation accompanying a spiritual vacuum is to fill the void with human work. Who will take Judas' place? The vacancy left by Jesus was too painful to live with, so the disciples opted for a problem they *could* solve.

As the disciples waited in prayer, Peter stood up and suggested that Judas' office be filled. Perhaps he thought they had waited long enough, or that some unfinished detail was precluding the fulfillment of Christ's promise. Remember, this is the same Peter who wanted to build three tabernacles on the Mount of Transfiguration, as if to concretize the mystical moment. Here, Peter appropriately quotes Psalm 69:25: "May his place be deserted; let there be no one to dwell in it." In so doing, he shows his gift for theologically reflecting on the unfolding story of the faith community. At that point, the community was experiencing the empty places left by Jesus and Judas. But then, Peter presumptuously finds the fulfillment of this verse in Psalm 109:8: "May another take his place of leadership." This is what Moltmann calls *praesumptio:* not waiting on God by attempting to usher in the future, presuming it is up to us to act. Peter's use of proof texts to support his presumption further indicates his confusing the *description* of Scripture from the *prescription* of Scripture. What Scripture *describes* is not necessarily what it *prescribes.*

"Therefore," reasoned Peter," it is necessary to choose one of the men who have been with us the whole time the Lord Jesus went in and out among us . . . for one of these must become a witness with us of his resurrection" (Acts 1:21-22). What Peter could not imagine was that Saul of Taurus was destined to become an apostle of Christ as Paul: the apostle to the Gentiles.

The election of Matthias to replace Judas is one of those recorded events in Scripture that receive no comment; no further acknowledgment. It drops like a faux pax at a dinner conversation when all the kind guests pretend they didn't hear. Matthias' election was little more than nervous busy work.

The disciples, still culture-bound and blinded by their messianic Jewish old-order doctrine, could in no way imagine a church that encompassed all people in a new order.

It is **an unimaginable fulfillment of promise** that comprises the fourth stage of the resurrection paradigm. It was unimaginable to expect God to choose Paul, a Pharisee Christian-hater, to become an apostle just as it was unimaginable to expect Jesus to be resurrected. It is part of the divine paradigm, or pattern, to not have a predictable pattern—to not have a paradigm. The resurrection paradigm is an oxymoron.

The temptation of limited imagination belies itself with words like "necessary" and "must." When we conclude that certain things *must* happen in order for God's will to be done, then we've just boxed ourselves in. God has a knack for operating outside of the boxes we build.

Disillusionment serves as a purgation, or emptying, of the soul of these paradigmatic expectations. The resultant space is available for the infilling of the Spirit of hope in a way we could never imagine. As the disciples waited in prayer, the Spirit came:

> Suddenly a sound like the blowing of a violent wind came from heaven and filled the whole house where they were sitting. They saw what seemed to be tongues of fire that separated and came to rest on each of them. All of them were filled with the Holy Spirit and began to speak in other tongues as the Spirit enabled them. (Acts 2:2-4)

While some groups seek to re-create this Pentecost event as a norm for the spiritual life, I suggest that one significance of the experience is its dramatic way of demonstrating the radical promise-fulfillment of God. The church is not an institution that safeguards the knowledge of God's behavior with predictable guidelines. The church is any community that lives out the faith of the wild Spirit of God with mind-bending innovations.

Disillusionment enables not only a good death for illusionary religion, but a dwelling place for the creative Spirit. For this reason I refer to this place on the spiritual journey with the juxtaposition of terms: death and dwelling. It has to be both. It is a strange, wonderful place where the end is but another way of describing the beginning.

A difference between disillusionment and death/dwelling is that disillusionment is when our illusions die and we experience no-thing-ness; death/dwelling is when we die and are reborn in the Spirit. Disillusionment is seeing Christ die whereas death/dwelling is dying in Christ—seeing ourselves die until nothing remains but Christ.

> I have been crucified with Christ and I no longer live, but Christ lives in me. The life I live in the body, I live by faith in the Son of God, who loved me and gave himself for me. (Gal. 2:20)

The Institutions Within

We do not—and cannot—appreciate what death means to us without considering what death means in the Trinitarian relationships of God like a Father, God like a Son, and God like a Spirit. In embodying the human experience and essence, God experienced death on the cross. For Moltmann, God cannot be contemplated as Trinity, or triunity, apart from the cross. It is the cross that expresses God in a Trinitarian way, a threefold experience of surrender. In the death of Jesus on the cross, God the Father suffers loss by surrendering the Son. God the Son surrenders to the Father to the point of Godforsakenness. The Spirit of God proceeds from this unity of self-surrender as the Spirit of abandonment and love who raises up the Abandoned as the Giver of life.

God is not out there. God is right here in the midst of life and death—and new life. The promise of the Spirit is the reality that God comes into the empty places of life: our losses, our disillusionments, our shame; our wounds.

When Jesus told Pilate that his kingdom was not of this world, I believe he meant that the Kingdom of God is not out there in the world, but within us. With the Kingdom within us, we change the world. Through the Spirit we are "in Christ" and Christ is in us.

This Trinitarian view of the cross provides a threefold model of mission in the world. Out of the facets of surrender experienced in the Godhead through the cross, we—as Spirit indwelt persons—carry on the mission of the death, burial, and resurrection of Jesus.

This mission entails first a *historical awareness* that questions the right of institutions to exist simply because they exist. Look at the manner in which institutions are formed: first as an organized response to a need and ultimately as an organization which takes on a life of its own, primarily protecting its existence and only secondarily serving its mission. Only as the organization is willing to surrender its very existence for the sake of its mission is it Spirit-led in its mission. God is like a Father who surrenders "his only begotten son" out of love for the world. We are to do the same with the institutions we build.

Now let's take this mission inside. In the interior life, where the real issue of sovereignty matters most, what institutions exist that no longer serve the life-giving mission of the Spirit? Another way of asking this question is to inquire about the nature of one's story. What is it that you believe about yourself? In what ways has your past experience become a script of present encounters? Our story contains the dogma upon which our current living is based.

A root of bitterness certainly qualifies as a self-perpetuating institution. There in the heart is an altar built for the service of a grudge, a wound; a resentment. Its root reaches out to the very ways in which we interact with others: defensively, aggressively, aloof, or dominating. Are you willing to surrender this institution with all its familiar patterns, expectations, and rewards that keep you safe from the scary prospect of learning new ways to relate to yourself, God, and others?

The childhood role we learned to play in our family often remains as an institution, unconscious but active. Perhaps in response to the chaos created by an alcoholic parent we learned to play the clown, distracting attention away from the tension between our parents. Our assumed role may have grown out of a variety of different family styles and influences: overly perfectionistic, neglectful, punitive, avoidant of feelings and affection, abusive, poor, affluent, small, large, first born, only child, religious, agnostic, divorced, remarried, widowed, orphaned, and so on. We tend to carry these styles into our marital and parenting styles. We even re-enact these dynamics in our workplace.

These roles may have served us well at one time. But, to live out these roles now in marriage, vocation, or congregation is to continually find ourselves disconnected, conflicted or unfulfilled. To challenge these internal institutions requires insight and courage: the self-awareness to identify the obsolete role or belief and the courage to face what is new and unknown. In Parker Palmer's words,

> Authentic spirituality wants to open us to truth, whatever truth may be, wherever truth may take us. Such a spirituality does not dictate where we must go, but trusts that any path walked with integrity will take us to a place of knowledge. Such a spirituality encourages us to welcome diversity and conflict, to tolerate ambiguity, and to embrace paradox . . . in the confidence that our search for truth, and truth's search for us, can lead to new life beyond the death of our half-truths and narrow concepts.[1]

In questioning the right of these internal institutions to exist, we open ourselves to re-writing the story. The story changes from a recounting of the events of our lives and the paradigms by which we live, to an open-ended witnessing of the renewal and innovation possible through faith. Our story changes from history to graced history, from a recounting of why things are the way they are to a recognition of the difference God has made on the journey.

At the moment of Christ's death, the Gospel writers declare that the veil of the temple was torn from top to bottom. This veil separated the innermost holiest place— accessible only by the high priest—from the outer sanctuaries. The Gospel declaration is that God is now accessible without the need for an institution to mediate. Through the surrender of the Son, God becomes accessible to us and replaces the old institution of Mosaic law with the dynamic of grace. Paul takes this image and applies it to the relations between persons who can be reconciled through Christ:

> For he himself is our peace, who has made the two one and has destroyed the barrier, the dividing wall of hostility, by abolishing in his flesh the law with its commandments and regulations . . . to create in himself one new man out of the two, thus making peace, and in this one body to reconcile both of them to God through the cross . . . (Eph. 2:14-16)

This interpersonal reconciliation is the second aspect of our mission: *a relational awareness.* Jesus surrendered to God to the point of a forsaken death. His travesty of a trial and execution served the interests of those who protected their institutions at any cost. In so dying, Christ becomes a citizen of this world: joining with all whose dignity and humanity are suppressed for the sake of political and economic—even religious— institutions. Jesus' trial and death is the trial and death of all people—a death for all.

This is the essence of Paul's theme in Ephesians. By bearing upon Himself the brokenness of humanity, Christ in turn bore gifts of salvation through His resurrection and ascension:

> "When he ascended on high, he led captives in his train and gave gifts to men." (What does "he ascended" mean except that he also descended to the lower, earthly regions? He who descended is the very one

who ascended higher than all the heavens, in order to
fill the whole universe.) (Eph. 4:8-10)

The resurrection of Jesus was a negation of all that
negates the Godforsaken and oppressed. Rather than
standing empty-handed on a dark margin of life, we
have gifts with which to serve one another in freedom
and power. Paul continues:

> It was he who gave some to be apostles, some to be
> prophets, some to be evangelists, and some to be pas-
> tors and teachers, to prepare God's people for works of
> service, so that the body of Christ may be built up until
> we all reach unity in the faith and in the knowledge of
> the Son of God and become mature, attaining to the
> whole measure of the fullness of Christ. (Eph. 4:11-13).

Moving this resurrection reality inside ourselves
means that our spirituality must eventually find an
expression in community. Our mission is not just a
personal mission; it is a community mission. It means,
for starters, that we stand with those whose human
dignity is suppressed. It means that we are world citizens, members of the citizenry of Christ.

This community mission becomes all the more important for our interior life as we become disillusioned
disciples. In the dark night we cry with Jesus, "My God,
why have you forsaken me?" God becomes unknown
and unknowable. The tendency of the disillusioned is to
withdraw from community; the tendency of faith communities may be to withdraw from the disillusioned.
But, God through the crucified Jesus calls us to band
together. In this regard, church life is really a forum
where we join others as abandoned children, sometimes
offering one another love and comfort, sometimes acting out our woundedness and fear. Like shell-shocked
disciples after Jesus' death meeting behind locked doors
or waiting in the upper room for the promised Spirit, we
wait together.

And the Spirit comes. Into our emptiness and darkness the Spirit's fresh breath and flame of love moves in. Our waiting is fulfilled, giving us a hopeful anticipation. We can face the future because there is hope. This third aspect of our mission is *a future awareness.*

Moving interiorly into a mission of hopeful anticipation involves the deepening of imagination. This imaginative mission has been historically carried on by prophets. Today we shy away from prophets, or those who claim to have a direct line to God. But a recovery of the prophetic tradition may help us to embrace the key role of prophets in community.

In the ancient Hebrew tradition, prophecy meant literally to "bubble over," an ecstatic communication of a message from God. Jeremiah found his message so unpopular that he restrained his prophetic impulse, but he found the message burning in his bones. He had to speak.

Prophecy involves two dimensions in its classical form: forth-telling and fore-telling. The prophet conveys a message from God: "Thus saith the Lord . . ." Here it is, people, God has spoken through me and wants you to repent. Forth-telling is usually a confrontational approach. Forth-tellers are the surgeons of the faith community. With their famous remark, "This is going to sting," they proceed to cut out whatever pathological masses they see.

Fore-telling, on the other hand, is a prediction of some future event. Often the prophets would receive a vision or locution that they themselves struggled to comprehend. But the sign of a true prophet was that their predictions came true.

Listed above in the text from Ephesians, prophets are one of God's gifts to the faith community. Have we lost the gift of prophecy? Or, do we no longer recognize the prophetic element?

I suggest that prophecy is the gift of imagination, the talent of conveying formative images of God and envisioning the way things could be. Prophets are the insightful, intuitive folks among us who seem to have an uncanny knack for getting to the bottom of things and a grasp of trends. Prophets see behind the words and actions to the dynamic—and often unconscious—levels of human interaction. Because of this, their observations often sound weird and off-base at first and may be rejected before the real truth emerges.

Faith is the capacity for imagination. It is an openness to conversion and change. In this world, we live between promise and fulfillment, between history and hope. History can only hold part of the equation, for in hope the story is always yet to be finished. The conclusion of the book is yet to be written. God invites us to the cutting-edge of life, to the cusp of the plot-unfolding, to become co-creator of the next chapter. This is our calling; our mission.

The Host of the Cross

> Oh, how everything that is suffered with love is healed again![2]
>
> Teresa

The cross, a Roman form of execution, was an instrument of punishment and intimidation. It had become a common part of the Palestinian landscape during the first century, used to publicly torture subversives and criminals. A horrible way to die.

Crucifixion was a means of preserving the control of Roman institutions by executing enemies of the state and making examples of those who dared to test the law. Jesus' death on a cross portrays the tension between personal authenticity and the power of institutions. The religious authorities used the government to accomplish their agenda. By making Jesus out to be an insurrectionist, the tyranny of Roman rule was employed to mask the threat he posed to those who depended on religious domination to preserve their specific version of the truth.

In this climate of ubiquitous death threat, Jesus emerges as a liberator from death. When society is controlled by its own fear of death, the brave heart who opts for death destroys the oppressor's threat and control.

The gospel zeros in on one of the countless crucified souls that pervaded the scenery and reveals the meaning of this one life and the relationships that formed its story. So long as the marginalized remain as a forest of unknown and indistinguishable trees, they may be more easily brushed aside from consciousness as a soul-less mass. By taking up his cross, Jesus invites us into the awareness that each life is a cosmos of beauty and meaning, formed into an individual created order. Each life is a graced history written from the elements of a unique experience: a grace story. Every person is a universe within themselves. When this awareness begins to settle over a society, differences and status cease to be a threat and become a cherished treasure.

By accepting his cross freely, Jesus becomes a host of freedom. By drinking the cup of political wrath, he became a mediator of peace. The cross as instrument of execution was transformed into a passage leading to life untangled from the attachments of greed and pride. Death's power is broken, for all it can take from us is our egocentrism. When we experience spiritual death—the surrender of all attachments—ours, too, is the freedom to live out our grace story.

In free death, the marginal becomes foundational. Peter refers to Christ as the cornerstone, "to you who believe, this stone is precious . . . but to those who do not believe, 'the stone the builders rejected has become the cornerstone' and, 'a stone that causes men to stumble'"

(I Pet. 2:7-8). Cornerstone; stumbling stone. Peter is picturing two different dispositions toward the innovations of God. The wind of the Spirit can refresh, but it can also blow your house down. The struggle between Jesus and the political institutions of Rome and Temple was warfare, a battle to the death. Either we kill Jesus or he will kill us (undermine our domination). The throne of the heart has room but for one sovereign.

> Christ says "Give me All. I don't want so much of your time and so much of your money and so much of your work: I want You. I have not come to torment your natural self, but to kill it. No half-measures are any good. I don't want to cut off a branch here and a branch there, I want to have the whole tree down. I don't want to drill the tooth, or crown it, or stop it, but to have it out. Hand over the whole natural self, all the desires which you think innocent as well as the ones you think wicked—the whole outfit. I will give you a new self instead. In fact, I will give you Myself: my own will shall become yours."[3]

The above description of spiritual death by C.S. Lewis is comparable to Bonhoeffer's: "The cross is laid on every Christian . . . the call to abandon the attachments of this world . . . when Christ calls a person, He bids them come and die."[4] To take up our cross is to give up what is vital to our way of life. "Vital" refers to that which we can't live without. In spiritual death we surrender what we feel we can't live without. Jesus asked some to leave lucrative careers, some their family ties, some their political loyalties, and others their religious practices. What our life is based upon may be a false foundation. Paul relinquished all confidence in the flesh for the sake of a sure foundation in Christ:

> But whatever was to my profit I now consider loss for the sake of Christ. What is more, I consider everything a loss compared to the surpassing greatness of knowing Christ Jesus my Lord, for whose sake I have

lost all things. I consider them rubbish, that I may gain
Christ . . . (Phil. 3:7-8)

Gift becomes threat and threat becomes a gift in this
topsy-turvy economy of the gospel. From disillusionment emerges a new clarity that enables our conversion
from the False Self to the True Self. The determining
factor is our willingness to die. Christ is a rock upon
which our illusions are dashed. If we remain rigid in our
attachment to illusory structures and self-images, then
we will be dashed like a clay pot along with our illusions—a life broken by rigidity and self-reproach.
Through spiritual death we can experience resurrection
and become as soft, pliable clay with which a new
reality can be fashioned on the cornerstone of the resurrected Christ.

Flora Slosson Wuellner recalls that stones rejected
by ancient city builders often wound up in the catapults
of besieging armies, and she draws the analogy of a
rejected cornerstone to a deprecated aspect of our personal power.

> When we reject that part of ourselves which was
> meant to be our most radiant gift, our deepest energy,
> we do, indeed, use those parts of ourselves as instru-
> ments of destruction against ourselves and others. Per-
> haps there is no more dangerous weapon than our own
> deep, unhealed, uncomforted, unreleased inner gift.[5]

Grace-story or death-threat? The stone of identity
cannot be denied. We will either approach it as a life-
giving source or as a destructive nemesis. For Simon
Peter, the stone was his identity in Christ—his name. In
response to his insight into Jesus' divinity, Jesus pronounced, "you are Peter, and on this rock I will build my
church, and the gates of Hades will not overcome it"
(Matt. 16:18). Jesus' word play was a promise that
Simon's character would be transformed from impulsive to bedrock stability. Simon would become Peter,

and Peter (literally "rock") would become the rock of
the church. This passage was the early church's way of
declaring that the foundation of life is the kind of faith
Peter demonstrated in Christ. For Peter, Jesus Christ—
crucified and resurrected—was the cornerstone of his
life.

A faithless life will encounter the stone of God as a
sobering reality. Paul referred to this immutable reality
as the law: "no one will be declared righteous in [God's]
sight by observing the law; rather, through the law we
become conscious of sin" (Ro. 3:20). You don't break the
law; it breaks you. Run stop signs and you may think
you break the law, but continue running stop signs and
you court disaster. The law will break you. Recall Peter's
statement: "But to those who do not believe, 'The stone
the builders rejected has become . . . a stone that causes
men to stumble and a rock that makes them fall'" (I
Peter 2:7-8). Without a foundation, a faithless life is
fragmented and adrift on a sea of meaninglessness, a
house built on sand.

Our Host bids us step onto the Rock, where our life
and identity can be grounded and guided. Just as a
cornerstone determines the primary angles of a structure, so our Rock forms us in character with Christ.
Spiritual death is a foretaste of physical death, the transformation of the soul into the True Self.

> Beneath your protecting banner
> Even the weakest are made strong!
> O life of our death,
> Reviving it so well . . .
> You are the freedom
> From our dread captivity;
> With so precious remedy . . .[6]
>
> Teresa

"Death is not extinguishing the light. It is putting
out the Lamp because the Son is here."[7] Nemeck and

Coombs aptly depict the transformation of death. This world's light pales as the inner light of God illuminates the soul.

Fear not death; fear only God. The journey will lead to a place of death in Christ, a sharing of the cross, commending our spirits into the hands of God. Once we have died in Christ, we relate to death differently. Perhaps mockingly, as Moltmann suggests. Perhaps gratefully, as Teresa suggests in "The Way of the Cross":

> The Lord of heaven and earth
> Is on the cross.
> On it, too, delight in peace . . .
>
> From the cross the bride
> To her Beloved says
> This is a precious palm
> Upon which she has climbed,
> Its fruit tasting
> Like the God of paradise . . .
>
> This sacred cross,
> An olive tree so dear,
> With its oil anoints us
> Giving us light . . .
>
> This cross is the verdant tree
> Desired by the bride.
> In its cool shade
> Now she is resting,
> Delighting in her Beloved . . .
>
> The soul to God
> Is wholly surrendered,
> From all the world
> Now truly free,
> The cross is at last her
> "Tree of Life" and consolation . . .[8]

"Take up your cross and follow me," Jesus declared. We are called to a cross-bearing community. Spiritual death is the requisite for continuing the journey, for the trail that Christ is blazing cuts straight through death into new life. The cross, rather than an object of fearful disgust, is our Tree of Life. Teilhard de Chardin believed that "For the Christian, it is not a question of swooning in its shadow, but of ascending in the light of the Cross."[9]

Dismantling the Old Structures

The Kickapoo Native American tribe has a history of migrating great distances in search of freedom from the domination of the New World Americans and other tribes. Now settled primarily in Mexico and Texas, their value of impermanence can be seen in their death rituals. When a Kickapoo dies, other members of the tribe take apart the house so the spirit of the dead won't return.

It is this deconstruction of the old structures that frees the living to go on with life and reconstruct the community with new meaning. By holding on to the old structures, a community is tied to the ground of the past. No movement can occur. The assimilation of new members would be increasingly difficult as the tribal society became cluttered with obsolete structures of obsolete roles. Remember Jesus' characterization of spirits:

> When an evil spirit comes out of a man, it goes through arid places seeking rest and does not find it. Then it says, "I will return to the house I left." When it arrives, it finds the house unoccupied, swept clean and put in order. Then it goes and takes with it seven other spirits more wicked than itself, and they go in and live there. And the final condition of that man is worse than the first. (Matt. 12:43-45)

A lacking in the discernment of spirits marks our society. The same old issues arise over again from generation to generation as if quickened by unseen spirits.

Prejudice, economic disparity, unfinished emotional business; family secrets. The unnamed spirits of society maintain a *quid pro quo*, a retaliation, a compensation; a debt to be paid by the next generation because the old structures remain. Shameful secrets are kept safe so that children are doomed to unconsciously repeat the dark behavior of parents and grandparents. The sins of the parents are passed down to the third and fourth generation. Structures remain that buttress inequality and allow the powerful to maintain power on the backs of the less influential. Foreign policy injustices return repeatedly to haunt us with ever-increasing insidiousness. Congregations and their denominations parlay their witness with divisive squabbles based on past offenses long unreconciled. All these, and more, are based on losses not grieved and old structures left as haunts for tomorrow. The old structures must be dislodged, or as the Kickapoo ritual suggests, dis-lodged, in the sense of removing the lodging.

For Gary Harbaugh, a loss that is not grieved dies a death for which there is no resurrection. Losses not fully integrated into life, feelings of grief left unacknowledged, and illusions disembodied but never buried, leave their wounds unhealed. "Where there is no death, there is no possibility of resurrection."[10]

Joining Christ in the cross work of our soul enables an uprooting of bitterness and dislodging of bitter vestiges of scurvy remembrances. This dis-lodging death is a delightful one, Teresa promised; we die "to the world so as to live more completely in God."[11]

Take up your cross and follow me, bids Christ. Just how far are you willing to go in this journey? The gentle Spirit senses our defensiveness—our willingness to make the sojourn, but at a deliberate and testy pace.

> Let nothing trouble you,
> Let nothing scare you,
> All is fleeting,

God alone is unchanging.
Patience Everything obtains.
Who possesses God
Nothing wants.
God alone suffices.

Teresa

Come to my cross, Jesus continues to beckon. See the world from the crossbeam of my tower. See in the eyes of passers by the haunting of death. Be this death that haunts them. Embrace this cross like a lover and surrender to its caresses. Then you will truly see and know what healing a life given in love can bring.

The wounded surgeon plies the steel
That questions the distempered part;
Beneath the bleeding hands we feel
The sharp compassion of the healer's art
Resolving the enigma of the fever chart.
Our only health is the disease
If we obey the dying nurse
Whose constant care is not to please but to remind
of our, and Adam's curse,
And that, to be restored, our sickness must grow
worse.
The whole earth is our hospital . . .[12]

T.S. Eliot

The True Self and the False Self

I have been crucified with Christ and I no longer live, but Christ lives in me (Gal. 2:20).

***

. . . the paradox of this transforming miracle within us is that never before have we so profoundly felt that we were our own true selves. For the love of God through Christ does not wipe out our sense of self, but wakens the self, espouses it, heals it, brings it to heights we never dreamed possible.[13]

Flora Slosson Wuellner

The giving over of ourselves to God is a huge cube of marble giving itself to the sculptor. What emerges from the stone at the point of the chisel is not what is constructed but from what is taken away. Bit by artful bit the form of pure imagination takes shape as the sculptor reveals the true form of the stone. "The treasure lies within our very selves," Teresa believed.[14]

In one of those south Texas droughts such as occurred in 1996, a local San Antonio newspaper presented a photo of the desiccated Falcon Reservoir. Revealed among the skeletons of barren trees was a lone stone cross emerging from the cemetery of Old Lopeño, which was a border village buried for forty-three years beneath the engineered lake. In like manner, we construct over our souls a basin of vitality—a life as we make it—capturing the run-off of accomplishments. Beneath the waves of our self-image await the shadowy remnants of our denied mortality, our identity connected to the earth. These vestiges of disturbing origins surface in the aridity of purgation and present themselves for claiming by their rightful owner.

Studying the photo's metaphors, I come face-to-face with my own roots often submerged. From my Anabaptist and Baptist predecessors, drowned in cold rivers and burned on obscene stakes of Reformation and Counter-Reformation assault, I find in my soul the generations of archetypal grief of cold steel oppression—an oppression that stamped out their flowers before they could blossom. Pushed from their home countries, harboring in tiny Rhode Island as a leper city of refuge, they drove ever westward until they scratched out a consortium with Comanches and Catholic Mexicans. Theirs was a *Pilgrim's Progress* penned in the prison of prejudice, libel, and freedom—fear. These pilgrim forebears fashioned a soul-free community out of state church stone with implements of humanistic enlightenment and stark biblical patterns. Their graves I cannot dishonor, buried beneath the sediment layers of my own identity.

This Baptist grief burns in the anger, often misplaced, of bony-nosed, crusty antagonists of bully pulpits and political machinations. Fiercely they defend the faith against a world depicted on mothers' knees as unjust and fallen, sometimes forgetting the subtler distinctions between religious liberty and politically-active religion. Cain and Abel siblings, they rival with their own kind for a sense of blessedness and acceptance, splitting off hairs of new shade-tree denominations like generations of self-defined children striking out on their own. They are wild flowers among the weeds of every American back road and highway, indigenous as Johnson grass and corn, and just as gangly, never again to be denied their Baptist-inspired Bill of Rights' freedom to worship as they see fit.

The anger smolders in my bosom from generations of gypsy tent roaming, longing for a cool and comforting arbor in which to mourn. I mourn the young ideologues, their lights snuffed out by persecution before they could systematize their faith into a Luther's *Theologica Germanica*, a Calvin's *Institutes*, or a sanjuanist's *Ascent*. Theirs was a faith never quite full grown, plateauing on conventionality and subservient to methodology. It was at times mystical, but fearing the mystic's report. It was at times prophetic, but to a fault. It was at times proud, but with a pride that injures. It remains autonomous, but seduced by conformity.

It is this heritage of the Reformation radicals of which I feel both shame and gratitude. My shame resides in the buzz saw tactics often used by ultraconservatives: using truth as a guide without regard for love. My gratitude is in the courage required to cut against the grain of comfortable institutionalization. In my mourning I take comfort in the self-honest pronouncement of Merton on the requisite of truth in developing true selfhood:

> What has to be healed in us is our true nature, made in the likeness of God. What we have to learn is love. The healing and the learning are the same things, for at the very core of our essence we are constituted in God's likeness by our freedom, and the exercise of that freedom is nothing else but the exercise of disinterested love—the love of God for His own sake, because He is God.
>
> The beginning of love is truth, and before He will give us His love, God must cleanse our souls of the lies that are in them. And the most effective way of detaching us from ourselves is to make us detest ourselves as we have made ourselves by sin, in order that we may love Him reflected in our souls as He has re-made them by His love . . . and in the end, we will find Him in ourselves, in our own purified natures which have become the mirror of His tremendous Goodness and of His endless love.[15]

For those willing to risk it, "disinterested love" is found on the journey inside where the generations of striving souls wear paths, where denied lusts and ambitions invent their devices for subverting the conscious eye, where all the fears, hopes, losses and treasures of a life are displayed. It is finding ultimately, like Teilhard de Chardin, the unfathomable source of our spirit's breath.

> . . . I went down into my inmost self, to the deep abyss whence I feel dimly that my power of action emanates. But as I moved further and further away from the conventional certainties by which social life is superficially illuminated, I became aware that I was losing contact with myself. At each step of the descent a new person was disclosed within me of whose name I was no longer sure, and who no longer obeyed me. And when I had to stop my exploration because the path faded from beneath my steps, I found a bottomless

abyss at my feet, and out of it came—arising I know not
from where—the current which I dare to call *my* life.[16]

This inner descent into the self to the point of en-
countering another Self gives us eyes with which to see
the Mystery in the everyday. An overwhelming uncer-
tainty captures us. How in the conglomeration of this
world's innumerable intersections of cause and effect
could I even continue to exist? What force sustains me in
such an enigmatically complicated cosmos? Am I so
insignificant? Teilhard answers:

> At that moment, as anyone else will find who cares
> to make the same interior experiment, I felt the distress
> characteristic to a particle adrift in the universe, the
> distress which makes human wills founder daily under
> the crushing number of living things and of stars. And
> if something saved me, it was hearing the voice of the
> Gospel, guaranteed by divine successes, speaking to
> me from the depth of the night: *ego sum, noli timere* (It is
> I, be not afraid).[17]

Behind the fabric of this cosmological tapestry is the
Weaver, the I Am—the eternally self-existent Creator
and Sustainer—the True Self that abides within us.
Beneath layers of the self-deceit, selfishness, and narcis-
sism of the False Self lies true being, the ground of
identity. The crucifixion of the self on Christ's cross, as
Paul says, is to allow this foundational energy of the
Spirit to be expressed.

The countenance of the Spiritual Self is manifold.
The spiritually-centered person has a posture of ***openness to a source within.*** Knowing that the Spirit Life
emanates from deep in the soul, we attend to emergences
from the unconscious, to images arising during prayerful meditation, dreams and daydreams, and to metaphors, parables and the unfolding of life's dramas—in
conversations, life passages, and serendipitous moments.

Another face of true Selfhood is its ***surrender to a
power beyond:*** beyond the horizon of our perception,
beyond all reason, beyond the grave, beyond self-deter-
mination to obedience. It is a surrender to a power
above and beyond our compulsions, which, instead of
giving change to our self-defeating instincts, give rather
a reinforcement of them. It is a surrender to a power
beyond self-improvement to Paul's discovery that "it is
God who works in you to will and to act according to his
good purpose" (Phil. 2:13).

A ***movement to the rhythm of the divine heartbeat***
further shapes our spiritual character: the ebb and swell
of compassion, grief, hope, and longing; the fruit of the
Spirit; the beatitudes of the "multifaceted grace of God,"
the brilliance of pure light through a clear eye:

> When a ray of light strikes a crystal, it gives a new
> quality to the crystal. And when God's infinitely disin-
> terested love plays upon a human soul, the same kind
> of thing takes place . . . the soul, left to its own natural
> level, is a potentially lucid crystal left in darkness. It is
> perfect in its own nature, but it lacks something that it
> can only receive from outside and above itself. But
> when the light shines in it, it becomes in a manner
> transformed into light and seems to lose its nature in
> the splendor of a higher nature, the nature of the light
> that is in it.[18]

Drawing from Teresa's metaphor is Merton's portrayal of the soul that not only reflects the light, but is
transformed into light—its own individuality not lost,
but refracted into the spectrum hues of grace.

The True Self's ***integration of transcendent meaning***
finds a deep vein running through the ever-changing
landscape of life and relationships. For example, Bellah's
study of American culture published in *Habits of the
Heart,* found that couples remain in marriage for a
number of reasons, many of which go deeper than just
the qualities of their partner. Couples find a transcen-

dent meaning for their marriage. The meaning of marriage may derive from a shared history or a shared commitment to a common ideal. They are married to marriage as well as one another.

Beginning with Tertullian in the second century, the concept of God as trinity emerged as a way to harmonize the various Scriptural statements regarding God's nature. By finding a transcendent meaning in our various experiences of God, the Trinitarian doctrine provides an integration of what Tertullian referred to as the "economy," or building up, of God's nature as unity: one substance, three persons (personae). Father, Son and Holy Spirit. Tertullian compared the three ways God relates to us to the actor's masks (persona)—one actor playing various roles.

God as trinity is a living dynamic in our lives: creation, redemption, and empowerment. God is in each new beginning as the Creator of life and possibilities. God is in each ending as a redeeming force, transforming what is inauthentic in our lives into the gold of true identity. God is in the pregnant moments of the present to empower and enable our sharing in the community of God's love, sustaining our spirits through the trials of life. God is the basis, potential, and presence of life. We stand, as it were, on the mountain of God seeing in the distant horizon the hope of our journey, encouraged to continue by the faith of our fellow sojourners.

In life we are beginning the journey toward spiritual, authentic identity. We are *becoming* human in a transformation that is completed only in death. For Jung, preparing for death is a primary task of the second half of life when we develop a consciousness detached from the world—continuing the process of individuation.

Why do we not see this process, this hope? Why do we continually revert our focus to the past and bind ourselves to institutions of archaic self-images? Perhaps it is because of our cultural antipathy toward solitude and contemplation. Many forces, both external and internal, conspire to delimit our experience of . . . ourselves. It is in silence and undistracted self-awareness that we experience the life of the Spirit emerging through our own death-to-self. What works against contemplation works against true selfhood. As Blaise Pascal is often quoted, "All human evil comes from a single cause, man's inability to sit still in a room." It is our inane compulsion for "diversion," a consoling busyness, which is ultimately our greatest misery. While we were made for contemplation, Merton picks up the thought, our diversions turn us aside from the one thing that can help us most: "the sense of our own emptiness, our poverty, our limitations, and of the inability of created things to satisfy our profound need for reality and for truth"[19]

The Womb Tomb

> Death occurs when my past has completely exhausted my future and all is now—my whole life and person are entirely present. Death is the transition of my whole being from time to eternity.[20]
>
> Nemeck and Coombs

Death does not take place in time. There is no "moment of death." Time is either past or future. Eternity is pure now.

The spirituality of toil is womb-to-tomb. What do you get for your tons of labor? "Another day older and deeper in debt," according to the old song. Our lives, laments Job, are "of few days and full of trouble."

The spirituality of promise, conversely, is tomb-to-womb. Creation groans with the "pains of childbirth"—a New Testament image of the end times—and we "groan inwardly as we wait eagerly for our adoption" (Ro. 8:23).

Both womb and tomb are a total abandonment. Helplessly, in birth as in death, we are thrust forth into a new realm of existence. From the warm, breathless, outgrown universe of the womb, we emerge into a cold, bright, stimulating world where all our illusions of being a universe unto ourselves are continually dashed as we learn to live with all the other universes on this planet. And at the end—or so we think—a new birth awaits, a comparable emergence into an existence just as unimaginable. "I am the resurrection," announced Jesus at Lazarus tomb, but no one emerges from the tomb until summoned. Death is abandonment.

It seems to have been popular at one time to pen prayers of abandonment. Jesus' prayer of abandonment was "Into your hands I commit my spirit."

A simple though scary children's prayer: "If I should die before I wake, I pray the Lord my soul to take."

From Teresa: "Let me die to myself so that I may serve you."

Ignatius of Loyola surrenders to God, "Take, Lord, all my liberty, my memory, my understanding, and my whole will."

We prayed with Merton in the last chapter, "My Lord God, I have no idea where I am going..."

And as a last sample of devotion, Charles de Foucauld's Prayer of Abandonment:

> Father,
> I abandon myself into your hands.
> Do with me what you will.
> Whatever you may do, I thank you.
> I am ready for all.
> I accept all.
> Let only your will be done in me,
>   and in all your creatures.
> I ask no more than this, Lord.
> Into your hands I commend my soul.
> I offer it to you with all the love of my heart.

> For I love you, Lord.
> And I so need to give myself to you,
>> to surrender myself into your hands,
>> without reserve,
>> and with boundless confidence.
> For you are my Father.[21]

Teresa likens self-abandonment to the fat and ugly silkworm spinning itself a cocoon in which it dies, only to emerge a little white moth. "Let's be quick to do this work," she advised her sisters, "and weave this little cocoon by getting rid of our self-love and self-will, our attachment to any earthly thing." Alluding to Colossians 3:4, "For you died, and your life is now hidden with Christ in God," Teresa encourages us to "Let it die; let this silkworm die . . . and you will see how we see God, as well as ourselves placed inside His greatness, as is this little silkworm within its cocoon." The results are spectacular: "Oh, greatness of God! How transformed the soul is when it comes out of this prayer after having been placed within the greatness of God and so closely joined with Him."[22]

The tomb-like cocoon we weave for ourselves is much like a womb in which we are reborn. This spiritual birth, as our natural birth, is an emergence into a new world and self-image. "It is a delightful union, the experience of seeing oneself in so new a life greatly helps one to die."[23]

Our initial perceptions of life are as fetuses-in-the-womb, with no conceptual framework, no way of comprehending the nature of ourselves or our environment. In time, nestled tightly in this elastic orb against which we kick and turn, our world begins to thrust us forth. With the contraction of the uterus and the squeezing off of the placenta and umbilical cord, we probably experience oxygen deprivation for the first time and the breathing reflex soon awakens—and with it our first gasps for air. In these moments, we may for the first time experience the physical sensations and affect we will later in our development associate with the emotion of fear.[24]

Is it unreasonable, then, to assume that much of our behavior is driven by the desire—albeit unconscious—to recreate for ourselves this comfortable womb? Would it not follow that another universal experience of life human is the perpetual thrusting forth from these womb-like places?

Our diversions, our narcoticizing obsessions with activity and amusement blunt the angst of this repetitive death-birth. By numbing our disillusionments, we perpetuate them; by giving ourselves to the emptiness they create, we open ourselves to the transformation of faith—an empty place for the Spirit to fill. "Unless a kernel of wheat falls to the ground and dies, it remains only a single seed. But if it dies, it produces many seeds" (John 12:24). The gospel promise, then, is sheer incongruity: those who love their life will lose it, while those who hate their life in this world will keep it for eternal life (v. 25). Jesus' hyperbole is not a call to self-flagellation, but to abandon our binding attachments to this world so that we may experience eternal freedom in union with God.

> There are three conditions which often look alike
> Yet differ completely, flourish in the same hedgerow:
> Attachment to self and to things and to persons, detach-
>   ment
> From self and from things and from persons; and,
>   growing between them, indifference
> Which resembles the others as death resembles life . . .[25]
>
>   T.S. Eliot

In the Greek underworld, the River Styx bounded the land of the living from Hades. The image of a river powerfully portrays the impassible barrier of mortality. Christian's final challenge in *Pilgrim's Progress* was to cross the river of death to reach the Celestial City. In

Revelation, the apocalypse of John, the Hebraic image of the sea depicts the place of death and the beast. At the conclusion of his vision, John triumphantly proclaims, "I saw a new heaven and a new earth, for the first heaven and the first earth has passed away, and there was no longer any sea" (Rev. 21:1). In the vision of transformation, John saw death transformed into life.

> . . . "the river of the water of life, as clear as crystal, flowing from the throne of God . . . on each side of the river stood the tree of life, bearing twelve crops of fruit . . . the leaves of the tree are for the healing of the nations . . . no longer will there be any curse" (22:1-3).

"You must be born again," Jesus told Nicodemus, "of water and of the Spirit" (John 3:5,7). Womb water and Spirit water. Baptism symbolizes passing through one and emerging into the other; from death into life.

We live on "the resurrection side of the cross,"[26] with lives integrating the transcendent meaning of love. Day by day we live out of gratitude for the Spirit life given to us in our identification with the death, burial, and resurrection of Christ, and even so this thankful awareness is a pure gift from God. Summoned from our tomb of spiritual death in God's good time, we find God in places we never imagined: in the ordinary. In dazzlement (and God knows how to dazzle) we found God in ecstasy or the spectacular. In contemplation, we see God everywhere: in nature, in relationships, in the souls of even the most annoying persons; in the most mundane of tasks.

A classic model for living in the ordinary is Brother Lawrence whose life is described in the seventeenth-century spiritual biography, *The Practice of the Presence of God*. Serving in the kitchen of his religious community, Brother Lawrence discovered the importance of acting "with God in the greatest simplicity, speaking to God frankly and plainly, and imploring God's assistance in our affairs, just as they happen." Eschewing the methods he read about in books on different practices of the spiritual life and prayer, which he claimed only puzzled him, Brother Lawrence sought a way of life in which he could "become wholly God's." "Our only business," he continued, "is to love and delight ourselves in God," which he experienced more in his "outward employments" and "common business" than in devotional prayer. Even in the noise and clutter of his kitchen, with several persons clamoring for different things, Brother Lawrence testified, "I possess God in as great tranquility as if I were upon my knees."

When so much religious programming is evaluated on the basis of the American success model, Brother Lawrence's spiritual simplicity sounds strange and insignificant. When megachurch-goers opt for bigger-is-better, nicely packaged, best-seller, top forty, and comfortable religion, the simple contemplative life remains obscure. But, often the ordinary virtues are also the deepest. The "Little Way" of Thérèse of Lisieux reveals the ordinariness of true spiritual living:

> Love proves itself by deeds, and how shall I prove mine? . . . I can prove my love only by scattering flowers, that is to say, by never letting slip a single little sacrifice, a single glance, a single word; by making profit of the very smallest actions, by doing them all for love.[27]

The Community of the Indwelling Christ

The call to death/dwelling is a call to depth. While some prayerful persons are farmers, scratching the whole surface of their field about six inches deep, contemplatives are welldiggers. They scratch only about six inches of the field, but they scratch it deeply to the aquifer, and with that depth they tap water for the whole field. Deep and wide flows the fountain of grace.

Deep and wide are the dimensions of the communal spirit. With breadth, we claim the land; with depth we nourish it.

Remembering Scott Peck's paradigm for community development, true community arises from the ashes of chaos and emptiness. The place of death/dwelling in the communal life is a relinquishment of the life made possible by illusion. When persons emerge from the desert of disillusionment, they bear a message to the community. Jesus came from the desert temptations preaching, teaching and healing as a witness to the coming reign of God. Moses came away from his desert burning bush experience with a call for Israel to drop their illusion of servanthood and return to the land God had promised.

As a community moves beyond disillusionment, it takes on a new form, a new identity; a new power. After the Pentecost filling of the Spirit, the disciples (followers) were referred to more often as apostles (messengers), even though Jesus referred to them as both disciples and apostles. It was only after they gave up the life and community based on following an earth-bound messiah that they were able to embody the authority and identity of the risen Christ.

Returning once again to Plato's allegorical cave, it is the role of the philosopher to return to the deluded prisoners in the shadows and show them the light. This process of enlightenment characterizes well the developmental journey I am describing in this book. In distraction, we see shadows. In dazzlement, we realize the shadows represent something. They fascinate us. In discipleship, we form paradigms for naming the shadows, speculating on what they represent and how they function. Out of this paradigm we form a culture, a way of life based on the meaning we derive from our shadow paradigm. In disillusionment, we realize the shadows are not real, but we can't see the reality from which they are projected. In death/dwelling, we give up the life that was based on the shadows and embrace the life based on light. In relationship with Christ, we fall in love with the life of light and long for it. Eventually, we become light to others.

What the cave depicts so well is our need, as unenlightened prisoners of this earth, for someone to descend into our cave-abyss and show us the light—to be our light. If we honor this courageous guide who risks life and limb to descend to us, we shall discover the true meaning of life . . . and our true selves as children of the light. We were, after all, created for the light. "You are the light of the world, " said Jesus. The question every person, every community, and every institution must eventually ask is: Why are we here? At a basic level, it is survival. We are here to be able to *remain* here. To live another day, to provide a place for our children, to stay in business, to keep the doors open, to make payroll; to preserve our way of life. But, the question still goes begging, So why are we here to remain here? Why did God create the world?

Moltmann suggests when we start asking these kinds of questions, we have quit living life simply for the sheer enjoyment of living. These, he says, are the questions of "an adult who doesn't want to play anymore but needs goals in order to make something respectable of himself." Could the advent of these questions signal our fall from childlike faith into a self-conscious pragmatism that enslaves us to the unfulfillable quest for success?

The Westminster Confession, a seventeenth-century Scottish Presbyterian statement of faith, declares with dignity our created purpose: to love God and enjoy God forever. We have been using God to enjoy the world, Moltmann observes, but faith leads us to use the world to enjoy God. Religion has been pressed into the service of political, economic, and even racial ends. Are our institutions serving the cause of living in the enjoyment of God?

Are our institutions life-giving? The budgets of our municipalities, the programs of our churches, the mission statements of the companies that employ us: are they worthy of our investment? Are they serving us as a world community, or are we serving them and by doing so enabling a system that makes the poor poorer and the rich richer? It may be time to dismantle institutions that are merely self-perpetuating. That kind of institution is worthy of our sheer neglect.

Followers of Jesus live in this kind of impermanence between the death of obsolete and self-serving structures and the new life of hope-centered, life-enhancing, Spirit-empowered service.

Not one stone shall be left on another, Jesus announced to the disciples as they admired the beauty of the Jerusalem temple. Jesus rebelled against the self-serving, exclusionary practices of money changers and animal merchants who made a profit off of pilgrims to the Temple: "It is written . . . 'My house will be called a house of prayer,' but you are making it a 'den of robbers'" (Matt. 21:13). And as predicted, years later, Roman legions ransacked the city in 70 A.D., leveling the temple, carrying away its sacred objects and desecrating the holy place with sacrifices to their emperor.

The house of God lying in ruins? Hardly. The structure had become obsolete in lieu of the new. Upon the foundation of the new reality in Christ, the cornerstone- a new community is built.

> As you come to him, the living Stone—rejected by men but chosen by God and precious to him—you also, like living stones, are being built in a spiritual house to be a holy priesthood, offering spiritual sacrifices acceptable to God through Jesus Christ. (I Pet. 2:4-5)

A new identity, a new community emerges built upon the brokenness of Christ and the brokenness of our lives to be a living house of God. We move through death to indwelling, through abandonment to the kinship of the community of faith, a living structure of the Spirit. Parker Palmer:

> ... the spiritual traditions offer hope that is hard to find elsewhere, for all of them are ultimately concerned with getting us reconnected. These traditions build on the great truth that beneath the broken surface of our lives there remains—in the words of Thomas Merton—"a hidden wholeness." The hope of every wisdom tradition is to recall us to that wholeness in the midst of our torn world, to reweave us into the community that is so threadbare today.[28]

Prayer of Death

Lord Christ, my musty gray Savior of the Dead, stand at my door today. Visit me in your grave clothes and beckon me to your station in death. I embrace your cold arms. Bid me die with you—not for the sake of new life, but for the sake of pure death.

> For by knowing you in death, I may know you in true life.
>
> > By knowing you in the grave, I may know you in the resurrection.
> >
> > > By knowing you in emptiness, I may know you in fullness.
>
> Into Thy hands I commend my spirit.

Amen.

Reflection

Are you following the teachings of Christ or are you following the voice of Christ?

Once you have lost all things and gained Christ, then what?

Have you come to the end of yourself in prayer? Are words and requests no longer enough?

What disturbs you? What consoles you? What sounds like the devil that used to sound like the Lord? (And vice-versa?)

Are you ready to consider that God wants you, and not just part of you all of the time, and not just all of you some of the time, but that God will not be denied?

Have you ever been aware of God introducing a wonderful "wild card" into your life? Reflect on the experience.

A Spirit-led group, organization, institution "is willing to surrender its very existence for the sake of the mission." Have you ever been part of such a group? What kind of lifestyle does such a stance require?

What does "community mission" mean for you? What community? What mission?

In what ways have you experienced freedom through abandonment, life through death?

Jesus said "I am the way." For Therese of Lisieux, union with Christ became concrete in her "Little Way." How would you name or describe your "way" of union with Christ?

What puts you in touch with the "hidden wholeness"— beneath the brokenness of our lives—of which Merton speaks? How is your hope nourished?

Endnotes

1 Parker J. Palmer, *To Know as We are Known* (San Francisco: HarperCollins, 1993), p. xi.

2 Quoted in Nemeck and Coombs, *The Way of Spiritual Direction* (The Liturgical Press, 1985), p. 96.

3 C.S. Lewis, *Mere Christianity* (New York: Macmillan Publishing Co., Inc., 1977), p. 167.

4 Dietrich Bonhoeffer, *The Cost of Discipleship* (New York: Collier Books, 1963), p. 99.

5 Flora Slosson Wuellner, *Prayer, Fear, and Our Powers* (Nashville: Upper Room Books, 1992), p. 71.

6 "To the Cross," *Collected Works*, Vol. 3, p. 394.

7 Nemeck and Coombs, *The Spiritual Journey*, p. 223.

8 "The Way of the Cross," *Collected Works*, Vol. 3, p. 395-396.

9 Pierre Teilhard de Chardin, *The Divine Milieu*, (New York: Harper Torchbooks, 1960).

10 Gary L. Harbaugh, *Pastor As Person* (Minneapolis: Augsburg Publishing House, 1984), pp. 97-98.

11 *Interior Castle*, p. 336.

12 T.S. Eliot, *Four Quartets* (New York: Harcourt Brace Jovanovich, 1971), pp. 29-30.

13 Wuellner, p. 43.

14 *Interior Castle*, p. 336.

15 Thomas Merton, *The Seven Storey Mountain* (New York: Harcourt Brace & Company, 1978), p. 372.

16 *Milieu*, pp. 76-77.

17 *Milieu*, pp. 77-78.

18 *Mountain*, p. 170.

19 *Ascent to Truth*, pp. 24-25.

20 Nemeck and Coombs, *The Spiritual Journey*, p.225.

21 Jean-Francois Six, ed., *Spiritual Autobiography of Charles de Foucauld* (Dimension Books, 1964), pp. 95-96, quoted in Nemeck and Coombs, *The Spiritual Journey*, p. 194.

22 *Interior Castle*, pp. 342-343.

23 *Interior Castle*, p. 350.

24 Robert Plutchik and Henry Kellerman, *Emotion: Theory, Research, and Experience* (New York: Academic Press, Inc., 1990).

25 *Four Quartets*, p. 55.

26 *Pastor as Person*, p. 140.

27 Thérèse of Lisieux, *The Story of a Soul*, XI, 158.

28 Palmer, *To Know as We are Known*, p. x.

6

DESIRED IN CHRIST

Black and sleek the body moves fluid-like through undergrowth. Silent steps pursue with cautious and intent eyes. Yellow eyes, orbs of harvest moonlight clear and bright, set like gems in a goddess face.

He catches her scent, but loses her shadow. Echoes of his call remember the passion but drown in the irrigation of a nearby stream. Distant hounds answer, tethered to nocturnal hunters. Come near; I must touch you. My love could move this mountain.

I am too dark, she speaks from the night. I am too dark for I work the sun, losing my beauty to the vines of my father.

He runs through dew-laden leaves, guiding his hands on branches and bark. Guiding his eyes in search of hers; gems in bronze. Cool dew and hot breath mingle on his lips, hinting of her taste. New wine rests on the vines. Sweet clusters stain his hands and lips as he searches the well-tended rows.

Songs of forest nymphs are rising with the stream's mist. Hope runs dimly beyond the wall. The moon, the vines and the fog converge to silhouette her shape beholding his.

A traveler handsome—sing the nymphs—
searches among the garden spirits.
She taunts him—the dark goddess—
luring him to the winepress.
A bride he seeks, a beauty unclaimed,
though she retreats in fearful modesty.
How can he escape her pursuit
if he knows not who is the pursuer?

MSJ

There is a place on the journey where we gain awareness of how Christ is pursuing us. We begin to see the unfurling dimensions of our own personal love story with God. Like asking a couple how they met, the story is borne on reminiscences of romance and surrender. The story unfolds in leaves of deepening revelation. First encounters. Infatuation. Falling in love. Making it work. Learning the language of the other's soul. Valleys endured; vistas shared. And now, a love that grows beyond imagination.

This place of desire is a cloudburst of love descending upon us in a supernatural flood of passion. It is not so much our values that change, but our motivations. A lover's motives are different from a servant's.

Jesus used the metaphor of marriage to describe his relationship with his disciples. He likened himself to a groom going to prepare a place for his bride. John the Apostle carried on the imagery in his apocalyptic vision of Christ united with the church at the marriage supper of the Lamb (Rev. 19). Paul conveyed this metaphor of the mutual relationship between husband and wife "... the two shall become one flesh," as mystically representative of the Christ-church union, "... This is a profound mystery—but I am talking about Christ and the church" (Eph. 5).

God invites us—pursues us—in this cosmic romance. Yet, we do not always feel free to succumb to the Spirit's wooing. For some, in fact, the sexual imagery of these mystical writings evokes unpleasant feelings of fear, anxiety, or shame. Images abound in our culture of sexual brokenness. Sex sells. Sexual power oppresses and power oppresses sexually. Our hope for sexual healing is in a bold, outlandish embrace of the incarnation of God into human flesh. Sexuality is a gift of God and fully embodied in Christ.

In this chapter, I will outline how we may heal the wounds of sexual brokenness by finding the source of our blessing in Christ, who incarnates the divine Spirit in human flesh. I will trace the origins of sexual brokenness to some sources that may be surprising to you, such as in the history of Christian doctrine that has largely framed human sexuality in negative terms.

Why this attention to *sexual* brokenness and healing? I suggest that our spiritual development eventually becomes limited by our inner conflicts: those unhealed wounds in our self-perception. Our woundedness is apparent in issues of anger, guilt, and shame over our sexual nature and close intimate relationships.

The battle between the sexes is more than just entertainment hype. True sources of anger exist in the psyches of men and women that are rooted in the historical and cultural dilemmas we create with gender inequality. Men have historically had the upper hand in political, economic, and social life. For women, this disparity remains as a lively dynamic in current male-female relationships. And for the men who seek to become more sensitive to this gender dimension of social justice, there is often a sense of guilt that drives the desire for change.

Healing these deep wounds in our souls and communities is the compelling challenge to Christianity today.

Run for the Hills!
There's a Sexual Being in Town!

Innocent faces gathered on the stairs of the sanctuary podium, spellbound as he carried the figurines of a woman and man making their way to a little village in the night. This woman was pregnant, he told them.

Their eyes darted among them, and bodies shifted uneasily.

It was the first week of Advent and during the pastor's children's sermon the mystery of incarnation unfolded before my eyes with a new reality. An anxious reality. The more he talked of angels telling Joseph to marry a woman who was with child by the Holy Spirit, the more those little Oedipal hormones raced until—without warning—his four-year-old daughter launched from the floor like Rocky the Flying Squirrel and landed in a headlock on the pastor's back!

Right smack dab in the middle of the Christmas story, replete with the nativity set, was sex. God sex. Virgin sex. Joseph without sex? Gosh, we won't even talk plainly to youngsters about where babies come from, and yet we introduce them to sex with supernatural stories about it. What's the message? Women—really good women—have sex only with God? Men—really good men—do without it altogether? I wonder if this influences the way we Christians are so conflicted about sexuality? Could our anxiety about sex be about this divine wild card? That little baby Jesus lays in a little manger with his little penis and all we see are the angels singing, the wise men bringing not-so-childlike gifts, and the shepherds kneeling? The lambs, ox, and ass were probably the only ones to really understand and not be anxious about it.

Should baby Jesus have been a hermaphrodite third-sexed hybrid, neither male nor female, but some kind of humanoid lacking altogether in genitalia? Can a testosterone-laden male Jesus save women? Did Francis of Assisi, founder of the celibate Franciscans, really want boys and girls to squirm at the sight of his nativity scene?

A healthy spirituality requires a healthy view of sexuality. Many heresies abound that carry on the historic anxiety of religious people about sexuality and

human nature. In spite of repeated councils and theological arguments affirming the full divinity and full
humanity of Christ, it is still easier for many to believe
that Jesus was divine than to accept his full humanity.
Images of a sexually-neuter, passionateless Jesus defy
the likelihood that in Jesus' Palestinian culture a celibate
rabbi would have been controversial big time. It is
possible that he was married, argue many scholars.

Robert T. Francoeur argues that attitudes about sexuality are not clearly delineated between various churches
or denominations but are on a spectrum that exists
across religious boundaries. His type "A" and type "B"
sects exists in virtually every religion. Type "A" beliefs
about sexuality hold to a literalistic and fundamentalistic
view of Scripture: sexuality is dangerous, and we need
religion to help us control it, specifically an authoritar-
ian, male-oriented religion. Type "B" theologies, in contrast, emphasize the positive value of sexuality and see
religion as facilitating healthy sexual expression through
self-awareness and ongoing reinterpretation of Scripture in light of our growth.

This division between type "A" and type "B" does
not necessarily classify groups between asceticism and
promiscuity but highlights the diversity of sexual attitudes. The difference is no more clearly seen than in
approaches to the most sexual book in the Bible, the
Song of Songs, in the Hebrew Scriptures. At one level,
the book is a love story between a couple and exalts their
romantic passions. But, the book has also been widely
hailed through its history as a mystical allegory of the
relationship between God (the Lover) and God's people
(the Beloved). The title is literally "The Most Beautiful
Song" and is believed to have originally been a love
song sung at weddings. The allegorical interpretation
emphasizes its spiritual nature and the song was often
used in this way during Passover in the spring. Rabbi

Akiva, who according to the Talmud was the only rabbi to enter Paradise and live to tell about it, referred to the Song of Songs as the holiest book in the Bible, "the holy of holies" of Scripture.

For Christians who took the Song as an allegory, it depicted Christ pursuing His church. Such a view is too erotic for many religious folks. Any passion of Christ, as with one's own libido, is best kept repressed and at a safe distance. Puritans avoided the book altogether as some sort of anomaly, and when it was referenced, the allegorical method was used. Since God is nowhere mentioned in the book, the debate has continued throughout Jewish and Christian history about whether it should be in the canon. Can anything sexual be spiritual?

The Levitical Law for religious life and worship required that a woman be considered ceremonially unclean during menses and after childbirth (twice as long for a daughter as for a son). Similar laws pertained to a man after an emission.

Even though purity laws expressed a type "A" view of sexuality, Judaism in general also enjoyed a strong type "B" positive view of sex. Beginning with the creation story, Eve was created from one of Adam's ribs and referred to as a "helper." Though traditionally the term has connoted an inferior status in relationship to Adam, the original Hebrew word is *azar*, partner or equal. The Hebrew words for man and woman are much closer in pronunciation than their English counterparts.

Under the rabbinical system, a positive sexuality had notable proponents. Rabbi Abba Aricha (third century A.D.) cautioned that we will have to render an account to God for all the good things our eyes have beheld but which we refused to enjoy.[1] Some rabbis encouraged sex on the Sabbath because it was favored by God.

Christianity's Sexual Wound

So, where's the rub? How is it that such negative views of sexuality pervaded the early church and remained throughout its history? Enter Plato and Greek dualism, one of the most influential philosophical systems in western human history. What orders the universe, said this fifth-century B.C. philosopher, is reason, or the logos. We humans live out of sorts with ourselves and the created order because we are spiritual beings imprisoned in physical bodies and have come to believe that the material world is real. Through enlightenment we come to see that the physical is only a shadow of the spiritual.

By the time of Christ, Judaism had inherited Platonism via Philo (whose lifespan predated and overlapped Christ's) and his integration of Plato and Judaism. An Alexandrian Jew, Philo sought to wed Greek contemplative philosophy with Hebrew faith in order to prove that Judaism was the true faith. He equated the logos, or ordering principle, with the Mosaic Law and Philo—and was regarded as both hero and villain for the attempt. In his day people used to wonder if Plato "philized" or Philo "platonized."

The Hebrew God was one God with two faces—a masculine Father-Creator and a feminine glory, the *Shekhinah* or divine presence and wisdom. Carl and Susan Raschke in *The Engendering God* discuss how Philo was able to conveniently correlate the two faces of God with the platonic dualistic model of matter and spirit: the Mosaic law as Wisdom to the Greek Sophia (and Plato's *philo-sophy*, "the love of wisdom").[2]

Unfortunately, Plato identified the material world with darkness and ignorance, and along with it sexuality and the female anatomy. Because of this, he disparaged any serious female-male relationships and created a system that disparaged women in general, as seen in the Greco-Roman culture. A "platonic" relationship, colloquially known as a friendship between members of the opposite sex without sexual behavior, originally represented a sort of male bonding.

The most avid of Philo's readers turned out to be Christians. John the apostle began his Gospel in platonic terms, referring to Christ as the logos: the Word. Through the influx of Greek culture and Platonism, the world that Jesus entered was largely colored by this world view and its attitude toward sexuality.

First-century Judaism was dominated by two groups: Pharisees and Sadducees. While both groups were strongly influenced by Greek thought, the Pharisees tended to be strict adherents to the law and the rabbinical tradition while the Sadducees aligned politically with the Romans. Pharisees believed in spirits, demons, the resurrection of the dead, and heaven and hell. The Sadducees denied all of these.

In Matthew 22, the Sadducees posed to Jesus one of their classic questions about the absurdity of the hereafter. According to the kinsman redeemer law, if a man died, his next of kin was obligated to care for his family and marry his widow. Suppose, the Sadducees questioned, that a man with six brothers died and his wife was married by his closest brother, who died . . . and so on until the woman had been widowed by all seven brothers. In heaven, whose wife will she be?

Jesus responded that the Sadducees knew neither their Bible nor the power of God. In the resurrection, Jesus declared, there is no marriage, but we shall be like the angels. Was Rabbi Jesus a Platonist? Did he not believe that sexuality is good enough to survive the resurrection and be a part of the new order?

How do you respond to the dilemma of the Sadducees' question? A type "A" response might be that since Jesus said there was no marriage in heaven, then there is no sex in heaven and therefore sex and sexuality are part of our sinful natures and limited to our existence in this material world of birth and death. A type "B" response, on the other hand, might imagine that Jesus' answer had something to say about marriage rather than sex. Perhaps our relationships with God and each other in the new order will be so much more intimate—sexual, if you will—than those in this life that marriage will be obsolete. Perhaps we will be united in Christ with each other in a way that transcends mere sexual union.

What is at stake is a well-developed spirituality of divine intimacy that encompasses our whole being. Without such a spirituality, churches blindly lead the blind into ditches of spiritual desolation and self-deprecation. We then become cut off from our bodies and become operational blasphemers of the incarnation, choosing not to believe in the flesh of Jesus.

The picture of Jesus that filters through the platonic lens of the New Testament writers is a person who took radical stands against the pervasive sexual norms. He was not an ascetic in the platonic sense, though he occasionally utilized ascetic practices. Apparently, Jesus lived anything but an ascetic lifestyle according to his detractors:

> For John [the baptizer] came neither eating nor drinking, and they say, "He has a demon." The Son of Man came eating and drinking, and they say, "Here is a glutton and a drunkard, a friend of tax collectors and sinners." (Matt. 11:18-19)

As a friend of sinners, Jesus repeatedly stood against the sexual culture of his day. For example, he refused to cast the first stone at an adulterous woman. Was he unconcerned about sexual sin? Or, was he more concerned about correcting the social injustice of punishing only the woman when a man commits adultery with her?

One of Jesus' closest companions was Mary Magdalene, out of whom he had exorcized seven demons. His relationship to her has been the topic of much theological discussion. She is a canonized saint. Some believe she is the best candidate for a Mrs. Jesus. Greek novelist Nikos Kazantzakis portrayed her as one of Jesus' temptations.

Who was the "sinful" woman who anointed Jesus' feet with perfume after washing them with her tears, hair and kisses? Jesus defended her against the insinuations of his male hosts as having "done a beautiful thing to me" (Matt. 26; Luke 7).

This Greek overlay of Jesus' teachings is further complicated by the fact that our only record of his teachings are in Greek, with all its platonic connotations. The Greek language provided a very specific and abstract vocabulary in comparison to the concrete language of Hebrew. Though Jesus' tongue was Aramaic, a Hebraic language, the Greek New Testament records his teachings and doctrine in all the color of Greek and the Hellenistic culture.

New Testament writers seized upon *agapeo* as a spiritual word for love: self-sacrificing love. Other terms for love, such as *phileo* (friendship) and *eros* (erotic), seem less than best. For example, in Jesus' reconciling breakfast conversation with Peter after the resurrection (John 21), the word play with "love" is usually lost in translation. Jesus asked Peter three times, Do you love me? And Peter replied three times, You know I love you, though he was grieved the third time, possibly because it corresponded to his three denials a few days before. What was actually happening was Jesus asking Peter about one kind of love—*agapeo*—and Peter owned a "lesser" kind of love, *phileo.* The first two times, Peter, do you *apapeo* me? Yes, Lord, you know I *phileo* you. The third time, Peter do you *phileo* me? Peter was grieved to hear Jesus ask the third time using the word *phileo* but responded, Yes, Lord, you know all things, you know that I *phileo* you.

To define spiritual love in purely non-affectionate, non-sensual ways is to ignore much of the passion of God's desire for us. The tradition of the Song of Songs as portraying the relationship between God and God's people is a sensuous, erotic one. Jesus' use of marriage as a metaphor for our relationship with Christ likewise entails all the facets of love that can be expressed in the Greek, and more: self-sacrificing, companioning and sensual. What kind of marriage lacks friendship and sensuality?

In our prayerful journeys, when we desire to snuggle God, crawl up in the lap of God, hug Jesus, feel God as a warm fuzzy—these may be expressions of the erotic in our spirituality. The biblical metaphors indicate that God likewise wants intimacy with us in all aspects of our being. The spiritual journey is about our growing into this relationship with God, not just in our ability to think properly about God or behave according to God's rules.

It is only in *relationship* that we can know God, says Martin Buber. We cannot know God as an *it*, but only as a *Thou*. Relationships that are I-It are merely utilitarian. It is in the I-Thou that we relate to God and others in a truly personal way. God is in the real, natural world, Buber insists, and we can know God if we remain open with our whole being to how God addresses us in it.

The first written witness of Jesus in the New Testament is Paul, a Pharisee steeped in Hellenism. He referred to himself as the "apostle to the Gentiles." The Greek name *Paul* became the Christian equivalent to his original Hebrew name, *Saul*. Paul's view of sexuality developed significantly over his life. Unlike his Hellenistic counterparts, he presented no preference for the unmarried state in his teachings or lifestyle. It is believed that Paul was married (though there is no mention of his wife in Scripture) because he possibly was a member of the Sanhedrin Court, Israel's highest legal-religious body, which required marriage for its members.

In his later writings, Paul radically applied to marriage the Levitical principle of "love thy neighbor," holding husbands and wives to "submit to one another" in their relationship, which symbolizes Christ and the church (Eph. 5).

Taken in context, Paul's teaching on sexuality mirror those of Jesus and present a balanced approach, neither ascetic or libertine. He deplored the Gnostic teachings that infiltrated the church with their neo-platonism and asceticism—and on the other extreme, promiscuity—and reaffirmed the Hebraic view of sexuality as God-given.[3] But, the context of Paul's teachings is a culture with some significant problems regarding the status of men and women. Women were considered second-class citizens, both legally and religiously.

Church and Sex: A Marriage Not Made in Heaven

Christianity has a long, sordid history of promoting a negative view of sexuality because it has failed to consistently refine the gold of the gospel from the ore of ancient paternalistic culture. Its platonic influences emphasized abstinence from materialism. While I do not wish to discount the positive contributions made by the early framers of the Christian mind, history also records their crusade for an anti-sexual philosophy. Origen tied redemption of the soul to rejection of the flesh. Jerome taught that the soul is masculine and the body feminine. Since the flesh is suspect, it follows that women and their opinions are not to be trusted. Augustine, conflicted with shame, equated pleasure with sin.

Emil Brunner—with ample double entendre—overviews the diminution of sexuality in Christian history:

> The argument for virginity which forced its way into the Christian church at a very early stage must be described as a serious distortion of the biblical idea of

marriage. Through Platonic Hellenistic mysticism the idea penetrated into the early church that the sex element, as such, is something low, and unworthy of intelligent man, an idea which . . . is in absolute opposition to the biblical idea of creation. This idea, actualized in monasticism, erected into a standard in the Catholic ideal of virginity, was not wholly overcome by the Reformation . . . An examination of second-century expressions of Christianity displays the impact of pagan asceticism and the way in which this moral dualism was projected back upon the literature and the personalities of the New Testament.[4]

Likewise, for Raymond Lawrence, Jr., in *The Poisoning of Eros*, the conflict was not between the "orgiastic classical pagan culture and the chaste church, but between a sex-affirming Hebraic and a sex-negating Greco-Roman culture."[5]

The Shepherd of Hermas, circa 130 AD, was the first Christian document to prominently express sexual asceticism. Hermas, a converted Roman, espoused "spiritual" marriage in the platonic ideal. Not only did Hermas consider celibacy the highest form of marital life, but raised to heroic proportions his ability to spend the night with a dozen naked seductive virgins while maintaining a prayerful spirit, totally lacking in sexual arousal.

"You will sleep with us," they replied, "as a brother, and not as a husband: for you are our brother, and for the time to come we intend to abide with you, for we love you exceedingly!" But I was ashamed to remain with them. And she who seemed to be the first among them began to kiss me. [And the others seeing her kissing me, began also to kiss me], and to lead me round the tower, and to play with me . . . Now the virgins spread their linen tunics on the ground, and made me lie down in the midst of them; and they did nothing at all but pray; and I without ceasing prayed with them, and not less than they. And the virgins rejoiced because I thus prayed. And I remained there with the virgins until the next day at the second hour.

Then the Shepherd returned . . ."On what," he asked, "did you sup?" "I supped, sir," I replied, "on the words of the Lord the whole night."[6]

Theological underpinnings were required to maintain the platonic forms that were warping Christianity. Justin Martyr and his pupil Tatian were highly influenced by the asceticism of their Platonist teachers. They resolved the philosophical absurdity between Greek dualism and the incarnation by arguing that Jesus Christ was not fully human. Justin, as Philo, allegorized the serpent in Eden as sexual intercourse and Eve's disobedience was her intercourse with "the logos of the serpent." Mary, conversely, was impregnated by the overpowering logos of God.

> Christ derives blood not from the seed of man, but from the power of God . . . Christ is not man of men, begotten in the ordinary course of humanity.[7]

Tatian went on to found the ascetical Encratite ("Self-controlled') movement, teaching that since sex is sinful, then marriage is sinful. Iraneaus condemned their doctrines as "setting aside the original creation of God" and "showing ingratitude to God who made all things."[8]

In countering platonistically-inspired sexual heresy, Iraneaus had his hands full, since other quasi-Christian groups took to the other extreme, such as the Basilides and Carpocrates, who promoted promiscuous sex and polygamy.

As the theological brawl over sexuality continued among the second-century church fathers, a more moderate group appeared with Gnostic tendencies, yet holding to a positive and chaste view of sexuality. The Valentinians held that it was the unmarried that were of lower standing morally since earthy monogamous marriage symbolized the heavenly union of Christ and Christians. They minimized the importance of Jesus' virgin birth and depicted Jesus as married to Mary

Magdalene. Apparently their short-lived influence was suppressed by rivaling factions.

It is hard for a student of church history to support the hypothesis that sexuality is no big deal in Christianity. In fact, much of the development of Christian doctrine and practice has centered around sexuality.

> "Heresies are themselves instigated by philosophy. . . . What indeed has Athens to do with Jerusalem? . . . Away with all attempts to produce a Stoic, Platonic, and dialectic Christianity!"[9]

The booming theological voice of Tertullian (160-230 A.D.) founded Latin Christianity. Though he loathed sex, he permitted marriage because he did not want to disparage the Creator. Since sex was voluptuous, he argued, Christians should outdo the pagans when it comes to asceticism. It was Tertullian who established celibacy as a norm for clergy. Schooled in the pagan classics, Tertullian, despite his resistance to platonism, sustained its influence of a negative view of women. A woman, for Tertullian, was a temple built over a sewer.

Tertullian ranked a person's lifestyle based on their sexual virtues, according to this order:

1. Perpetual virginity
2. Perpetual virginity in marriage without intercourse
3. Sexual intercourse in marriage only for conceiving children
4. Sexual intercourse in marriage for pleasure
5. Sexual intercourse in polygamist marriages and/or extramarital relations

His obsessions about sex and his poor opinion of women are evident in his essay *On the Apparel of Women:*

> And do you not know that you are [each] an Eve? The sentence of God on this sex of yours lives in this age: the guilt must of necessity live too. You are the devil's gateway: you are the unsealer of that [forbidden] tree: you are the first deserter of the divine law:

you are she who persuaded him whom the devil was not valiant enough to attack. You destroyed so easily God's image, man. On account of your desert—that is, death—even the Son of God had to die. And do you think about adorning yourself . . . ?[10]

A rare voice of balance for this era spoke from Alexandria, where Clement (150-215) espoused a view of women and men as equals in knowledge, character and spiritual potential. Though Greek in culture, his sexual ethic reflected the influence of his Palestinian Jewish mentor: a balance between promiscuity and asceticism. His treatment of sexuality and marriage was surprisingly balanced and open, so open that his treatment of sexuality in Book Three of his *magnum opus, Miscellanies,* was left in the original Latin by Victorian era (and later) translators, so that it would be available only to scholars.

Clement gauged the doctrinal soundness of groups in his day by their views on sex. Heresy was marked by licentious or ascetical practices. His response to those who taught against marriage: "Fornication and marriage are . . . far apart as God is from the devil."[11]

In spite of Clement's sound and sane approach to sexuality, most influential church fathers were proponents of asceticism, including Clement's brightest student and successor. So absorbed was Origen (185-254) with his shame over his libido, that he castrated himself, an act that later drew the humorous bead of Martin Luther. Later in life he regretted this, partly because it was ineffectual in dissipating his sexual drive and partly because he realized his sexual attitudes were founded more on neoplatonism than on Jesus. Even so, he advocated separating worship and prayer from sex and prohibited taking communion following sex.

Origen's allegorization of the Song of Songs converted it from one of the most embarrassing biblical texts to an asset for ascetical Christianity. He did this by spiritualizing love in true platonic fashion, which allowed him to circumvent the full-bodied sensual nature of the book. He considered any desire of the flesh to be of Satan and stated that "God made the present world and bound the soul to the body as a punishment."[12]

The view of marriage in Origen's day became so negative that it was considered adultery by Cyprian and Jerome. Because of their ascetic interpretations of the Song of Songs, the Christian was considered the spouse of Christ. In fact, Chrysostom considered marriage worse than adultery "in proportion as God is greater than man."[13]

Celibacy became the norm for religious persons in subsequent years. Methodius, Bishop of Olympus, pronounced Jesus the Archvirgin, his favorite title for Christ. Because of the importance of celibacy, Methodius believed that only virgins could receive pure doctrine. Gregory of Nyssa (330-395) compared his longing for pure contemplation to a parched man gazing at a stream from which he could never drink because he was married.

In the four centuries between Jesus and Augustine (354-430), Christianity moved from its Hebraic roots to a pervasively Stoic and Gnostic philosophical base. Schnarch puts it none too mildly.

> The sex-affirming Hebraic roots of Western civilization have been masked by Augustine's legacy of eroticism-hating sexual dualism, perpetuated by authoritarian-oriented Christian dogma, which negated the basic worthiness of human beings. The evolution of Western culture is a history of theologically based sexual oppression.[14]

Augustine took sexual negativism a dramatic step further. He endorsed virginity to the extent that he hoped for human extinction and the advent of the City of God, his vision of the triumphal reign of Christ. Not only did he consider sexual desire to be sin, but he equated it with Original Sin. In other words, it is the sexual act as pleasurable that conveys the sinful nature from one generation to another. Sexual libido became known as a monster in the groin that must be restrained.[15] Intercourse is a depraved act which results in our birth "between the feces and the urine," reflecting his view of the female as a "defective male." His conclusions were in part drawn from the doctrine of the virgin birth of Christ, assuming that Christ had to be born of a virgin to bypass Original Sin.

Julian of Eclanum, a married bishop, considered Augustine's view of Original Sin an uncivilized slander against God. Furthermore, for Julian, sexual desire is no more obscene because of fornication than hunger because of gluttony.[16]

By medieval times, Christian moralists argued that Christ is absent during sex so Christians were encouraged to refrain from sex in proximity to any holy day, including Thursdays through Mondays, all feast days, a month preceding Easter, Pentecost, and Christmas, and during pregnancy, menstruation, and until babies are weaned. All totaled, abstinence was prescribed for five months out of the year.[17]

Penitence lists reflected the relative seriousness of some sins over others, revealing the current attitudes regarding sexuality. An eighth-century list prescribed by Theodore, Archbishop of Canterbury, listed the following guidelines for penance:

Abortion	120 days
Premeditated murder	7 years
Oral sex	15 years to life

Likewise, the thirteenth-century *Codex Latinus Monacensis 22233* equated with murder a wife's agreement to deviate from the missionary position in sex. A manual of the Middle Ages on moral doctrine by Vincent of Beauvias, *Speculum doctrinale* warned that "a man who loves his wife very much is an adulterer . . . The upright man should love his wife with his judgment, not his affections." In the thirteenth century, a woman had to be "reconciled with the Church" after childbirth because of the desecrating power of childbirth blood, and a woman who died in childbirth was allowed no funeral or burial in consecrated ground. By the seventeenth century, sex during menstruation was considered a venial sin and communion was disallowed during her period.[18]

The Reformation brought a radical change in theological positions on sexuality. Martin Luther went from being a celibate Augustinian monk to a married pastor and soon a married clergy became the norm in Protestantism. For Lawrence, the Reformation was a defeat of "salvation through sublimation or suppression of the sensuous and the sexual, and a victory for the body and sex and for a religion that affirms both."[19]

The Divine Healer is Our Divine Lover

Teresa and John were romantics, and this is reflected in the romantic imagery of their depictions of God. Teresa's *The Interior Castle* is based heavily on the themes of medieval romances: the fair maiden wooed to the castle of the great king through many dangers, toils, and snares. How is it that a nun was so acquainted with love stories and the ways of amour? Perhaps it is those who are most integrated in their spirituality—body and soul—who are most able to speak to us about intimacy.

Teresa describes the passion of spiritual lovers, "where the soul is now wounded with love for its Spouse and strives for more opportunities to be alone."[20] This tumultuous passion is variously compared to a fallen comet, a thunderclap, the blazing sun, and a cannonball so that "the soul dissolves with desire" in this "delightful pain."[21]

"All burnt up, the soul is renewed like the phoenix," Teresa observes with pathos.[22] The afflictions of this wound of love "are meant to increase one's desire to enjoy the Spouse."[23] So powerful is God's seduction that resistance is futile: to resist at this point, she warns, only makes matters more unbearable for the lovers. They cling to the promise that their love is destined to be consummated in the innermost room of the castle, His Majesty's bed chamber.

> Oh, God help me! Lord, how You afflict Your lovers! But everything is small in comparison with what You give them afterward.[24]

No journey for the weak hearted, this place in Teresa's castle requires courage. Over and again she makes this point and finally concludes, "Here you will see, Sisters, whether I was right in saying that courage is necessary, and whether when you ask the Lord for these favors He is right in answering . . . *are you able to drink the chalice?*"[25]

Courage for what? Union. Authentic knowing and being known. Loving and being loved.

John's *The Dark Night of the Soul* is based on his love poem of mystical embrace that depicts the divine-human drama:

> Into a dark obscured night,
> warmed by love's passion,
> —What an enrapturing adventure!—
> I went out unnoticed
> from a house grown silence.

> Obscure and secure in my darkness,
> disguised in my secret passage,
> —What an enrapturing adventure!—
> I furtively escaped
> my house grown silent.

> On that blessed night,
> in secret; seen by no one

—and seeing nothing—
with no light or guide
except the one in my ardent heart.

That heart flame guided me
more clearly than the midday sun,
to where he waited for me
—the one I know so well—
in a place secluded from everyone.

My guiding night!
A night more gentle than the dawn!
The night that joined
Lover and beloved;
transforming one into the other.

Upon my breast's bouquet,
reserved for this very moment,
there he laid his sleeping face
upon the gifts of my caresses,
while the cedars softly swayed.

The breeze down the tower wall
parted his locks of hair
with its calm hand.
My neck, too, it touched,
suspending my senses.

Remaining there, oblivious to myself,
reclining my face to my beloved.
I left everything behind.
Even my cares were left,
forgotten and fading, among the lilies.[26]

Notice how John's movement in love takes him through the darkness of disillusionment to intimacy with God. The journey to loving and knowing God passes through unknowing. It is not in comprehending God that we have faith and relationship with God, but in experiencing God. Since westerners are so Greek-minded, we tend to think of knowledge, *gnosis*, as understanding while in the Hebrew mind knowledge and experience are one. Theology (literally, the study of God) is our common language in talking *about* God. Spirituality, on the other hand, is our experience of God.

Plato separated the mind from the body and his influence on early Christian thought resulted in Gnosticism, an elaborate philosophy which tried to map a means of transcending this evil material world to the spiritual realm of God above. To the Hebraic culture of Jesus, however, this dualism was an alien spirituality. God is experienced in the flesh. Theirs was an earthy, visceral spirituality. The center of emotion for the Hebrew was the bowels. God was to be experienced, not figured out. In fact, the Hebrew word for "knowing" was used to denote sexual union, as with Adam knowing Eve.

When Moses sought to know the name or essence of God, he was ironically given the Hebrew verb "to be": I AM. God isn't known; God is. God is perpetually is-ing. The shift in the spiritual journey to the interior life moves us from knowing and doing God's will to un-knowing and being in God. This transformation in our journey is marked by transformation in our images of God.

Three distinct movements in our imagery of God throughout our spiritual development are charted by Nemeck and Coombs. First, we relate to God as **Creator and Savior**, as God's redeemed creatures. God at this point is a doing God: God creates and saves. Second, the relationship transitions to a *friendship*; to communion with God. And finally, we and God become **Beloved and Lover.** We go from praying to being prayed, from talking to listening, from praying about one thing and then another to praying about nothing, from praising and loving God to being in love with God.

Unlike Teresa, John leaves little to the imagination in his voluptuous recounting of this love affair with God. His portrayal of consummation describes an intense mystical intimacy in *O Living Flame of Love!*

> O passionate flame of love,
> that touches my soul
>   in its deepest center!
> Now, without shyness,
>   let your desire guide you.
> Join me in this sweet encounter!
>
> Your cauterizing sweetness
> regales me with sensation!
>   Your gentle hand,
> Your delicate touch,
>   tastes of eternity
>   and total forgiveness!
> This death gives me a new life.
>
> Lamps of fire!
> In your splendor
>   the deepest caverns of sentiment
> —once cold and dark—
>   now give an exquisite
> warmth and light to my Beloved.
>
> Softly and tenderly
> you awaken my heart
>   —where you alonedwell secretly—
> with your sweet breath,
>   graciously and delicately
> soothing my heart with love![27]

The ecstasy of love as a "little death" is a romantic notion but expresses for John an even more profound transcendence: a taste of heaven. As McGinn puts it, "Ecstatic mystical experience and personal immortality are two sides of the same coin—the former the foretaste of the latter, which serves as its completion."[28]

To be enamored with God in prayer is a common motif in the mystical spirituality of many religious traditions, as in these lines from the *Kabir:*

> Since the day when I met with my Lord
>> there has been no end to the sport of our love.
> I see with eyes open, smile and behold
>> his beauty everywhere.
> I utter his name, and whatever I see
>> reminds me of him.
> Whatever I do
>> becomes his worship.
> Wherever I go
>> I move round him.
> All I achieve
>> is his service.
> When I lie down
>> I lie prostrate at this feet.
> Whether I rise or sit down
>> I can never forget him.
> For the rhythm of his music
>> beats in my ears.[29]

Augustine, who struggled long with his sexuality and the pious life, had a heart aflame for God:

> Late have I loved you, O beauty so ancient and so new.
>> Late have I loved! You were within me while I have none outside to seek you . . .
>>> You called,
>>>> you cried,
>>>>> you shattered my deafness.
>>> You sparkled,
>>>> you blazed,
>>>>> you drove away my blindness.
>> You shed your fragrance, and I drew in my breath, and I pant for you. I tasted and now I hunger and thirst. You touched me, and now I burn with long ing for your peace.[30]

Love does what obedience and faith cannot: it transforms. In the Love Chapter of I Corinthians 13, Paul
concludes that of the three chief virtues—faith, hope
and love—the greatest is love. There comes a point
when faith turns to love.

Joan Timmerman, in *Sexuality and Spiritual Growth*,
maps out the spiritual journey through five transformative stages. Our first challenge is *living in the world of
things,* learning to effectively link means to ends, manage nutrition, technology and personal energy. The goal
of this stage is to be normal. But, at some point in our
youth we experience a *conversion to a world of people,*
where we reach out to form meaningful relationships.

Purification is the third stage, where we let go of old
patterns and seek balance in life. This balance and as-
sessment enables a fourth stage, *enlightenment and illumination:* a revisioning of life and a movement into the
unknown. At this we come to live out our humanness in
mystery and mysticism, the fifth stage: *union.*[31]

We are at once propelled along this time line toward
union by the force of love and at the same time repelled
from it by fear. We live constantly in the tension between desire for the world of things and spiritual union
with God. Though the world of things is our familiar
home, we discover it to be fallow ground for fruitful
living and find ourselves lost in its superficiality. Centering our lives in God leads us inwardly to finding our
True Self, but entails a fearful stripping away of the
dead layers of pretense and defense. The fallow soil
must be broken. The seed, said Jesus, must die in the
earth in order to come alive.

Daniel Helminiak, in *Spiritual Development*, defines
spirituality as "authentic self-transcendence," the paradox of finding true selfhood by focusing our life on the
divine reality which is beyond us. As Teresa noted, this
is a journey that requires more than desire: it demands
courage. In reflecting on Helminiak's spiritual selfhood,

David Schnarch, in *Constructing the Sexual Crucible,* points to the existential anxiety which is aroused by such a proposition:

> . . . we fear transcending ourselves . . . we all face the crisis of faith in which we expose ourselves to life through self-willing spiritual desire. This is what desire based on fullness looks like in its fledgling state. Faith is what drives us to face the fear of successful self-evolution, brought about by our own desire. We fear the unknown, we fear becoming someone we don't know and yet, this is exactly why people enter therapy: to escape the problem-maintaining solutions that are known, and to become someone other than who we know ourselves to be.[32]

Yet, it is only by proceeding with the current of the Spirit toward the breakwater of spiritual union with God that we can hope to celebrate the foretaste of divine union in authentic and loving human sexuality. Otherwise we remain in an intermediate state of development in which relationships can only be a means to an end, or at best, sheer commitment and obligation. Without authentic self-transcendence, the loss is too great to risk basing relationship on freedom. Our lover becomes an object of dependence, a possession, a source of self-affirmation, or an extension of our psyche rather than a free, volitional individual. And as such, we can never become more than this to another.

It is toward a willingness to trust that love thrusts us into the unknown. This is the first dilemma of life, according to Erik Erikson: basic trust versus mistrust. In our infantile experience, do we perceive the world as a loving place to which we can give ourselves, or a dangerous place against which we must helplessly cower? It was upon our mother's breasts that we learned to trust (Ps. 22:9), from that first nurturing love we build a like of trusting in the goodness of life.

Like Erikson, many have noted that the primary nature of trust is the capacity to love. Sebastian Moore: "To not trust life is to sink into a pathology." Bertrand Russell saw that to fear love is to fear life and those who fear life are already three parts dead.

Or as Stratton asks, "When your life beckons to you like a lover, do you reach out with faith and desire or with suspicion and defensiveness?"[33]

Love is foolish; it follows no reason. The rational methodology of discipleship creates a strong box for faith. Love opens the box and throws away the padlock. Sam Keen refers to this developmental stage as Lover/Fool, "For the lover, the world has ceased to be a problem to be solved and has become a mystery to be enjoyed." And when that mystery becomes painful, "the lover is also a fool because s/he can look at the tragedy of history and say: 'Nevertheless . . . I trust.'"[34]

It is the compelling power of a vision that "inspires people and leads them to fulfillment in their lives," says Alfred North Whitehead. "For a Christian, the final authority is the love of God in Christ, and love is not love if its power is anything but inspiration."[35]

What we can trust is our capacity to please God: not from any accomplishment or sacrifice, but from our being that desires to please God. It is what Fromm calls "response-ability," the ability to be responsive to the needs of the other. Love, he says, is the power to produce love.

Love is "the yearning to serve God, which is a thing very pleasing to God," said John. Merton echoed these words in his prayer of abandonment: The desire to please God is pleasing to God. From this please-ableness we find freedom to give ourselves fully in relationship to God and others. Our basis for intimacy is established not on our loving abilities, but in our inherent capacity to be loved. We love God, after all, because God first loved us (I John 4:19).

Healing the Disparity
Between the Haves and Have Nots

The gospel of spiritual freedom and healing has long been housed in church dogmas that can harm as well as heal. The structure of Christian society has too often reflected a male-dominated culture, which derives more of its form from Plato than Jesus. Because of this, power and influence have been afforded to males and denied to females.

Jesus' teachings raised the status of women in a time when women had no status. For Jesus, this injustice is rooted in the brokenness of human nature. His ministry was aimed at healing this brokenness and restoring the divine order to relationships at all levels.

From its Judaic roots, Christianity inherited a concept of salvation as integration. The word most commonly used for salvation in the Christian scriptures comes from the same root as healing or restoration. Salvation, then, restores the integrity and wholeness of a person. Body and soul, female and male, mind and heart, past and future, friend and enemy; all the dehumanizing and fragmenting splits in the human experience are healed through the love of God. This is our hope in Christ.

The nature of human disintegration is projected onto the screen of history in the story of Adam and Eve. The creation story is a drama of integration and imaginative tensions. Day and night, heaven and earth, land and sea, man and woman; the tree of life and the tree of knowledge. It was all very good. When Adam and Eve partook of that disintegrating power of the knowledge of good and evil, the whole cosmos began to unravel. They felt ashamed. They projected their guilt onto another by blaming each other, the creation, and ultimately God. An alienation set in which destroyed the original goodness of their sexual difference.

From then on, it was the haves and have nots, a system which, says Tina Beattie, "makes women born losers in the system that governs our fallen world."[36]

Cast Down the Male Idol

Can a male savior save women? In arguing the full divinity and full humanity of Christ, the early church fathers stated that whatever aspect of human nature Christ did not assume is therefore not saved. This being the case, is femininity saved since Christ became a man? This masculine Christ is inadequate for women, some would say.

Others would argue that while Christ became a man in the person of Jesus, Christ is not a male, *per se;* Christ transcends gender. For this reason, the Christa figure— a crucified female Christ—is more appealing.

Beattie asserts, more cohesively, that Christ assumed maleness in order to take on the fundamental nature of humanity, which is sexually-oriented. By taking the form of a man specifically, Christ was then able to redeem masculinity from its hierarchical and aggressive roots through His sacrificial death at the hands of the patriarchal system of this fallen world. To cast Christ in the form of a crucified woman, Beattie continues, is to only reinforce the images of this patriarchal social order with yet another depiction of a punctured, violated woman.

Patriarchy, "the rule of the fathers," is a masculine dominance of social and political structures. David James defines the chief assumptions of the patriarchal system. First, only patriarchal ways of thinking and viewing the world are valid. Second, those outside the dominant class, namely women and minorities, are inferior and dangerous. Third, dominance is maintained by control and power.[37]

> Man corrupt everything, say Shug. He on your box of grits, in your head, and all over the radio. He try to

make you think he everywhere. Soon as you think he everywhere, you think he God. But he ain't.

Alice Walker, *The Color Purple*

Patricia Lynn Reilly, in *A God Who Looks Like Me*, uses this quote to help make her point that women are excluded from the divine in traditional male language and imagery. These same traditions, she suggests, "also teach that God is beyond human naming and imagination," and in that tradition she challenges the stronghold of patriarchal God-words.[38]

In that same vein, the Raschkes point out that exclusively male language and images regarding the divine is tantamount to idolatry, since none of our concepts of God are inalterable. Furthermore, there is no Scriptural basis for an exclusively male image of God.[39]

In celebrating the historical basis for worshipping God as female as well as male, Reilly echoes the commonly held hypothesis of the *Magna Mater* (Great Mother) cult:

> In my search for the truth I began to explore the historical and archaeological evidence supporting the fact that the most ancient image of the divine was female and that this image reached back 25,000 years. There was a time when God was imagined, known, and worshiped as a woman.[40]

Furthermore, Reilly discovered in her research that there are in fact two accounts of creation in Genesis, not one. Genesis 1:26-28 pictures a simultaneous creation of man and woman in which they both dominate the world together. Another version, Genesis 2:18-23, describes man being created first, and then woman from one of his ribs. The Sumerians worshipped this prototypical woman as the goddess Lilith, the Divine Lady. This version of creation, Reilly asserts, was suppressed through rabbinical legends to the effect that God's first attempt in creating a wife for Adam was unsuccessful since she was rebellious and autonomous.

These ancient goddess religions were not all they are depicted to be by zealous feminists, the Raschkes point out. In fact, *Magna Mater* cult worship was often characterized by orgiastic rites, violence, mutilation, and living sacrifice. Ancient Judaism's rejection of the goddess cults was not based so much on misogyny (hatred or distrust of women), but a rejection of worshiping with human blood and orgasm. And besides, even in cultures that worshiped female deities, women still had inferior status compared to men. In historical contexts, the Judeo-Christian tradition offered a relatively high status for women, providing for humane treatment of wives, feminine dimensions of worship and a theology that sexual divisions will not persist beyond this life.

It is natural and good that we struggle with our God images and have ongoing public debate about them. Our imagination about God powerfully influences the way we view ourselves and others in the world. Negative and restricting God images often correspond with dysfunctional patterns of behavior and relating. Perfectionism and compulsivity are usually accompanied by judgmental images of God, for example.

David James identifies some of the salient issues regarding gender-borne images of God. First, God-images are profoundly significant because they "reflect the paradigms of those doing the imaging." We tend to unconsciously project onto God our own distorted feelings of what is acceptable or unacceptable about ourselves.

Second, justice requires that we not limit our God images to those groups that are in the dominant power class. Jesus often challenged the power base of his day by offering iconoclastic images, e.g., the kingdom of heaven is of children, wanting to protect Jerusalem like a mother hen protects her chicks, or talking to a "sinful" woman of another race.

Third, when we begin to cling to our sacred images of God we are in danger of idolatry—the worship of images. Disillusionment is about losing our images of God: any illusion that we think we have a handle on the nature of God.

Fourth, our ever-developing understanding of human nature should influence the way we image God. Imaging God as a king may have spoken to the people of ancient cultures but may not relate so well in our present democratic society.[41]

If exclusive masculine God-images are idols, then some want to burn the whole village to be rid of them. To them, patriarchy is to blame for virtually all social, political, economic, environmental, and spiritual ills. Misogynists lurk in every alley and behind every bush. We would be better off without men altogether.

Various aspects of the feminist movement have powerfully affected men. No doubt, male chauvinist pigs are still hanging out in their favorite misogynist sties bemoaning the good old days when the good old boys ran everything. What has arisen, however, in response to misogyny and patriarchy is clearly yet another form of dehumanization: *misandry* (the hatred or distrust of men). A toxic and militant feminism marches with the cry, Let's castrate the males!

As a counter-movement, both to salve the wounds inflicted by misandrists and to reconstruct a redeemed masculinity, the men's movement has been a favorite joke butt, with such caricatures as urban New Age men beating drums in the woods. Misandry, James observes, is now a household phenomenon.

> . . . with the evolution of the masculine identity and the ascendance of feminist influences in society, there is more than a little misandrist, or anti-masculine opinion evidenced in both the popular culture and the

academic world. From the critical spirit of television talk shows to some feminist literature, a myriad of derisive masculine images have flooded our collective awareness. These suggest that being a man is, for the first time, more of a deficit than a benefit.[42]

In Timmerman's discussion of masculinity, she posits two basic types of responses on the part of men who acknowledge the inequality between the sexes in remaining patriarchal structures. One, those who become feminist, taking on an irrational guilt for their gender. Two, those who focus on the harm done to themselves and seek to break out of masculine stereotypes. She castigates both groups, one as inauthentic and the other as inadequate, in a manner all too typical of the blind-alley emasculating, doubly-binding approach of some feminists that denies men an affirmative response except self-deprecation or silence. Theologians who attempt to update masculine God images, she warns, produce a God image that is "a better male, but still male." She prohibits men from developing a more expansive and healthier masculinity while inviting women to cast off male-defined roles of femininity. Why not grant men the same option: to cast off female-defined masculine roles? After all, from whom did we learn them, if not from our mothers?[43]

When parents are caught in the misogyny / misandry split, their children are wounded. Esau and Jacob, for example, were the twin sons of Isaac and Rebekah; their story is told in Genesis 24-35. Rebekah was well experienced in the wiles of the ancient patriarchal culture, which treated women as little more than property. Esau was a hairy hunter, a real Daddy's boy, since he was technically the first born. He shamed the family, though, by marrying outside the clan. Jacob was a home body, who stayed around his mother. But, he was smart. He had already outwitted his impulsive brother out of his inheritance in exchange for a bowl of soup.

Before Isaac died, he wanted to pass down the patriarchal blessing to Esau, so he sent him to kill some wild game and prepare his favorite food. Overhearing the conversation, Rebekah plotted for Jacob to trick his nearly-blind father into blessing him instead. Bringing in his mother's best recipe and with head and arms covered with lambskin to mimic his woolly brother, Jacob convinced his father to bless him instead of Esau. Had Jacob not fled for his life, his brother would have surely killed him.

The misogyny/misandry dynamic is embodied in these two forms of reaction: the manipulating Momma's Boy Jacobs and the macho Daddy's Boy Esaus. They are two extremes representing both sides of the same depersonalizing coin. Men who manipulate women are at some level ashamed of their masculinity and have difficulty claiming their power. They have to control others in more indirect ways and need powerful women to help them feel affirmed. Macho men are also anxious about their masculinity and compensate by sexualizing women. They feel affirmed by relating to subordinate, compliant women.

Those who react to masculine images of God, as if they were de facto injurious or offensive, send the message that there is something injurious or offensive about masculinity itself. One form of victimhood begets another. A femininity that needs to bash men in promoting itself offers little hope for spiritual healing and is ultimately no better than the patriarchy it castigates. Following in the steps of Robert Bly, various authors and speakers have raised the issue of male woundedness and foster what is meaningful, positive, and wholesome about masculinity.

Sam Keen advises men to sort out the healing treasures of prophetic feminism from the toxic trash of ideological feminism. In *Fire in the Belly: On Being a Man,* Keen defines Prophetic feminism as a model for change.

Ideological feminism, on the other hand, is characterized by enmity and scapegoating. The ravaging fires of
the great patriarchal Satan, assert the feminist ideologues, must be met with fire.[44]

Healing the Anger, Guilt and Shame

Most of us are at best confused about our sexuality.
What kind of woman or man do we desire to be? What
is a desirable woman and or man? Let me restate that
last sentence, because the word *desirable* might connote
a sexual desirableness that will place too much emphasis on sex appeal to the exclusion of a more holistic view
of human nature. What, then, is the kind of woman or
man that we feel we ought to be? Oops, I probably
should have not used the word *ought*, since it may
convey an imposed moralism on the issue.

Beyond my feigned pickle with language and gender, let me try to define the issue I'm seeking to address
as one of gender image. What image of femininity or
masculinity do we define as wholesome, healthy, or
meaningful?

Let me offer the requisite disclaimer that I am a man
writing about gender. As such, I seek to follow two
principles in my writing. First, I am choosing to be self-
disclosing in my own attempt to work out some clarity
of my masculinity. Take it for what it is worth: good
comedy or tragedy. Second, I want to address some
issues for female spiritual development as I see them.
After all, no one can speak to the issue apart from their
own sexual identity.

Where is my Feminine Side?

I've looked in the mirror, had my testosterone level
checked from both sides of my body, attempted to sing
the soprano and alto lines during congregational singing, and had my handwriting analyzed. The results
have all been negative: no recognizable signs of femi-

ninity. I've got big male bones, a balding male head, hairs in my male nose, and absolutely no signs of female reproductive organs. So, when I hear my male friends talk about getting in touch with their feminine side, I just scratch a few more hairs from my bald spot and discreetly count my ribs (as a boy I used to think I had more on one side than the other due to Adam losing a rib).

According to Michael Kimmel, in *Manhood in America*, I'm not alone in my conundrum about men having female characteristics and vice versa. In 1936, Lewis Terman, developer of the Stanford-Binet IQ test, decided to create an instrument that would separate the men from the boys. Along with his very feminine assistant, Catherine Cox Miles, he came up with the "M-F" scale (that is, masculinity-femininity). The test was a grand success, as far as popularity is concerned. As far as internal validity (one of those terms statisticians use to talk about a test's reliability), the results of the M-F scale were a bit ironic. For example, boys brought up primarily by their mothers scored higher in masculinity than boys raised by their fathers or both parents. Likewise, girls reared by their fathers rated as more feminine than their mother-reared counterparts. And the big kicker: male heterosexuals and "active" male homosexuals scored equally high in masculinity.[45]

> We have genitalized so much of our masculine spirituality with the values of the phallus, the prized male erection, the quintessential symbol of manliness. Ideally, the phallus is big, hard and up. So we have accented those values in the divine. God, too, must be big, hard and up: sovereign in power, righteous in judgment, the transcendent Wholly Other . . . but, when we finally realize how one-sided this is, a new revelation comes . . . we men are not big, hard and up very much of the time . . . more of the time with are small, soft, and down.
>
> James B. Nelson, *On Doing Body Theology*[46]

"Our sexuality is not incidental to our humanity," cautions Beattie, "It is the focus of our identity." God became male, in essence, to disempower the big, hard, up fallacy. Through the fall, Adam became disconnected from his own body. God came in flesh to restore that connection.[47]

Men need to find their power, not over women or under women, but with women and with one another. It is our power to plant the earth with a hopeful seed. It is our power to reap a harvest and provide richness to our communities. It is our power to engage the world and make our place in it. It is our power to bless our daughters and sons and teach them how to find their powers.

If beating a drum in the woods helps you to find your power, then go beat the hell out of a drum in the woods and don't come back until you've broken the drumstick. If saying No to your father's curses helps you find your power, then go find a mentor who will bless your deep desires. If saying No to your mother without feeling guilty helps you to find your power, then come tell me how you did it, because I haven't found that much power yet.

It is over the ideologies of the feminine that men get stuck in their relationships with women, says Keen. Men, in order to find their powers, must reckon with three primary images of WOMAN. The Goddess and Creatrix challenge a man to justify his existence. For what purpose are we here? Who defines our purpose? The Mother and Matrix hold the power of approval. Men struggle with power by either trying to please women or by demeaning them as a way of denying their power. The largely unconscious feminine archetype of the Erotic-Spiritual Power is the feminine active power. It is this sexual power that we tend to split off from God: the God who desires us and who seduces us with desire. From this power men find their artistic, creative abilities.

The struggle of the male psyche with WOMAN is a life-or-death battle. Too often swallowed up by poisonous messages from their female idols and fellow strugglers, men may find little grace to heal their wounds in the misandrous culture of many academic and religious communities. For example, in *Manhood in America: A Cultural History*, professor Michael Kimmel leads any reader seeking positive or hopeful images of manhood down a blind alley of 336 pages of articulate critique and exactly two pages of broad brush prescriptive vision in an era and subject matter that is already 99.4% criticism and 0.6% solution. Kimmel's thesis is that a profeminist masculinity, or what he calls a "democratic manhood," is the cure for masculine anemia, which comes across like a Leninist text on democracy. Virtually every expression and context of masculinity however noble or feeble, however mythopoetic or savagely survivalist, is written off as a poorly inadequate solution or shameful failure, leaving men where too many feminists leave them: emasculated, demeaned, stereotyped, blamed, and cut off from history and legend.

This kind of masculine definition splits manhood into a Jacob-Esau rivalry: two kinds of men: a Momma's Boy and a Daddy's Boy, both seeking a blessing in ways that are only alienating. Rather than men honoring Mother and Father, these boys split them into manipulative shrewdness and blind naïveté. Women smart but weak; men strong but dumb. It takes little smarts to see the problems in the gender world; what we need are some insightful, courageous solutions. Kimmel comes off ironically in character with his own insulting terminology: wimpy and whiney.

In contrast, James offers a discussion of masculine spirituality which

> . . . examines the use of masculine images of God from a participatory perspective. It is a spirituality that is personal, evocative, challenging and compelling. Since

men's approach to life is rooted in "doing, direction
and definition," theological reflection upon experience
becomes an important element of a man's spirituality
…images of God that communicate deeply to men will
pursue the connection between the masculine and the
divine in two dimensions: connection and challenge.[48]

I've already outlined some of the challenges that
face the development of a compelling masculine spirituality in terms of misandry and the hostility that exists
to the generation of new male spiritual images and
reclaiming new ways of understanding traditional ones.
But, the deeper challenge that faces men and women
today—brought to the fore by the movements of feminism and masculinity—is the whole notion of a personal God. Imaging God in more inclusive and less
culture-bound ways offers freedom to relate to God in a
more life-giving way. Through the painful valleys of
Disillusionment, and the burial of our outmoded images of ourselves and God, we find empowerment
through the indwelling Spirit to allow God more intimately to reach out to us. The challenge of spirituality is
connection.

Movements in masculine spirituality that deal with
connection focus on a number of relational issues. James,
from whom I draw heavily in this section, traces the
psychic numbing that men experience in relationships
to two sources. One, the relationship of woman and son.
Research is demonstrating how men are socialized from
infancy regarding their feelings by the way they are *not*
held and the ways they *are* held in comparison to female
babies. Two, in the relationship of man and son, boys
commonly receive what Bly described as the Father
wound, which contributes to the macho-addicted male
persona.[49]

The "sensitive man" model of spiritual development idealized by Philip Culbertson guides men in their
liberation from gender stereotypes, who "seek a more

sensitive self-understanding in light of the feminist critique." Rejecting the Iron John myth, Culbertson insists that "instead of seeking the wild man within, sensitive men should seek to nurture and facilitate."[50]

Patrick Arnold, in contrast, is concerned that "masculinity itself is under attack, and not only in its negative shadow, but in its most positive qualities, too." In *Wildmen, Warriors and Kings: Masculine Spirituality and the Bible*, Arnold outlines the masculine spiritual path in four movements. Beginning with the *static feminine*, males exist in a maternal world. In his first connections with the outside world as a "man," the *dynamic masculine* is born. Eventually, the man settles down in the world and builds institutions, a stage Arnold calls the *static masculine*. But, if a man is to develop depth and attunement with his inner wisdom, beauty, and art, he will eventually enter the *dynamic feminine*.[51]

Richard Rohr and Joseph Martos trace *The Wildman's Journey* through a similar development of spirituality, beginning with the *common masculine*, wherein a man has a natural confidence, self-assurance, independence, resourcefulness, but lacks vulnerability and sensitivity. Along the way, a man's spiritual development can become arrested or proceed to another level. At this juncture, he may move either toward the tough guy of the *shallow masculine* or grow into the empathy and intuition of the *common feminine*. In the latter stage, the man then has the capacity to grow further toward either the soft man of the *shallow feminine* or into the *Journey of John the Beloved*, Rohr's and Martos' title for the independence, assertiveness, focus, and strength of the *deep masculine and inner feminine*.[52]

The Androgyny Myth

Notice the prevalence of construing spirituality as developing inner masculine and feminine qualities. All three of the masculine spirituality models discussed above direct a man to the development of his feminine side. Reflecting the pervasive influence of Carl Jung in modern spirituality and his concepts of anima and animus to denote feminine and masculine aspects of the psyche, the paradigm of androgyny (masculine / feminine) is perhaps one of the greatest and least addressed challenges facing spiritual development today.

The concept is appealing, I must admit. Finding the feminine in my own shadow-side suggests that the solution to the gender war lies within. Jung drew heavily from the beliefs of ancient alchemy in developing his notion of the feminine soul—the anima—and masculine worldly aggression—the animus. Alchemy sought to transform lead into gold through a series of chemical reactions. It was all metaphorical, Jung insisted, for the marriage of the feminine and masculine spiritual forces in the universe.

For years, I felt inferior to my male counterparts who related their growing integration with their feminine side. My lead never turned to gold. Was I slow? Was I too stupid to get it? Or, was I just hopelessly male chauvinistic?

When I began reading authors like Keen, I was relieved to find that other men—quick studies with smart wits and open minds—weren't turning lead into gold, either.

> . . . I find the whole notion of the marriage within the psyche between "masculine" and "feminine" qualities . . . confusing . . . I can locate nothing that feels "feminine" about holding my daughter in my arms, allowing myself to be comforted, weeping for the pain of the world, or exercising my intuition . . . As nearly as I can tell, I being a man, have nothing feminine about me.[53]

That men believe they can turn masculine lead into androgynous gold says a lot about the depth of self-doubt in the male psyche. Is this an illusion, made appealing by the guilt and shame men feel about their masculinity? We're a bunch of Charlie Browns at the mercy of the Lucys of the world.

Androgyny is a concept seized by men in the throes of the feminist movement as a way of dealing with not only the movement's valid prophetic confrontations of patriarchy, but with the crisis of misandry as well. Androgyny offered a way for Momma's Boys to overcome their anxiety about being different from women— their mothers and sisters—by being able to talk about their own feminine side.

Likewise, the concept of androgyny was seized upon by feminists to demarcate feminine and masculine characteristics, so as to lay claim to masculinity as something attainable by women, since femininity had such limiting connotations. In this way, Jung was pressed hard into the service of gender struggles without the full Jungian meaning of anima and animus being taken into consideration. Jung never saw the marriage in the psyche as a 50/50 proposition. It was more like 90/10, reflecting perhaps the nature of his own marriage and multiple mistresses: women should be about ninety percent anima; and men ninety percent animus. Jung's favorite term for women with predominant assertiveness, self-confidence, and other so-called "masculine" traits was "animus hound."

Isabel Briggs Myers and Peter B. Myers developed an instrument to measure significant personality traits based on Jungian psychology. The Myers-Briggs Type Indicator has become enormously popular and helpful in developing self-awareness and understanding interpersonal dynamics. While the M-BTI does not directly measure femininity or masculinity, it is based on a primary Jungian principle that personality traits appear in opposites, such as introversion and extraversion. Sound psychological health is not merely a balance of the two opposites, but paradoxically, a more developed trait indicates an increased capacity for balance. A score midway between poles can indicate that neither aspect is well-developed.

A dominating, aggressive man is not a strong man but a very weak man who lacks the capacity to express his human qualities more fully and freely. He has a limited masculinity. A strong man is a man with a fully-developed masculinity, who can be his own person, know his own self, have his own feelings, and initiate and maintain meaningful relationships. He is what Terrence Real calls the "strong, big-hearted guy."

I began my pastoral ministry in an open country farming community where I encountered a very clear cultural distinction between male and female. Men were men with all the cultural socialization thereof and women were women in like manner. Yet, there in the rural black dirt counties of north Texas, the theory of androgyny caves in on itself. Listening to the reflection of men who spent hours a day alone on a tractor, walking their fields, or tending their livestock, I came to appreciate how interior their world was and how contemplative they were in a very earthy way. They were contemplative in the sense of inner exploration, a flair for the symbolic, and the meaning of church bells and special seasons. They were contemplative in the sense of self-awareness and honoring their own feelings of being sad in their sadness, angry in their anger, excited in their enthusiasm and gladness. They knew far better than many folks in urban areas about the realities of disillusionment and the shadow-side of God. They were intimately in touch with the cycles of death, burial and new life, fallow earth and growth; harvest and sowing. Perhaps we city boys with our thin socks, fashionable shirts, and trendy conversation topics could learn much about the range of masculinity from our rural counterparts.

And those women, who left cold raw milk for me in the parsonage frig every week and a brown sugar-cured pork shoulder (the best part) with the cold fall "north-ers" at hog-killin' time, were real women. At fifth-Sunday dinners they brought peach and plum pies and cobblers from the fruit of the trees in their front yards— canned food had an altogether different meaning from the nicely-labeled commodities found at the grocery stores in town. Like their men, they knew their Bibles like the back of their hands, and although some had difficulty pronouncing Bach, they knew the finer points of local and national politics. After all, it was Sam Rayburn country.

Christian spiritual writers often swallow whole the dogma of Jung's androgyny without first consulting their Bibles. Where is androgyny in Scripture? To para-phrase Tertullian, what has Zurich to do with Jerusa-lem?

The Bible is largely ignored by many feminists and approached suspiciously by others as a patriarchal docu-ment regarding a patriarchal religion in a patriarchal society. Since Scripture is patriarchal, it is obsolete, goes the reasoning. The Raschkes call this "de-canonizing" of Scripture the "sociological fallacy" of mistaking the images of Scripture for the essence of the divine and the nature of the divine-human relationship.[54]

Jesus was a man, but that doesn't make God a man. Jesus also referred to himself as a gate (John 10:7), but that doesn't endue God with a latch. To toss aside the canon upon which the Christian faith has been based for two millennia because its metaphors are dated is to throw out the baby with the bath water.

The Bible is the witness of God's people throughout the ages of the reality of God in their lives. That histori-cal witness is the word of God. As God's children, we all are that spoken word. Our bodies are the revelation of God in the world, and we receive that revelation as it is in its contextual form—male or female—as our human-ity.

Just as feminists have advocated a departure from and deconstruction of patriarchal institutions as a way of finding their feminine soul, likewise there is a growing consensus of men's movement and masculine spirituality writers that men need to come away from women in their journey toward individuation. James, for example, quoted anthropological evidence of this in the initiatory rites of many cultures where pubescent boys are taken through the rite of passage from boyhood to manhood.

So, how can we have it both ways? How can we have an androgynous masculine spirituality that equates maturity with getting in touch with one's feminine side, on the one hand, and a coming apart with other men to find our masculine voice, on the other hand? Should men come away with men, sit around in the woods gazing into their navels searching for their inner feminine?

The biblical witness bears out an *Imago Dei* that transcends gender. Human nature, however, does not transcend gender, even though we have sociologically mislabeled some traits and energies as masculine or feminine. Men will be men, women will be women, and much of who we are is just plain human.

Erik Erikson, another of Freud's disciples, mapped out human development along psychosexual modes. Erikson noticed that boys and girls take different routes in certain aspects of their psychological development, observable during play. Playing with blocks, for example, Erikson saw girls building houses and walls and boys building towers. Erikson related the images to the womb and phallus. While differences in boy-girl behavior can be explained by socialization, Erikson believed some basic differences to be genetic, a part of the biological fabric of personality. It is interesting to parallel Erikson's observations with the primary metaphors for the spiritual life employed by Teresa and John. For

Teresa, the journey is like exploring a castle, while for John, it is climbing a mountain. Coincidence?

Rather than this whole business of masculine and feminine sides, it is more psychologically accurate to speak of introjects. An introject is the record of messages we have received from significant persons in our lives, which have become a part of our thinking. For example, a maternal introject may contain the parental messages we received from our mothers, which we have internalized and continue to maintain through our own self-talk. These messages may be helpful: "Look both ways before crossing the street" or toxic—"You're lazy and will never amount to anything."

Significant aspects of these introjects have to do with our gender roles and self-image. If a woman's paternal introject is of a father who consistently reminded her of what girls are not supposed to do, she may have toxic feelings about her own femininity: subordinate to men, weak, irrational, etc. It is not that these messages are hard-wired into the brain, but rather that they remain as unconscious and unchallenged beliefs.

The World According to Garp portrays a man's struggle with some negative introjects from his mother who wanted nothing personally to do with men. The developmental results were disastrous: a man who could not relate deeply to women.

As the work of Ana Marie Rizzuto shows, these introjects have powerful bearings on our developing God images. Just as our parental introjects may be the source of sexual conflict in our self-image and relationships, so these issues will impinge on our faith.

John embodied in many ways the Platonic ideal of love as same-sex and spiritual.[55] Neoplatonists were distrustful of heterosexual relationships and viewed the soul as feminine. John dealt with the gender issue in his God images by posturing himself as feminine in relationship to a masculine God. In "O Living Flame of

Love!" John graphically depicts the soul's passion for divine union with unmistakable feminine imagery: "break the membrane of our sweet union . . . my breasts . . . my soul in her profoundest core!" Did John actually transcend his sexuality in relationship to God or merely repress it?

The contemplative life is historically associated with monasticism and celibacy: the downplaying of sexuality. Religious life is often a haven for those with gender-role ambivalence and unconventional sexual identities. Solitude should not be equated with withdrawal, nor spirituality with the fringe of human nature. Our relationship with Christ defines our gender more sharply rather than more ambiguously. Men become more fully masculine, and women more fully feminine in relationship to Christ. Christ enlivens our humanity, heals our sexual wounds, and empowers our personalities. Our relationships to Christ is the transcendent key to reconciliation both with God and others as sexual beings.

> For he himself is our peace, who has made the two one and has destroyed the barrier, the dividing wall of hostility . . . His purpose was to create in himself one new man out of the two, thus making peace, and in this one body to reconcile both of them to God through the cross. (Eph. 2:14-16).

> There is neither . . . male nor female, for you are all one in Christ Jesus. (Gal. 3:28).

It is not that Christ has destroyed identity or difference, but that Christ transcends our differences. The tension of masculinity and femininity does not find resolution in our intrapsychic inner world, but in our relational world. One ancient creation myth was that the human being was cut in half, resulting in male and female. The two halves spent their lives longing to be reunited with the other. There is truth in that myth: finding wholeness is a relational task.

John Bunyan, in all his cultural limitations, recognized the unique spiritual journeys of men and women, describing the *Pilgrim's Progress* in two separate parts of his book: Christian and Christiana. Both had their unique challenges and graces, but both were drawn to God by the same Spirit.

Pilgrim's Progress contains the account of not only Christian's pilgrimage to the Celestial City, but the later journey of his wife Christiana and their four children in a sequel. Christiana has her own hazards to overcome, namely the Genesis curse and her dulled spiritual conviction. Though very much couched in seventeenth-century English convention, Bunyan attempts a depiction of the unique spiritual journeys of men and women rather than a common pilgrimage.

The world is full of evil polarities that split us into two exclusive parts and bind us from any middle ground of integration. A polarity of liberal constructionism and conservative behaviorism, between Democrat and Republican, between Protestantism and Catholicism, between Jew and Gentile—the split runs right down into the very soul of community and psyche of individuals. In dying with Christ and living the new life of conversion, we come to a place where we deconstruct the old structures of discipleship and methodology in the spiritual life. We embrace structurelessness, we embrace being that transcends these evil polarities—religious polarities, economic polarities, geographical polarities; sexual polarities.

Jesus poignantly dramatized evil polarities in his parable of the unjust steward. A man who owed his master an unimaginable debt was graciously forgiven but immediately went out and foreclosed on his debtors. What the parable depicts is how some people remain locked into seeing the world in terms of evil polarities: either oppressed or oppressor. As Erikson discovered, this polarity translates to the male-female issues of initiative-openness. Fear drives the polarities: fear of domination; fear of intimacy. For women, it is the fear of intrusion and the challenge to trust being open. For men, it is the fear of initiative and the challenge to trust entering and exiting. Religiously, for women it is the fear of an oppressive father-god; for men, the fear of a church-mother who is manipulative and dominating.

Teresa seems to have never confused the two. She knew very well what it was like to be a woman of faith in the patriarchal Spanish Inquisition, which made her automatically—by virtue of her femininity and faith— suspect. As a *conversos,* she knew the evil polarities of a Christian faith that worshiped a Jewish Messiah but persecuted anyone with Jewish blood. Because she did not confuse oppressor with oppressed, she was largely able to transcend the demeaning evils of her culture and blaze a trail of a new spirituality of the inner Christ. She would allow nothing to come between her and her passionate Christ.

Because her mystical theology was so self-affirming, Teresa could let go of much of the neurotic sexual conflict, which characterized much of her early life. She was a vivacious, intelligent woman who loved the com- pany of well-educated men. Unlike John, she was able to celebrate her gender in relationship to God, a maiden pursued by His Majesty, her favorite image of God. Her spirituality was not austere, but full of opulent images of spaciousness, wealth, innovation, and grandeur.

For me, however, Teresa's most endearing spiritual trait was her playfulness. She didn't take herself or others all that seriously. Even the grand hierarchy of the Roman Catholic Church and the frightful specter of the Spanish Inquisitional courts were taken with a grain of salt, as she wrote with a dry wit about frail, uneducated women not quite getting the finer points of theology as a way of mocking the religious establishment. She cleverly maneuvered her way among the ecclesiastical pitfalls in promoting her radical—and politically un-popular—reforms.

It is because of Teresa's playfulness that it is hard to find any clear parallel in her seven dwelling places of *The Interior Castle* and John's *Dark Night of the Soul*, even though they were close associates. Disillusionment, for Teresa, is more akin to the Latin root of illusion, which is *en utere*, "in play." In this sense, we think of the playfulness of an illusionist. As such, Thomas Moore plays with the term as indicating the heightened perception of one moving toward romantic or sexual intimacy.

Jeremiah's complaint to God had this air of playfulness as well as the sting of the more vernacular meaning of illuse, which is "to mistreat."

> O Lord, you deceived me, and I was deceived;
>> you overpowered me and prevailed.
> I am ridiculed all day long;
>> everyone mocks me. (Jer. 20:7)

His word "deceived" could be translated "per-suaded" or "seduced."

Teresa was constantly being surprised by God and undone by God's way of casting her life in such different light. This was her Disillusionment, a playful, seren-dipitous, ongoing process of losing one illusion about herself and then another.

Through Disillusionment we can let go of our illu-sory and binding sexual images of ourselves and others and learn to play with the process, as Timmerman suggests:

> I think the spiritual issue at stake in gender rela-tions is reconciliation . . . A certain playfulness about gender, a rejection and reordering of elements, belongs to the stage of transition . . . This process of forgiveness and renewal typically takes place privately in indi-vidual sexual relationships and households. At this point there has been little exchange of ideas or experi-

ence in the public or religious arenas. When there is, it will chart a development of the spirit. There are historical moments when the possibilities of overall transformation of consciousness and culture depend more crucially on the dynamic of gender relations than on any other social force. It can be argued that we are in such a moment now.[56]

Teresa emulates a moving beyond an other-defined sense of self and into a self-defined, interior-oriented identity where we find healing and come to be at peace with ourselves. And as Frederick Bueckner points out, peace biblically is more than just the absence of conflict...

> ... in Hebrew peace, *Shalom,* means fullness . . having everything you need to be wholly and happily yourself.[57]

Desired in Community

We look to relationships to bridge the separateness we feel. Relationships, however, that are dehumanizing, manipulative, objectifying, or depersonalizing leave us vulnerable to despair, as unknown faces in a soulless, nameless mass. Loving, affirming, dignifying and free relationships, on the other hand, facilitate our growth as individuals.

Christ our Lover brings to focus the love of God in a laser-dot beam of brilliant light squarely on our soul. Our intensely intimate, passionately jealous and exclusive relationship with God heightens our sense of individuality to a perspective from which we see the world not as a disordered mass of human plasma, but as a household; an immediate family.

This house of God is no longer a temple of stones, but a temple body of living stones, a cosmic cathedral whirling through space and time cradling the timeless, limitless love of the Universe, at once indwelt by Love and simultaneously dwelling in Love. Our bodies are living temples, love-in-us and we-in-love, composing together a community of love in which we dwell.

In our very fleshly fabric, our engendered incarnation of the creative Word, we are, in our most fundamental nature, relational beings. One part of two, female and male, both comprising the image of God, who exists in eternal loving communion within the Godhead.

It is a powerful vision and no academic language will do justice to the beauty of what God has in store for the church at the Marriage Supper of the Lamb. John the Apostle likened the new creation to a wedding:

> Then I saw a new heaven and a new earth, for the first heaven and the first earth had passed away, and there was no longer any sea. I saw the Holy City, the new Jerusalem, coming down out of heaven from God, prepared as a bride beautifully dressed for her husband. And I heard a loud voice from the throne saying, "Now the dwelling of God is with men, and he will live with them. They will be his people, and God himself will be with them and be their God. (Rev. 21:1-3).

What began in a garden, ends in a city. Beattie finds significance in this twist of fate: "The city, symbol of all that we hold dehumanizing in this urban age but also symbol of humanity's greatest creative endeavor, will be caught up in the transformation that will make 'the whole of creation new.'"[58]

What does it mean to live as a community-in-love? First it means that we are not only equal, but each of us uniquely special. What Fromm calls the "equality of individuality" is the biblical model of body-faith. We are not just all members of the body of Christ, Paul maintained in 1 Corinithians 11, but each of us a *different* part of the body with "equal concern for each other."

There are none of us above or below the others. There are no "Very Important Persons," for we all are very important persons.

Secondly, living as a community-in-love centers each of us in a focus both within and beyond ourselves. The Christ we discover as Lover in the centermost chambers of the Interior Castle of our soul—and the Christ who indwells all of God's children—is the Christ in whom we dwell. I, therefore love the Christ in me and, therefore, love the Christ in you and, therefore, am loved by the Christ in whom we are. Relationships can no longer be casual, for all persons we meet are universes within themselves, and in that universe God is the center.

We offer to one another as a community what none of us can have alone. The "in the midst" presence of Christ where two or three are gathered is greater than the sum total of the parts. There is always an added dimension in community, an greater presence, a sharper concentration, a more permeable prayer.

I have sat in amazement as other members of a contemplative prayer group have shared the images from their meditation. The similarity, common theme, and synchronized movement of the spirit in our midst was experienced by each one in unique, yet related ways. And the more vulnerable those group members become in sharing what was really going on within them during that meditation, the more obvious it is that we were all plugged into a common reality.

If such commonality can be experienced in a small prayer circle, what are the common movements of the Spirit in our faith communities as a whole? Our world as a community in space?

Thirdly, to what destination are we all as a world community moving? The biblical writers struggled to describe this Omega Point, but all metaphors failed to convey its breadth as surely as they offered some light. A new creation, a new body, a wedding, a banquet, a judgment, a reward, a rest; an inheritance. Wherever it is, we are all going there together. Whatever it is, we are all together a part of it.

What place will there be at that final point for our pain, our joy, our regrets, and satisfactions?

Since we are all characters in, as well as co-authors of this incredible story, it seems that we can never again take one another as a totally unknown, unrelated, and irrelevant member of the big family. Our story lines will all someday intersect, because they all revolve around the main plot of God's love.

Prayer of Desire

Dance with me! Hold me in your embrace as we step
    through swirling galaxies,
Dizzy with love and the
    scent of your breath.

Lay with me
    under clouds of stars
    with the breeze of starlight
    and your fingers through my hair.

Gaze with me;
    eyes filled with laughter
    swollen with tears
    raining sweet drops of passion.

Stay with me! Let our moments never cease
    but fill with love and hope,
Resting on the air
    of our living.
Amen,
    Amen.

Reflection

Can you imagine yourself being totally, completely loved by Christ? That Christ makes over every little detail of your physical appearance and character? That Christ loves things about you that you love and also loves things about you that you hate? In loving things about us that we hate, Christ perhaps sees these characteristics for what they are: not unlovable, horrible qualities, but undeveloped, overextended, or distorted forms of truly good characteristics.

In the Song of Songs, the brothers of the beloved became angry (1:6). Who might feel threatened by your intense love for Christ?

Romance could be seen as going through these phases of development: infatuation, commitment, disenchantment, and establishing a new kind of relationship. Where are you in your relationship to Christ?

"God wants all of you all of the time." What meaning does this sentence hold for you?

Teresa states that courage is required for one who seeks union with God. How would you describe this courage from your own experience?

Theology and the experience of God: in what ways are these two realities complimentary? In what ways have you experienced them as contradictory?

One definition of a mystic is a person who lives in the awareness of God's first-love. In what ways may this simple definition "say it all"?

Can you relate to the following definition of prayer: "Prayer is letting God love you"? In what ways might this present a challenge for you?

What images of God are most comfortable for you? Most uncomfortable? What value might you derive from exploring your lack of comfort with these latter images?

"Men become more fully masculine, and women more fully feminine in relationship to Christ." Do you agree that this is the key to our integration as complete persons?

Does the fact that everyone you meet is a VIP affect the way you relate?

In what ways have you integrated your sexuality with your spirituality? Can one exist without the other?

Endnotes

1 Jerusalem Talmud, *Qiddushin* 4:12.
2 Carl A. Raschke and Susan Doughty Raschke, *The Engendering God: Male and Female Faces of God* (Louisville: Westminster John Knox Press, 1995), pp. 27f.
3 Here I am drawing from William E. Phipps, *Was Jesus Married? The Distortion of Sexuality in the Christian Tradition* (New York: Harper & Row, 1970), pp. 117-118.
4 Emil Brunner, *The Divine Imperative* (Philadelphia, 1947), p. 364, quoted in Phipps, p. 124-126.
5 Quoted in David M. Schnarch, *Constructing the Sexual Crucible* (W.W. Norton & Company, 1991), p. 562.
6 Hermas, *Similitude*, 9, 11, *The Anti-nicene Fathers, the Writings of the Fathers down to A.D. 325*, the Rev. Alexander Roberts, D.D., and James Donaldson, LL.D., Editors, *American Reprint of the Edinburgh Edition* Printed *July, 1975*, Volume 2, Fathers of the Second Century, Sage Digital Library, 1996.
7 Justin, *Dialogue with Trypho*, quoted in Phipps, pp. 131-132.
8 Irenaeus, *Against Heresies*, 1, 28, 1, quoted in Phipps, p. 132.
9 Tertullian, *On Prescription Against Heresies*, 7, quoted in Phipps, pp. 143f.
10 Tertullian, *On the Apparel of Women*, 1, 1, Sage Digital Library.
11 Phipps, pp. 146ff.
12 Phipps, pp. 149ff.
13 Phipps, pp. 152ff.
14 Schnarch, p. 548. 15 Francoeur, quoted in Schnarch.
16 Phipps, pp. 173ff.
17 Schnarch, p. 563.
18 Schnarch, pp. 570-573.
19 Quoted in Schnarch, p. 573.
20 *Castle*, p. 359.
21 *Castle*, p. 368.
22 *Castle*, p. 379.
23 *Castle*, p. 378.
24 *Castle*, p. 424.
25 *Castle*, p. 426.

26 *The Poems of Saint John of the Cross*, translated by Mark Sibley Jones.

27 Ibid.

28 McGinn, *Foundations*, p. 18.

29 Rabindranath Tagore, translator, Poem 41, *Songs of Kabir* (New York: The Macmillan Company, 1915).

30 Quoted in Richard J. Foster, *Prayers from the Heart* (HarperSanFrancisco, 1994), p. 50.

31 Joan H. Timmerman, *Sexuality and Spiritual Growth* (New York: Crossroad, 1992), p. 19.

32 Schnarch, pp. 591ff.

33 Quoted in Schnarch, p. 587.

34 Sam Keen in Jerome Berryman's dialogue with Sam Keen and James Fowler, *Life Maps: Conversations on the Journey of Faith* (Waco: Word Books, 1978), pp. 123-124.

35 Quoted in Deborah Hanus, *A Book of Readings, Questions and Spiritual Exercises* (Incarnate Word College, undated), pp. 145-146.

36 Tina Beattie, "Sexuality and the Resurrection of the Body," in Gavin D'Costa, ed., *Resurrection Reconsidered* (Oxford: One World, 1996), p. 139. I'm indebted here to Beattie for her general treatment of the subject in my discussion.

37 David C. James, *What Are They Saying About Masculine Spirituality?* (New York: Paulist Press, 1996), p. 41.

38 Patricia Lynn Reilly, *A God Who Looks Like Me: Discovering a Woman—Affirming Spirituality* (New York: Ballantine Books, 1995), p. 58.

39 Raschke and Raschke, pp. 5ff.

40 Reilly, p. 83.

41 Cf. James, pp. 34ff.

42 James, p. 12.

43 Timmerman, p. 41.

44 Sam Keen, *Fire in the Belly: On Being a Man* (New York: Bantam Books, 1991), pp. 195ff.

45 Michael Kimmel, *Manhood in America* (New York: The Free Press, 1996), pp. 206-210.

46 Quoted in Beattie, p. 141.

47 Beattie, pp. 141ff.

48 James, p. 48.

49 James, pp. 14-21.

50 Quoted in James, pp. 25-26.

51 James, pp. 27-28.

52 James, pp. 22-24.

53 Keen, 213-124.

54 Raschke and Raschke, p. 2.

55 John was likely influenced by the Gnostic and Neoplatonist sources of the Cabala, cf. Catherine Swietlicki, *Spanish Christian Cabala* (Columbia: University of Missouri Press, 1986), pp. 1-3, 6, 145, 158-186, esp. 170, "In both the *Bahir* and *Zohar*, the human soul is sometimes referred to as the *Shekhinah*. with one small step, a Christian Cabalist could easily substitute the individual soul for the *Shekhinah* as the Bride of Canticles. The Christian Cabalist could thus apply all the divine mysteries and images associated with the *Shekhinah* to the soul in union with the Godhead."

56 Timmerman, p. 47.

57 Frederick Bueckner, *Wishful Thinking: A Theological ABC* (New York: Harper and Row, 1973), p. 69.

58 Beattie, p. 147.

7

DESTINED IN CHRIST

***

The stillness of predawn hazes the heavy air. Mauve tints of glowing sky slowly illuminate the Mirror Lake and the inverted landscape matted on sleek waters. Nestled, barely eyed in the still darkness, a traveler cautions and then peers across. What is seen in her haunted stare?

As sunbeams burn orange the desert forms beyond, doves coo a daybreaking chant. She startles to a step, then a shielded vantage behind huge boulders. No intruder had invaded her.

Expanding vision with the daylight reveals who watches her across the mirror. Orbs in a black sculpture comfortably poised and peering without alarm, without intent; without self-consciousness.

The forest waits.   MSJ

In ancient Christianity, the unimaginable reality of Christ's incarnation fueled the movement that within three centuries had revolutionized the Roman Empire. Heretical and radical, the notion of God becoming human ignited a persecutory firestorm against the early Christians. To refer to Jesus of Nazareth as Lord was considered blasphemy by the monotheistic Jews and treason by the pantheistic, Emperor-worshiping Romans. To accept such a doctrine would undermine both the Jewish faith in which Christianity was born and the political allegiances of the Roman Empire, along with its Hellenistic religious and philosophical base.

Yet, the more these first-century Christians were driven underground the more their subterranean faith shook the foundations of the Roman world. One of their symbols was the fish, a fitting secret passkey for Christian greetings. The Greek word for fish, *ichthus*, formed an acronym for Jesus Christ Son of God Savior. Faith in Christ was the Fish that swam the deep currents of the human sea, revealing the profound and disturbing realities of the spiritual underworld-realities that form the source of life.

But, an even more compelling mystery dawned on those early followers of Jesus. By virtue of the incarnation—God in human flesh—we humans are not only confronted with the divine on our terms, but we are invited to share in this divine nature.

God became like us, so we might become like God, pronounced Clement of Alexandria, the second-century Church father. It was Clement who first expanded upon the biblical teachings of union with Christ in his references to Jesus' statement in Luke 20:35-36, "those who are considered worthy of taking part in that age and in the resurrection from the dead...can no longer die; for they are like the angels...They are God's children..."

Humans becoming like God? Before I recount the more logical meanings of this ancient riddle, I want to just let it stand a moment in its wonderfully outrageous simplicity.

In the creation story, we are told that God created humans in the divine image; the *Imago Dei*. Mark Twain quipped that ever since, we have been returning the favor, creating God in our image. This natural tendency to anthropomorphize God is the root of all sorts of human evil, but also reveals a basic characteristic of God's relating to the human race—to put on the human garment and live the human life.

A human God creating divine humans? Historically the doctrine is known as *divinization*, or in the orthodox tradition, *theosis*. Divinization—humans taking on the divine—is actually a central tenant of the Christian faith, if not one of its most illogical and unintelligible mysteries. Divinization is transcendence, according to the author of *The Cloud of Unknowing*,

> I say you have transcended yourself, becoming almost divine, because you have gained by grace what is impossible to you by nature, for this union with God in spirit, in love, and in oneness of desire is the gift of grace. Almost divine—yes, you and God are so one that you (and any real contemplative) may in a sense truly be called divine. The Scriptures, in fact do say this [Ps. 82:6, "I said, 'You are gods'; you are all sons of the Most High.'"]. Yet, of course, you are not divine in the same way as God himself is; he without origin or end is divine by nature. You, however, were brought into being from nothingness at a certain moment in time. Moreover, after God had created you with the almighty power of his love, you made yourself less than nothing through sin. Because of sin you have not deserved anything, but the all-merciful God lovingly re-created you in grace, making you, as it were, divine and one with him for time and eternity. Yet, though you are truly one with him through grace, you remain less than him by nature.[1]

For many of us, divinization may best be understood in terms of *glorification*. Glory is synonymous to
many with heaven and the mystical moments along the
way that give us a taste of glory. New Testament writers
used the term to denote the ultimate state of God's
children in Christ:

> Now if we are children, then we are heirs—heirs of
> God and co-heirs with Christ, if indeed we share in his
> sufferings in order that we may also share in his glory
> . . . and those he predestined, he also called; those he
> called, he also justified; those he justified, he also glori-
> fied. (Ro. 8:17, 30)

"Then the righteous will shine like the sun in the
kingdom of their Father," said Jesus in Matthew 13:43.
And John the Apostle scratches his head at the mystery
of God's love,

> How great is the love the Father has lavished on us,
> that we should be called children of God! And that is
> what we are! . . . now we are children of God, and what
> we will be has not yet been made known. But we know
> that when he appears, we shall be like him, for we shall
> see him as he is. (1 John 3:1-2)

Why do you think the choir sings "Glory, Glory,
Hallelujah!" and "When the Saints Go Marching In"?
Don't make divinization more complicated than it has
to be. Warren Wiersbe, in *Back to the Bible*, brings glorification down to this basic notion:

> When the Child of God
> Looks into the Word of God
> And sees the Son of God,
> He [or she] is changed by the Spirit of God
> Into the Image of God
> For the Glory of God.

For folks who have never heard the term, *divinization*
sounds suspiciously like divination. At my first hear-

ing, divinization sounded like a New Age spiritual pig-in-a-poke until it finally dawned on me: Why they're just talking about glorification!

Divination (unlike divinization) is the occult practice of manipulating the spirits into revealing the future or other truths known only to those in the other world. It is a practice rooted in Jewish apocalyptic and Greek traditions. Divination is unfettered Dazzlement. It is awe at the power of the spiritual. Related dazzling phenomena include the psychic, paranormal, extra-sensory perception, and clairvoyance.

A consensus of classical and modern Christian writers on spiritual development is that these powers may accompany spiritual growth but are not necessary for it. Furthermore, these abilities may be used for evil as well as good. Paul downplayed supernatural abilities. Teresa and John placed little stock in them, believing they could be demonically inspired as well as divinely produced.

Part of my personal fondness for the term *glorification* lies in its ability to remind me that the goal of spiritual growth is the glory of God. A spirituality not based on a Discipleship of wanting nothing but the will of God is a misbegotten journey into self-delusion and megalomania.

Divinization, on the other hand, is union with Christ. It is partaking of the divine nature. In teaching divinization, Clement drew heavily from the biblical teachings on participation in the divine nature as a way of counteracting the pagan notions of the divinization of their Greek heroes, such as Hercules, who became a god by choosing the hard life of virtue. Unlike Hercules, a mortal who became divine, Jesus Christ is God becoming fully human as a way to reveal to us both the otherwise unknowable nature of God and the nature of true humanity. In the Christian tradition, divinization is not about becoming God, but becoming godly.

His divine power has given us everything we need
for life and godliness through our knowledge of him
who called us by his own glory and goodness. Through
these he has given us his very great and precious
promises, so that through them you may participate in
the divine nature and escape the corruption in the
world caused by evil desires. (2 Pet. 1:3-4)

Knowing and Loving

Unable are the Loved to die
For Love is Immortality,
Nay, it is Deity—
Unable are they that Love—to die
For Love reforms Vitality
Into Divinity.

Emily Dickinson (809)[2]

My college philosophy professor spoke of "getting
down to the bottom of things." When he got down to the
bottom of things, he found no God. I didn't quite grasp
his concept until years later when, in a dark night of
disillusionment, I got down to the bottom of things in
my life. There I lost the God of my illusions. Nothing
made sense in this life where pain and suffering co-exist
with goodness. But I did find one single golden thread
of faith in that crucible. Though this life made no sense,
God in Christ gets down into the senselessness with me.
That is a God I can believe in. Not a God who offers a
tight package of explanation, but a God who loves
enough to participate in the human experience. That is
love. And because of that in-fleshed love, I can then
participate in the divine experience through knowing
the love of God.

What we come to know of the otherwise unknowable God is love. In the midst of his well-known chapter
on love, Paul speaks of the full knowledge we shall
attain of God in contrast to the partial knowledge we

now have: "Now we see but a poor reflection; then we shall see face to face . . . Now I know in part; then I shall know fully . . ." (1 Cor. 13:12). But, as Paul went on to write to the Corinthians in another letter, this fuller knowledge is not just to be experienced in our future state, but in this present life: "And we, who with unveiled faces all reflect the Lord's glory, are being transformed into his likeness with ever-increasing glory" (3:18). "Reflect," in this verse can also be translated "contemplate." Thus McGinn sees a linking of contemplation and the restoring of the image of God in us: "that it is by contemplation of the glory of the risen Christ that the image of God in us . . . is being conformed to the Word, the Father's perfect Image."[3]

Daniel Helminiak, in *Spiritual Development*, describes divinization as taking on the characteristics of the divine. We do not take on all the characteristics of God, but only two—knowing and loving—to a certain extent.

Helminiak makes a number of logical points about divinization. We as created humans cannot become God, though the uncreated God became a human. As Christ was human and yet had divine characteristics of knowing and loving, so we humans may share in those characteristics. The concept of human divinization is not understandable since it presupposes something beyond human ability, but it can be accepted by faith.[4]

This brings us to what John of the Cross and the whole tradition of the dark night is all about, coming to a point in faith that goes beyond knowing. Divinization is a transformation to a state that we cannot conceptualize now.

Drawing heavily from Bernard Lonergan, Helminiak sees spiritual development as constantly unfolding the basic human quest for truth and goodness in the process of *authentic self-transcendence*. Sounding similar to a journey that begins in Distraction and Dazzlement, he locates the starting point of the process with the "primordial curiosity or wonder."

In the awe of my experience, I become aware of realities beyond myself (transcendence). In responding to these realities in a way consistent with my understanding of them and my sense of self, I become authentic. So, the dynamic is an ongoing tension between awareness and response. I transcend myself to the extent that I become aware of what is beyond me, ask questions about it; discover if it is so or not. Then, in my response-ability to what I know, I decide what I am going to do about it. If my actions are in keeping with who I am and what I know, then I achieve another facet of self-transcendence: authenticity.

But, here's the catch. My response may not be an authentic one—or what I commit myself to may not be authentic—and my self-transcendence becomes an inauthentic self-transcendence. These are the major concerns of Discipleship: knowing and doing the right thing in commitment to the true reality.

So much of what we identify as self may actually not be so, but as John insisted, merely attachment of self to things, even righteous things or good things. While Helminiak rejects the notions of "deeper self," or "true self," "inner" or "outer" selves and contends there is only one self that is lived either authentically or inauthentically—yet we may misidentify or mistrust what appears to us as reality. Becoming aware of significant illusions about our self and our world usually precipitates a dark night of Disillusionment.

Several years ago, I had been reading Helminiak's book when I attended a seminar on grief. The hosts were unable to get the teleconference equipment to function, so Debbie James, R.N., the education coordinator for the event, agreed to pinch hit with a presentation based on her master's thesis on near-death experiences. It was an amazing synchronicity with what I was reading at the time. In her research from interviews with six hundred patients, a corollary emerged out of these conversations concerning their experiences: while out-of-body, they had a sense of *unlimited knowledge and love!*

While knowing and loving are key attributes of divinization, love is the primary force in our growth in godliness. And the knowing is more of an unknowing, as described in the *Cloud of Unknowing*, in which we come to understand that it is not by the power of intellectual understanding that we can attain an experience of God, "By love God may be touched and embraced, never by thought."[5] And for Merton, "The life of the soul is not knowledge, it is love."

I therefore surrender my struggle to comprehend divinization to the wisdom of the old hymn: "We'll understand it better by and by."

* * *

This tension between knowing and loving is reflected in two major movements of spirituality today, the deeper life and the contemplative movements, to borrow the designations of Gary Furr.[6] Deeper life proponents define spirituality in discursive terms typical for Discipleship: knowing and doing the will of God. They prescribe Bible study and prayer as means of discerning God's will and developing a godly character. Contemplatives, on the other hand, focus on being in God, self-awareness, and interior growth. They may pray utilizing their Bible as a way of communing with God. Paradoxically, one is about fruits while the other is about roots. Discipleship is about growing up, while contemplation is growing down.

I suggest the different sides of this polarity are not two extremes, but merely two aspects of the spiritual journey. Like the rain forests, it is what grows up—the branches, leaves, and vines and all the ecosystems that are supported by this up growth—that produces the

byproducts that fall to the forest floor, enriching the soil
for down growth. There is the Discipleship aspect of
getting into the method of serving God—of getting God
into one's life—and there is the contemplative aspect of
getting into God. One is the natural foundation of the
other; and the latter the natural outgrowth of the former.
This is the main thesis of this book. Too often, however,
disciples continue to define the deeper life in a way that
is unnecessarily shallow. Conversely, a true contemplative life bears fruit in response-able action in the world—
a contemplative life that lacks loving service is what
Teresa referred to as "castles in the air."

Salvation, as taught to me on the Baptist knees of my
spiritual mothers and fathers, entails three broad movements: justification, sanctification, and glorification. Past-
tense salvation, present-tense salvation, and future-tense
salvation. You have been saved. You are being saved.
You will be saved.

Justification is a transaction, a passive response to
grace; Distraction. God gets our attention and we accept
the invitation. Come to my party, God compels. Justification is a legal term. Through grace we are made right
with God. It is a conversion from our self-willed life to a
God-willed life. Paul describes the process in Ephesians,
"For it is by grace you have been saved, through faith—
and this not from yourselves, it is the gift of God—not
by works, so that no one can boast" (2:8-9).

Sanctification is a collaborative process: our working with God in living out the new nature we are
endowed with at conversion. In fact, sanctification—
being made a saint or holy one—is an ongoing series of
conversions. "For we are God's workmanship, created
in Christ Jesus to do good works, which God prepared
in advance for us to do . . . that you, being rooted and
established in love, may have power, together with all
the saints, to grasp how wide and long and high and
deep is the love of Christ" (2:10; 3:17-18). Sanctification

is about the moment-to-moment decisions we make to live authentically or inauthentically. This is Discipleship—the discursive life—knowing and doing the will of God.

But, even our own collaborative actions can only carry us so far. We come to the end of ourselves eventually. The work that God initially began, God ultimately finishes: "Those he justified, he also glorified" (Ro. 8:30). *Glorification* is the fulfillment of our longings for union with God. John called it the passive night. It is something God does in us as we allow. It is not something we do, it is something we become. It is not just knowing the love of God, it is being the love of God: "that you may be filled to the measure of all the fullness of God . . . Now to him who is able to do immeasurably more than all we ask or imagine, according to his power that is at work within us, to him be glory . . ." (3:19-21).

Being Fully Human

Our destiny in Christ is not about becoming God but becoming fully human. The most divine act of God is becoming human, the mystics say.

The development of true humanness can be seen as a three-fold process. First, there is *human knowing,* where we gain an awareness of our humanity. So much of religion is about denying our humanity: our bodies, our sexuality, our hungers and desires. Spirituality is about claiming who we are, not suppressing it.

The second step is *human doing.* Once aware, we become more intentional in our humanness. What this means to me is living humanly on purpose. Rather than human qualities being an afterthought or accidental lapse in our piety, to live well is to add richness and meaningfulness to our living and relating. It is what Thomas Moore calls soulfulness, which "is not about cutting ourselves off from our problems and symptoms, but about embracing the full experience of being human."[7]

The third step is *human being:* connecting who we are with who God is. This is seeing the divine in ourselves. Dazzlement is when we are in awe of God. Divinization is when we are in awe of who we are becoming. We have this hope in our very being, in our *Imago Dei.*

Ireneaus made a distinction between our being created in the image of God (*imago*) and being created in the likeness of God (*similitudo*). Through the fall, we have lost our likeness to God, namely our immortality, but not the natural image, because it is this natural image that makes us human.

Unlike the Platonic view of the created material world as evil, the Judeo-Christian view, according to Tillich, is that humans were created good but have fallen by our own choice. Humans, "who [are] mortal by nature [were] supposed to become immortal through obedience to God, remaining in paradise and participating in the food of the gods, in the tree of life." Immortality must be received as a gift, said Tillich, from the realm of the eternal.

Ever since I was a child, I heard my pastors talk about God's "plan of salvation." I imagine this concept likely originated with Irenaeus and his view of history as *recaptilulatio,* or recapitulation—the history of salvation. History, for Irenaeus, is about the unfolding story of our estrangement from God and God's saving initiatives. Through the first Adam we inherited our fallen state—our mortality. But through Christ, the second Adam, the fulfillment of all that humans were to become is achieved.

> The childish innocence of Adam has been lost; but the second Adam can become what he was to become, fully human. And we can become fully human through participation in this full humanity which has appeared

in Christ. This includes eternal life, similitude with God with respect to participation in infinity.[8]

In reflecting on our participation in this full humanity and the mystery that John the Apostle referred to "what we will be has not yet been made known,"Flora Slosson Wuellner wonders:

> What immensities and depths will be revealed in us as we increasingly enter into not only the love of God, but also the indescribable mystery of God?
>
> Already we know, even on this earth, that we use only a tiny percent of the total capacity of our brains. Already we have experienced our amazing capacity for creative work, for clear, efficient thinking in an emergency situation. What sorts of giants are sleeping within us? What mysterious powers lurk there? What will happen if they get out?
>
> We feel this fear with special poignancy if we are not yet in touch with or aware of a strong, central identity within us that can set reasonable day-by-day goals for ourselves and maintain healthy boundaries as we grow and relate to others. Is it this lack of awareness of the inner guiding power that makes us so afraid that we will go, and grow, out of control once we start growing?[9]

A helpful distinction for me at this point is between our actualization as being open to our unimaginable potential, on the one hand, and *authenticity* as being true to ourselves, on the other hand. In the language of humanistic psychology, human growth leads ultimately to self-actualization. An actualization by oneself, however, is not the same as an actualization of one's self. I'm not referring to an up-by-your-own-bootstraps self-improvement course. The transcendent focus of divinization reveals that the source of self-actualization is beyond the self. It is in God. Through Christ we can become more than who we are.

Paul located human authenticity "in Christ," his chief expression. It is through the incarnation of God in Jesus Christ that we have the vision of true humanity. Jesus taught us how to be human. And for William of St. Thierry, that humanity is the best reflection of the divine: "Know thyself . . . and you shall know me." It is a reflection in which we see the glory of God in our divinely-formed image.

> But we all, with open face beholding as in a glass the glory of the Lord, are changed into the same image from glory to glory, even as by the Spirit of the Lord. (2 Cor. 3:18 KJV).

Let the person who thirsts to see God clean their mirror, Richard of St. Victor suggested.

Authenticity begins with an awareness of who we are now and our ability to respond with integrity to the discoveries we make. Here again is the transcendent focus on what is beyond us: the revelation of God to us. All the serendipities of life can be viewed as the all-wise, self-revealing God bringing us to a point of awareness just at the moment we are ready to become aware. The teachable moment is a learnable moment. The Christian, according to Ruysbroeck, is resolved to this paradox of self-revelation and discovery "What we are, that we behold; and what we behold, that we are; for in this pure vision we are one life and one spirit with God."

For many Christians, the goal of the spiritual life is to transcend their humanity in the sense of being free from their bodily-ness and corporeality. "That was just my humanity," they say apologetically. To show God's love to the world, they believe, is to somehow step out of their skin. This is the pervasive Gnostic heresy that matter is evil and spirit good. This is an inauthentic self-transcendence. How odd that God's way of showing love to the world was to step *into* skin.

Self-actualization, it follows, is the vision of becoming love, of having the divine quality of unconditional love.

> . . . that you, being rooted and established in love, may have power, together with all the saints, to grasp how wide and long and high and deep is the love of Christ, and to know this love that surpasses knowledge that you may be filled to the measure of all the fullness of God. (Eph. 3:17-19)

Divinization as self-actualization is further portrayed in the biblical hope of the wise who "will shine like the brightness of the heavens, and those who lead many to righteousness, like the stars for ever and ever" (Dan. 12:3, cf. Phil. 2:14-16), whose destiny is to reign with Christ (Rev. 3:21) and to be like Christ (1 John 3:2).

In spite of all the language of glory, divinization looks very mundane. It is about being very human. Divinization begins with the acceptance of humanity— ours and Christ's. Divinization is sharing in some of the attributes of God—knowing and loving—but not in a supernatural way. We bear the image of God in a very natural way. "That which was from the beginning," John the Apostle remembers about Jesus' *natural* glory, is that "which we have heard, which we have seen with our eyes, which we have looked at and our hands have touched" (1 John 1:1).

Jesus is God with feet, hands, ears, eyes; a body of many members. And we become that body, said Paul in First Corinthians 12. It is this mystery of the body of Christ that Symeon the New Theologian, a tenth-century mystic, extolled in *Hymns of Divine Love.*

> We become members of Christ—and Christ becomes our members, Christ becomes my hand, Christ, my miserable foot; and I, unhappy one, am Christ's hand, Christ's foot!

It is truly a marriage which takes place, ineffable
and divine: God unites Himself with each one—yes, I
repeat it, it is my delight—and each becomes one with
the Master. If therefore, in your body, you have put on
the total Christ, you will understand without blushing
all that I am saying;[10]

The glory of God is found in the person who is fully
alive, said Irenaeus. Teresa was one of those fully alive
persons in whom the glory of God was found. She knew
how to connect faith with life, admires Tessa Bierlecki,
and the more we learn of her winsome qualities, the
more we are attracted to her vivacious faith. Bierlecki
notes that "there is an intimate and ineradicable connection between life and prayer. When we really live fully,
exuberantly, and divinely, we inevitably pray."[11]

In divinization the tension between the sensual and
spiritual is alive in divine ways as our passions meet the
passions of God who is not ashamed to be like us and
frees us from any shame of living the authentically
human life. Spirituality is about longing, money, food,
the ambiance of our living environment, art, relationships; becoming. Spirituality is about baths, clothes, and
dishes. Baths are not about cleansing our filthy flesh
from its perpetual corruption but grooming our bodies,
which are "fearfully and wonderfully made." Clothes
do not cover our shameful parts, but adorn our frames
with dignity and express our creative individuality.
Dishes are not mere conveyances of sustenance for our
metabolism, but means for honoring our life's richness,
for celebrating the flavors and spices of our sensual
palate, and for accommodating the uniquely human
ways we commune with the world.

Union with Christ: Being the Miracle

Love is most nearly itself
When here and now cease to matter.[12]

T.S. Eliot

Creation has no purpose but God's goodwill, states Moltmann in *Theology of Play*. Creation is not based on any need of God's, or else God would not be the self-sufficient, self-existent I AM THAT I AM. God has no need to reveal. God has no need for fellowship. It is God who says of Adam, "It is not good for man to be alone," not Adam who said of God, It is not good for God to be alone. The creation is meaningful, but not necessary—it serves no use whatsoever. It is *play*. It is of sheer desire.

Why are we here? Not to be useful, but to be. Why did God become human? Because of "uncaused love."

One of the grave illnesses of American spirituality is pragmatism: the belief that faith must provide some useful, practical purpose. Studies abound about the healing properties of prayer and worship. Religion will help you live longer, healthier, wealthier, and more successfully. We have no use for a useless religion. Give us the Giving Tree, not the Useless Tree.

When spirituality is used for some purpose, it has no purpose in itself. It is not God who helps us enjoy the world, Moltmann insists, but we who use the world to enjoy God. To enjoy God, for me, is the same as enjoying life, which is the epitome of the Christian journey.

Institutions have long sought to annex faith for institutional goals. State religion, or the state's use of religion, is still formally prevalent in many countries and informally prevalent in ours. Even churches, as institutions, often use faith to maintain themselves as institutions. Institutions eventually have their own survival as their chief mission; some are simply more honest about it than others.

The more we focus on institutions' need of us and allow ourselves to be co-opted to these institutional agendas, the more depressed, angry and fearful we may become. We become bearers of the institutional anxiety over its own potential demise. It becomes a symbiotic sadomasochism of both needing the other to survive

and ensuring that survival by domination and subjuga-
tion. And what is the threat that keeps us subjugated?
Death. Not death per se, but the fear of death as represented in all our attachments. You'll starve if you lose
your job. You won't be the same without this relationship. You'll go to hell if you leave the church. Without
these possessions, your life will become meaningless
and boring. And so goes the list of fears.

"The first thing liberated beings do is to enjoy their
freedom and playfully test their newfound opportunities and powers," observed Moltmann questioningly:
"Why are we seeing so little of this?"[13]

Why do we yet live as if bound to institutional
domination when Jesus died at the hands of institutional oppression and was resurrected as a Liberator
over it? The eternal Easter is life-as-rejoicing. Our attitude toward death, then, becomes mockery, as Paul
jeered at death with an Easter Hymn, "Where, O death,
is your victory? Where, O death, is your sting?" (1 Cor.
15:55). Moltmann longed for the spirit of orthodox Protestant pastors who began their Easter sermons with a
joke. "Easter indeed becomes the beginning of the rebellion of the liberated against the bonds of their slavery."[14]

Those favorable forces, which free us toward self-
actualization, and those hostile forces, which obstruct
us, Teilhard de Chardin refers to as *passivities of growth*
and *passivities of diminishment.* Birth and death are both
passive experiences to Teilhard, they happen to us—
they are given to us and received by us.

It is our response that determines whether these
gifts are authenticated or squandered. As Teilhard had
written earlier in his life,

> . . . the soul has hardly arrived at the heart of things,
> when if finds itself ready to be detached from them.
> Having taken its fill of the Universe and of itself, the
> soul one day discovers that it is possessed by an intense
> need to die to self and to be led beyond itself. Moreover,

this is not the effect of disillusionment, but rather results from a logical development of its own effort.[15]

What, then, is our response to life and death? *Amen,*
an ancient benediction which means "So be it," is an
acknowledging and receiving of God in the moment.
Says John, "Not only do we have to say *amen,* but we
must especially be *amen.*"[16]

Death is ultimate healing, the restoration of wholeness. It is in death that we receive our divinization, say
Nemeck and Coombs,

> Our personal death occurs when our past has com-
> pletely exhausted our future, and our entire life is now.
> Stripped of all our mortal limitations, we then fully
> encounter God who is pure Love . . . pure Light . . . and
> pure Spirit . . . Such divine love and light are engen-
> dered within us that their sheer intensity purges us in
> that instant of whatever is not transformable in God. In
> the moment of personal death, God's love so divinizes
> us that that very love consumes everything in us which
> has not yet been spiritualized. Death is the point where
> the two arms of God's all-embracing love meet, and our
> whole being and life end up fully transformed in God
> with nothing left to be purged.[17]

My life is not really mine. It is not of me, but given to
me. What is mine has been received, and what has been
received is destined by God for transformation. As John
states, "My self is given to me far more than it is formed
by me. In the ultimate analysis the interior life, life at its
source . . . completely eludes my grasp."[18]

This most interior life Teresa calls the seventh dwelling place. Here the soul, "In the extreme interior, in
some place very deep within itself, the nature of which
it doesn't know how to explain . . . perceives this divine
company."[19]

It is before this Life within our life that we must
stand in sheer honesty, in bare vulnerability and grate-
ful openness. In this transformative awareness of life-

as-gift, we self-transcend into a consciousness of one-ness with God. It is not so much that God is *in us*, but that we are in God. Conforming into the image of God gives way to a transformation *into* divinity, akin to what the Quakers call "centering down."

Divinization is the sense that God is in us and we are in God and all things are in God. It is the union of our true self with the true Christ.

The seventh dwelling place, for Teresa, is a trans-forming marriage to God. Drawing from the mystical tradition of seeing marriage as symbolic of God's rela-tionship with us, John refers to First Corinthians 6:17, "he who unites himself with the Lord is one with him in spirit." The marriage metaphor was commonly used by Paul in this way, such as in Ephesians 5:31-32, "'For this reason a man will leave his father and mother and be united to his wife, and the two will become one flesh.' This is a profound mystery—but I am talking about Christ and the church."

In John's *The Spiritual Canticle,* stanza 22, "The bride has entered the sweet garden of her desire." Based on the imagery of the *Song of Songs,* John explains this verse as "like saying: She has been transformed into her God." "The union wrought between the two natures," he continues, ". . . is such that even though neither changes its being, both appear to be God."[20]

The log becomes indistinguishable from the fire, says John. "The very fire of love that afterward is united with the soul, glorifying it, is what previously assailed it by purging it, just as the fire that penetrates a log of wood . . . so that it can be penetrated and transformed into the fire."[21]

And for Teresa,

> Oh, knot that binds
> Two so different . . .
> Bind the one without being
> With being unending[22]

This union, for Wesley, is "the Great Privilege of those that are born of God," to receive the breath of God and return that breath to God.

For Moltmann, in *The Spirit of Life,* Wesley captures the essence of divinization: "a divine act through which God chooses something for himself and makes it his own, thus letting it participate in his nature." "God is continually breathing, as it were, upon the soul, and the soul is breathing unto God," Wesley is quoted. But, unlike Wesley and most orthodox theologians who envision the Spirit from above, Moltmann maintains that the Spirit comes to us "from below," from the human level—from within our experience of life.[23] The spiritual breath and the bodily incarnation of that breath are a mutual revelation of God: the breath enables the spoken word which resonates the breath.

"God is a Word that speaks itself," wrote Meister Eckhart. "The Father is a speaking work, and the Son is speech working . . . To the extent that I am close to God, so to that extent God utters himself into me."[24]

This union of breath and breathing is the movement from discursive prayer to contemplative prayer. Discursive prayer is talking to God. Contemplative prayer is being in God. The movement of divinization is *from* praying, to *being* prayed, to being *prayer.*

I grew up with the rich tradition of the centrality of the Word of God. We read it, preached it, sang it, prayed with it, argued about it, and sometimes came dangerously close to worshiping it as we sought to incarnate it. We believed the Word became flesh and dwelt among us. So, for me, the great question of life is How to incarnate the Living Word in my life?

One of my favorite Old Testament images is that of Elijah meeting God on Mount Horeb. A great wind tore the mountains apart, but God was not in the wind. Then came an earthquake, but God was not in the earthquake. After that a fire. But God was not in the fire. And after the fire came a gentle whisper. Then Elijah heard the Word of the Lord.

One of my favorite New Testament images of God is that "the Spirit intercedes for us with groans that words cannot express."

I've come to believe that if I hear God's Word at all, it is in gentle whispers and wordless groans; and, if I incarnate the Word of God at all, it is in providing a listening presence in which another soul can perhaps hear the gentle whispers of the Spirit. There is a mystery in that moment—when the Word listens and the listener becomes the Word.

It is illusionary to speak in terms of "my life" or "your life." It is not *our* life, but the life of God in us that we speak. I am an observer of and listener to the life of God in me and in you. Therefore, the basic Christian disposition toward others is reverence. It is an awareness of the oneness of all things. It is the breath of God's life that dwells in you and me and all living things. Paul expressed this in his many references to greeting one another with a holy kiss. More than just a custom, the holy kiss conveyed an honor and affection, and an acknowledgment of the divine breath. In rabbinical legend, Moses died with the kiss of God on his lips. It is from God and to God that our life-breath flows.

* * *

My great-great-grandmother was a six-foot tall widow, among the first white folks to settle in Comanche County, Texas in the 1880s. A historical marker today in DeLeon acknowledges the history behind her legend. Aunt Fanny Brown was a healer, midwife, rancher and source of spiritual strength to a sparsely-settled community and to a family of Browns, of which the men were typically either weak-minded, unruly, or both. With a bullwhip in her strong hand, she feared neither men nor the panthers, which occasionally approached her on her long rides to deliver a baby or serve as a frontier hospice nurse for the dying.

Strapped for water by those frequent west Texas droughts, Aunt Fanny began digging a well using her apron to carry dirt. Legend has it that after hitting solid rock at twenty-five feet, she abandoned the project to care for a homeless family with scarlet fever. As it turned out, one of the men was a "Powder Monkey" and used some of her black powder to blast through the rock, breaching the aquifer below.

With my tall frame, I bear the image of Aunt Fanny (*Imago Brown*). It's no wonder I chose ministry in a health care setting as a vocation. Her spiritual legacy lives in me with Baptist roots that run deep in Texas soil, rock and all. Reminiscent of Teresa's four waters, Aunt Fanny teaches me much about prayer. Prayer is about going deep and connecting to the Source of Life. Words are not enough; we need the dynamic of the Spirit to go the distance. We begin the prayer, but God finishes it. The process begins with receiving the water of Life and moves to our becoming the water of Life to others.

One With Nature

> For since the creation of the world God's invisible qualities—his eternal power and divine nature—have been clearly seen, being understood from what has been made . . . (Romans 1:20).

> [Christ] is the image of the invisible God, the first-born over all creation. For by him all things were created . . . all things were created by him and for him. He is before all things, and in him all things hold together (Colossians 1:15-17).

The ancient practice of meditating on a Scripture passage—the *Lectio Divina*—can be expanded by "reading" nature. M. Basil Pennington, while emphasizing the special qualities of praying the Scriptures, remembers that nature is also the text of God's revelation.

> The whole of creation bespeaks its Maker. As the Greeks would say, the whole of creation is full of *logoi*, "little words," that give expression to the Logos, the Word . . . Yes, all that the Word has made and keeps on making bespeaks the Word and is to be heard, if we have but the listening.[25]

Teresa echoes the age-old maxim that "the Creator must be sought through creatures," and in spite of her ascetical emphasis, which led to an impugning of all things material, she allows a rejoicing "in considering God's creatures and the power He had in creating them."[26]

"Apprehend God in all things, for God is in all things," advises Meister Eckhart. "Every single creature is full of God and is a book about God."[27] A "nonverbal book," for Richard J. Foster:

> So give your attention to the created order. Look at the trees, really look at them. Take a flower and allow its beauty and symmetry to sink deep into your mind and heart. Listen to the birds—they are the messengers of God. Watch the little creatures that creep upon the earth. These are humble acts, to be sure, but sometimes God reaches us profoundly in these simple ways if we will quiet ourselves to listen."[28]

Nature asks us to simplify. An earthy life is a basic life, a life of balance and ground. A natural life is based on the lessons of the earth's rhythms and seasons, boundaries of water and land, sky and canyon, time and timelessness; birth and death. It is, as Annie Dillard reveals in *Pilgrim at Tinker Creek*, a receiving the present.

> My God, I look at the creek. It is the answer to Merton's prayer, "Give us time!" It never stops. If I seek the senses and skill of children, the information of a thousand books, the innocence of puppies, even the

insights of my own city past, I do so only, solely, and entirely that I might look well at the creek. You don't run down the present, pursue it with baited hooks and nets. You wait for it, empty-handed, and you are filled. You'll have fish left over. The creek is the one great giver. It is, by definition, Christmas, the incarnation. This old rock planet gets the present for a present on its birthday everyday.[29]

Divinization terms our oneness with the Creator, in creating and being a part of the created whole. The dark night strips us of attachments that have sequestered us in the illusion that we are over-and-apart from the whole and releases us to the grandeur of being in the whole, just as a dark, clear night hundreds of miles from civilization releases the Milky Way to display its glory and our glory in being a necessary part of such a grand universe. It is a universe, which comes alive to us in the nearest of limbs and blades; a mysticism—speaks Dillard—of our participation in the divine calling to be.

One day I was walking along Tinker Creek thinking of nothing at all and I saw the tree with the lights in it. I saw the backyard cedar where the mourning doves roost charged and transfigured, each cell buzzing with flame. I stood on the grass with the lights in it, grass that was wholly fire, utterly focused and utterly dreamed. It was less like seeing than like being for the first time seen, knocked breathless by a powerful glance . . . I had been my whole life a bell, and never knew it until at that moment I was lifted and struck.[30]

By participating in nature we become participants in the divine nature. Our participatory divinity grants us the nature of an unashamed soul, celebrating our very existence; a gift to the world. That shameless is-ness, for Meister Eckhart, proclaims our glory, "Now the moment I flowed out from the Creator all creatures stood up and shouted: 'Behold, here is God!'"[31] Claiming our station in God's heart is to commune with the family of all God's creations, of which we are not least or greatest, but simply a part; a member. Our place in God is not found in withdrawing from the world, Eckhart insists, but by being most present in it.

> Such persons find far greater merit with God because they grasp everything as divine and as greater than things in themselves are. Truly, to this belong zeal and love and a clear apprehension of their own inwardness, and a lively, true, prudent and real knowledge of what their disposition is concerned with amid things and persons. We cannot learn this by running away, by shunning things and shutting ourselves up in an external solitude; but we must practice a solitude of the spirit, wherever or with whomever we are. We must learn to break through things and to grasp our God in them and to form God in ourselves powerfully in an essential manner.[32]

Our communion with nature is an act of worship and sanctification. In Christ, God came to our world, taking on its substance. Or so it seems. To envision the spiritual God donning human flesh is to see incarnation from a limited perspective. This makes Jesus different from the rest of us in respect to his humanity and his incarnation a sort of hiatus in the natural order. Jesus came not to break the natural order but to reveal God in it. In his baptism, Jesus immersed himself in the fluid of our existence. In his crucifixion, Jesus offers us his flesh and blood for food, that we may eat and drink full humanity. As believer priests we offer to God our communion with the world and our place in it as proclaimers of its being in God.

Moltmann locates the presence of God in the world as God's participation in human suffering. This relationship of heaven and earth is not the Neoplatonic dualism between matter and spirit that depicts a gap between Creator and creatures, but rather the specifically Christian doctrine of creation based on the incarnation of the Son and the indwelling Spirit. "In Christ's death on the cross, God took evil, sin and rejection on himself, transforming it into goodness, grace and election in the sacrifice of his infinite love. All evil, all sin, suffering and damnation is 'in God.'" The Spirit has been poured out on all flesh (Acts 2:17) and now the creation is alive with the power of God's love.[33] It is for this unity that all creation has groaned (Ro. 8:22).

Therefore, Moltmann envisions spiritual development occurring along five points of growth, which occur on a horizontal level on earth rather than a vertical level between heaven and earth.

1. Action and meditation
2. Meditation and contemplation
3. Contemplation and mystical union
4. Mysticism and discipleship
5. The vision of the world in God

Discipleship, for Moltmann, is virtually synonymous with martyrdom. Similar to the first century early church father Ignatius of Antioch, who viewed mystical union as attaining God in death, specifically the death of martyrdom, Moltmann sees the cloister cell as preparatory for the prison cell. The dark night is not just about the purification of the soul, but sharing in the sufferings of Christ. John's dark night was not just an introspective journey: it was imprisonment. For Thérèse of Lisieux, "her experience of dying in the absence of God links the mysticism centered on Christ with martyrdom and with everyday life. Believers are not simply the passive recipients of the fruits of Christ's passion. They are counted worthy to suffer with Christ, so that like him they may become fruitful for the kingdom of God . . ."[34]

> The person who believes that God is to be found in the Godforsakeness of the crucified Jesus believes that he sees God everywhere, in all things; just as after we have experienced what death is like, we experience life

more intensely every moment, because every moment seems unique.

This vision of God's world is alive in the experience of the persecuted and the martyrs who feel God's presence in prison. It is alive in the mystics, who find God's presence in the dark night of the soul. It shines in the devotion of the simple, to whom God is present in the darkness of the lived moment.[35]

In her youth, Teresa's desire in life was to be a martyr at the hands of the Moors. She was likely influenced in this regard by Kabbalistic beliefs and teachings upon which she based so much of the imagery of the *Interior Castle*. In the *Zohar* mystical union was depicted as a marriage with the *Shekhinah* of God at death. For Teresa, the mystical experiences of oneness with God along the way are the "wounds of love" and "little deaths," which are a foretaste in this life of our fully-divinized state in the next.

This view that we attain a divinized divine nature at death may be based, in part, on Paul's elaboration on our eternal state in First Corinthians 15:44 in which he indicates that our natural bodies are transformed into spiritual bodies.

All creation is moving toward spiritualization, according to Teilhard. We are created as *becoming*, with all creation moving toward the Omega Point of becoming Christ. He termed it *Christogenesis*—matter is evolving into spirit—the *Christification* of matter. What Nemeck and Coombs call "the spiritual direction of creation" is reflected in the biblical syllogism: "The Word *became* flesh and bestowed upon us the power to become children of God (John 1:14,12), so that in him we become a new creation (2 Cor. 5:17)."[36] "Our personal death . . . is our salvific moment *par excellence*," Nemeck and Coombs conclude.

> . . . only in death does each of us become fully human. Until death, we are becoming human. In death, we

attain the completion of our individual humanity and personality . . . the "moment" in our lives above all others of maximum consciousness, optimum freedom, definitive decision and perfect encounter with god.

. . . Death is an integral part of our life. It is essential to life at its fullest. Death is the point of transition between the two basic modes of our one life in Christ Jesus: mortal and immortal . . .[37]

Inasmuch as we live fully humanly, we embody Christ. Divinization, though an ultimate reality, is experienced in our most mortal moments, in our most fleshly encounters with the whole of creation. We can look forward to an eternal existence beyond our deepest abilities to imagine. Yet, we are now in the midst of life—a life becoming. To reiterate my three-fold progression of spiritual development toward divinization: first, we awaken to creation, then we come to worship the Creator; and ultimately we become creators—as a part of creation, as all creation is in God—we become co-creators.

The future is now. While so much of the present is lived simply carrying out plans made in the past, our present lives much more reflect our visions of the future—future stories both of grace and that which works against grace. A past that obstructs a free future works against grace. Grace is the gift of the present, a free present in which we may create with God a future worth living into. The purpose of history, says Moltmann, is to give us a future.

Through our experience of the history of the world as a history of passion do we become painfully aware of the moments of this future which as prevision, foretaste, and preplay of a totally-other reaches into our mortal life. For this reason we find pain and happiness, suffering and love, hope and mourning, so closely tied together that one cannot be without the other.[38]

In Christ, our future is not merely time, but eternity. "The man who through suffering is aware of the endlessness of time can love eternity of which he has received a foretaste in unending joy."[39]

How are our grace-ful future stories constructed, and how may our grace-less future stories be deconstructed? Utilizing the concepts of linguistic systems theory, Andrew Lester points us to the spoken word—that our futures are created in conversation. "Rather than assuming that social systems create language and symbols, this theory claims the reverse, that language and communication create the social system . . . we construct the realities that shape our existence through [language] . . ."[40]

But, the spoken word is in some ways the essence of divinization: the paradox between the spirit-breath enabling speaking the word which resonates the breath. Creation, proclaims Genesis, was *spoken* into existence: "And God said, Let there be . . ." When we speak about our future, we participate in the divine creative activity. Perhaps this is one meaning of the cryptic statement of Jesus to Peter in Matthew 16:19, "I will give you the keys of the kingdom of heaven; whatever you bind on earth will be bound in heaven, and whatever you loose on earth will be loosed in heaven." It is through our inbreathed futures that we bind or loose ourselves.

Again, divinization does not mean that we attain divinity, but that we participate in certain divine characteristics: knowing and loving. When we speak authentically what we know, when we speak authentically our love, we co-create with God a future that transcends the present moment and our present limitations. We become the prayer that God answers.

About four in the morning I awoke to a carried-over frustration from yesterday's Friday-at-work. I felt frustrated that I was lying awake disturbed about something rather than slumbering away like my wife beside me. Feeling stressed, tired, and empty, I scolded myself for not attending more to my soul. In my twilight sleepiness I let my imagination go in a prayerful return to some perspective in life and found myself in outer space.

Some of my favorite contemplative images are views of outer space. It is as if meditating on outer space gets me into inner space. There is something about the expanse of the night sky and my knowledge that what I see when I look up at the stars, or ponder the latest view from the Hubble telescope, is only an infinite fraction of what is to be known or seen of the universe. That almost immediately and profoundly places me in a mystical state. A sense of the infinite handwork of an infinite God out there and the infinite presence of an imminent God within me coming together in a richness of awe, amazement, and love.

The galaxy of my world stretched out before me; swirling clouds of stars. Then swirling clouds of galaxies. Soon, from my mystical vantage point, I beheld the universe in all its cohesiveness and entirety as, I often fantasize, a round orb. My spatial image met a temporal twin when I began to imagine, from the standpoint of infinity, the expansion of the universe from one single point in space to its full form, and then its contraction over a similar mind-boggling breadth of time back into that single point. A constant recurrent exploding and imploding so quickly to the view of the eternal eye that the universe pulsated as a single point of dazzling light, much as an incandescent light bulb pulsates with sixty cycles of electricity a second, appearing as a constant beam of luminescence.

There before me was all that is spatially and temporally in this one point of light, hanging in the air like a cottonwood seed floats in the warm humid air of Texas summers. This bright, white, delicate, and downy seed lay rested and admired in the hand of a young boy, sitting in a pasture of soft grasses. In the purest of all innocent benevolence and the sheerest of all curiosity, the boy blew the seed into the air from his inverted flat hand and watched its course.

Into the currents of the breeze drifted the seed light until it rested in the soil of the grassy pasture. Germinating into a seedling, it soon grew into a magnificent tree with the smoothest of low branches, which stretched to the sun. On these branches climbed the playful child as the air was filled with airborne seeds of light, which likewise found their footing and produced a huge forest where seeds blew and the boy played.

Divinization and Community

Divinization is about embracing life and community with zest and hope. We become Christ in the world. We become Christ to others and they become Christ to us. It is an other-centered way of relating because it is a God-centered way of living. It is not self-denial; it is self-transcendence. It is not self-negating; it is authenticity.

Our journey in relationship to community may take either of the two historical paths to divinization, according to Deborah Hanus. The movement of immanence positions us in the center of community, immersed in the social milieu. From the center we participate as *part of* the members of the community.

The movement of transcendence pushes us to the edge where we speak—prophetically—from our solitude as *apart from* the community.

Jesus embodied both of these movements. He often drew away from the crowds and even withdrew for a forty-day fast in the wilderness. From those retreats, he returned with a clear word to the world—differentiated, powerful, and clean-cutting.

On the other hand, he was often the life of the party, right in the center of the crowd. Approachable, touchable, reachable, and empathically affected, Jesus rubbed shoulders with sinners, priests, children, women—anyone in his presence.

In our "Christification" we also may find both the need to withdraw in contemplative solitude and the passion to engage in the most intimate and public of relationships.

Divinization is not an outgrowing of discursive devotion and the disciplines of discipleship; but rather the outgrowth. The footings of discipleship must be maintained. When I lead retreats or classes in contemplation, I like to conclude the series of lessons or experiences with an emphasis on old-fashioned devotion: a piety of regular Bible reading, prayer, and the methods of spiritual routines. My more contemplative friends remind me by their simple actions of the value of meal-time prayer, systematic readings, intercession, and church involvement.

In the individualistic journey of the spiritual life, many of us tend to become only marginally connected with a religious community. In fact, being on the fringe feels about right. But this kind of do-it-yourself-by-yourself spirituality was virtually unknown to the earliest Christians. The deeper consciousness of the presence of God for them was most likely experienced in the life of the *ekklesia*—the New Testament term for church, literally the "called out ones."

> Let us hold unswervingly to the hope we profess, for he who promised is faithful. And let us consider how we may spur one another on toward love and good deeds. Let us not give up meeting together, as some are in the habit of doing, but let us encourage one another . . . (Heb. 10:23-25)

At this point I wish not to get caught in defending the "institutional church" or "organized religion." What is "church," in its basic form, but community? What is it that enhances soulfulness in the institutions and ambiance of a community? In community, divinization is about the continual in-breathing of the renewing Spirit into structures and organizations.

While the Spirit is a Comforter, the Spirit also convicts. A church, biblically, both comforts by attending to the needs of people and also disturbs its community by challenging injustice and institutional oppression and corruption.

Ironically, it is often the churches that emphasize discursive spirituality and its concomitant evangelistic zeal that provide the most well-funded and potent social services to the community. Too often, the contemplative life is paralleled with personal introversion and detachment. It becomes a comfortable spirituality of self-exploration.

While social activism is the natural outgrowth of contemplation, as Teresa insisted and Merton demonstrated, it is an authentically self-transcendent activism that truly represents Christ to the world. Activists who serve out of their own need to be needed, Moltmann warns, "will only pass on . . . the infection of their own egoism, the aggression caused by their own anxiety, and the prejudices of their own ideology."[41]

To ask with Paul, How can we believe in the one of whom we have not heard (Ro. 10:14)? "That which we have heard," John the Apostle answers, "which we have seen with our eyes, which we have looked at and our hands have touched—this we proclaim concerning the Word of life" (1 John 1:1).

The journey begins as we see Christ's true selfhood and love in others. We may not call it Christ, we may not know it to be Christ, but in the Dazzlement of that beautiful Christ, we come to have a relationship with that which is beyond us, which has come from beyond into our world. In that relationship, Christ becomes more than a guiding principle or method for success. Christ becomes a reality when all else comes to be seen as illusion. In Christ we find ourselves and to Christ we lose ourselves in a cosmic romance. And in the world we become Christ to others.

Prayer of Destiny

Christ has no body now but yours;
No hands, no feet on earth, but yours.
Yours are the eyes through which
He looks with compassion on this world;
Yours are the feet with which
He walks to do good;
Yours are the hands with which
He blesses all the world.
Christ has no body now on earth but yours.

Attributed to Teresa of Avila

Reflection

How human is your Christ? What aspect of your humanity could Christ not have assumed? This is the part of you that needs healing (saving). In what ways is Christ coming to you with "healing on His wings"? (Mal. 4:2)

How do you imagine yourself being in heaven? What will be different or the same?

What was a recent experience of feeling that what you really wanted and what God really wanted was the same?

In what ways are "you" and Christ interchangeable? "Others" and Christ?

Discipleship is about growing up, while contemplation is grown down. Discuss these two movements in your life.

Can spirituality be private? In what ways does the call to become fully human stretch you?

If you really believed and accepted the fact that you are in God (rather than only that God is in you), how might your vision change?

How does Christ romance you? How do you romance Christ?

When was the last time of "read" nature? Pick some "simple" item of nature-a weed, a bug. What does God reveal of God's self-or of yourself-to you through this creation?

As a believer priest, what do you most often offer to God on your chalice?

In you family, workplace, community, what graceful story are you able to construct? What grace-less story are you required to deconstruct?

Endnotes

1   *Cloud*, p. 135.
2   From *Complete Poems of Emily Dickinson* (1955)
3   *Foundations*, p. 71.
4   Daniel Helminiak, *Spiritual Development: And Interdiscipli-nary Study*, (Chicago: Loyola University Press, 1986), pp. 22-33, 166-176.
5   *Cloud*, p. 54.
6   Gary Furr, "The Road of Ashes: Spirituality and the Pros-pects for Disillusioned Baptists," *Ties that Bind: Life To-gether in the Baptist Vision* (Macon: Smyth & Helwys Pub-lishing, Inc., 1994), pp. 127ff. While parochial to Baptists, I find Furr's designations to be fairly applicable across the board in American Christian spirituality.
7   Thomas Moore, *The Care of the Soul.*
8   Paul Tillich, *A History of Christian Thought: From Its Judaic and Hellenistic Origins to Existentialism* (New York: Simon and Schuster, 1968), p. 45.
9   *Prayer, Fear, and Our Powers,* p. 32.
10 George A. Maloney, trans., *Hymns of Divine Love by St. Symeon the New Theologian* (Denville, New Jersey, Dimen-sion Books), pp. 54-55.
11 Tessa Bierlecki, "Saint Teresa: The Grand Wild Woman of Avila," *Fellowship in Prayer*, Vol. 46, No. 5, Oct. 1995, p. 31.
12 *Four Quartets*, p. 31.
13 *Theology of Play*, p. vii.
14 *Theology of Play*, p. 30.
15 Both quotations of Teilhard are from Nemeck and Coombs, *O Blessed Night: Recovering from Addiction, Codependency and Attachment* based on the insights of St. John of the Cross and Pierre Teilhard de Chardin (New York: Alba House, 1991), pp. 132-133.
16 *O Blessed Night*, p. 134.
17 Nemeck and Coombs, *The Spiritual Journey*, p. 164.
18 *O Blessed Night*, p. 135.
19 *Interior Castle*, p. 430.
20 *The Spiritual Canticle*, p. 561.

21 *The Living Flame of Love*, p. 648.

22 "Oh Exceeding Beauty," Vol. 3, p. 381.

23 Quoted in Jurgen Moltmann, *The Spirit of Life: A Universal Affirmation* (Minneapolis: Fortress Press, 1992), p. 331. Other references to Wesley, pp. 161, 174. Cf. Gerard Reed, Notes of Books, No. 52, August 1995.

24 Edmund Colledge and Bernard McGinn, trans., *Everything as Divine: The Wisdom of Meister Eckhart* (Maywah, New Jersey: Paulist Press, 1996), p. 23.

25 M. Basil Pennington, *Lection Divina: Renewing the Ancient Practice of Praying in the Scriptures* (New York: Crossroad, 1998), pp. 28-29.

26 Vol. 1, p. 195; Vol. 3, p. 126.

27 Fox, Meister Eckhart, p. 14.

28 Richard J. Foster, *Celebration of Discipline* (Harper-San-Francisco, 1988), p. 31.

29 Annie Dillard, *Pilgrim at Tinker Creek* (New York: Bantam Books, 1974), p. 104. 30 Ibid., pp. 33-34.

31 Matthew Fox, Meditations with Meister Eckhart (Santa Fe: Bear and Company, Inc., 1983), p. 12.

32 *Everything as Divine*, pp. 22-23.

33 *Experiences of God*, pp. 78-79.

34 *Experiences of God*, p. 74

35 *Experiences of God*, p. 79

36 Nemeck and Coombs, *The Way of Spiritual Driection*, p. 29.

37 Nemeck and Coombs, *The Spiritual Journey*, p. 224.

38 *Theology of Play*, p.36.

39 Ibid., p. 37.

40 Andrew D. Lester, *Hope in Pastoral Care and Counseling* (Louisville: Westminster John Knox Press, 1997), p. 103ff.

41 *Experiences of God*, p. 60.

To Order Copies
OF *DAZZLING AND DIVINE*

Contact Mark Jones at
www.dazzinganddivine.com

or call
LangMarc Publishing
1-800-864-1648
www.langmarc.com

Printed in the United States
17855LVS00004B/43-204

9 781880 292693